India has embarked on an ambitious goal of digitising the economy through multiple pathways—'Broadband For All'; National Public Digital Platforms in key sectors; positioning India as a global hub of electronic manufacturing; catalysing Indian software and digital products; and nurturing an innovation, incubation and start-up ecosystem to harness emerging technologies to solve problems for the next billions of people. This book by industry leaders, who are partnering with the Government in many ways to achieve the trillion dollar Digital India goal, is an asset for the industry and policymakers.

—Shri Ajay Sawhney, Secretary, Ministry of Electronics and Information Technology

The appetite for Digital Reengineering ignited by the pandemic is similar across the globe, but the strategies required will vary, based on digital maturity of organisations. Further, the ability to deliver a measurable return on technology investment quickly and acceptable to all stakeholders will be central to CEOs/CXOs roadmap for Digital Reengineering. This book by seasoned practitioners will prove to be a prescription for success for organisations in the post-pandemic Digital Era.

—Dinesh Khara, Chairman
State Bank of India

ACCELERATING DIGITAL SUCCESS

ACCELERATING DIGITAL SUCCESS

Reimagining Organisations for a Post-COVID-19 World

Ganesh Natarajan
Uma Ganesh
Lavanya Jayaram

BLOOMSBURY
NEW DELHI • LONDON • OXFORD • NEW YORK • SYDNEY

BLOOMSBURY INDIA
Bloomsbury Publishing India Pvt. Ltd
Second Floor, LSC Building No. 4, DDA Complex, Pocket C – 6 & 7,
Vasant Kunj, New Delhi, 110070

BLOOMSBURY, BLOOMSBURY INDIA and the Diana logo
are trademarks of Bloomsbury Publishing Plc

First published in India 2021
This edition published 2021

ISBN: PB: 978-93-88912-74-7; eBook: 978-93-88912-76-1
2 4 6 8 10 9 7 5 3 1

Typeset in Manipal Technologies Limited
Printed and bound in India by Thomson Press India Ltd.

MIX
Paper from responsible sources
FSC® C010615

To find out more about our authors and books visit www.bloomsbury.com and sign up for our newsletters

We dedicate this book to the indomitable spirit of Indian entrepreneurs who are able to rise above all the odds and enable a renaissance time and again. With digital on the rise, this is our opportunity, and I am sure we will inspire our countrymen to deliver a new India that is in all our dreams.

Contents

Foreword

Post-COVID-19, the world is in a reset mode, recovering but at the same time reimagining and reinventing. Achieving accelerated inclusive growth in the face of the devastation of lives and livelihoods and also sudden rise in inequality will need disruptive and not incremental innovation.

Digital transformation can be a great force multiplier here. Here are some illustrative examples.

Take education. Post-COVID, one-third of the 1.6 billion children around the world, who suddenly went out of school, do not have access to online learning due to digital deprivation. We need innovations that will provide digital access equality despite income inequality. India had made headway during 2001–2005, innovating to create extremely affordable indigenous tablets, such as Simputer, Akash and Mobilis, but then missed the journey from ideas to impact. We need to restart this innovation journey with renewed zeal.

Take health. Look at the illustrative example of the challenge of shortage of ICUs during the pandemic and the power of Indian inclusive innovation. Start-up Dozee, using IoT, set up a continuous contact-free vitals monitor with remote monitoring capabilities and alert system that converts any bed into a step-down ICU quickly (a few minutes) and affordably (5% of the cost of a full-fledged ICU system). It has a proven medical-grade accuracy of 98.4%. The data is uploaded to the cloud to give remote access so that the clinicians can access the data from a safe distance. The data is further analysed using advanced machine learning and artificial intelligence algorithms.

Not just the coronavirus pandemic but the perennially persisting pandemic of poverty will need innovations. The start-up JioVivo created an IoT-based solution, SaveMom, with a culturally aligned user-friendly wearable maternal healthcare device, which (together with a suite of apps) monitors a mother's health and uploads the data to the cloud for doctors to view remotely. It saves the lives of pregnant women in remote villages. Their solution is already deployed in 100+ villages in southern states. The cost? Just one rupee per day!

Innovation in digital India will accelerate due to four powerful drivers, namely the exponential nature of technology in terms of sharply rising performance and simultaneously plummeting costs, creative convergence of technologies into new combinations, the emergence of digital platforms and declining entry costs thanks to affordable cloud-based computing and open-source software. India will have to use DARQ power to drive innovation. That means a combination of distributed ledger technology, artificial intelligence, extended reality and quantum computing. India will have to leverage innovations based on DARQ technologies, not only for creating new Indian businesses but also powerfully executing businesses cutting across the diversity of business models, customer segments, distribution channels, business processes, products and services and workplaces.

In this new amazing digital world, this book shows the massive transformational power of digital reengineering. It shows how exponential technologies will dramatically change the extended workplace, how processes will get reengineered, how design thinking will enable a complete rearchitecting of the customer and other stakeholder journeys, touchpoints, new skills and how cultural change is becoming the essence of this new norm.

The book rightly emphasises that we require digital reengineering with experimentation, with new ideas, with continuous innovation. And then the challenge is not just about changing the skill sets, but changing the mindsets, that will embrace innovation as a way of life.

What should a true digital transformation be like? George Westermann of MIT Sloan Initiative on the Digital Economy has famously said that when digital transformation is done right, it is like a caterpillar turning into a butterfly, but when done wrong, it is really a fast caterpillar. The book provides ideas that will guide you so that you do not end up with a faster caterpillar but a truly transformed beautiful butterfly.

Let's first look at the contextualisation of this wonderful book.

Business transformation using digitalisation was traditionally focused on productivity improvement—better, faster, cheaper being the keywords.

Going further, the advent of disruptive digitalisation posed challenges by asking a fundamental question as to what is the business that one is really in? Where is the value shifting? What are the opportunities at the inflexion points? In the authors' own words, how can we move from merely a better business to a new business?

Going even further, to achieve truly successful business transformation, a dramatic shift in culture, business practices and strategy and even in the nature of the work becomes a must.

And all this intricate business transformation has to be now done with hardly any time on hand! Why?

It is because of the COVID pandemic. It woke us up rudely, and by the time we were fully awake, the world was in a radical reset mode. The COVID transformation brought in a dramatic new normal and indeed a new imperative and that too with stunning rapidity.

Microsoft Chief Satya Nadella summed up this unprecedented rapidity well when he said that during this pandemic, two years of digital transformation took place in two months. E-commerce, fintech, edtech, telehealth, online gaming and entertainment—all of these grew rapidly. What would have happened in x years happened in x weeks or x months!

And some of the rapid exponential growth was so spectacular.

Can you imagine a young company providing just video communications surpassing the oil major Exxon Mobil in less than 200 days? Yes, it is Zoom. Beginning the year with a market cap of $19 billion, on 29 October it crossed a market cap of $139 billion, exceeding Exxon Mobil's $138.9 billion!

Most importantly, the book shows that digital transformation isn't just about investing in digital infrastructure and then turning on a switch. It shows how the customers, employees and supply and demand chain partners have to become the stakeholders of the enterprise to undergo a successful transformation with speed, scale and sustainability.

After a fascinating tour of technologies, processes, domains, customer journeys, data and analytics, skills and culture, the book offers something that I was very impressed with—a robust Digital Capability Maturity Model, identifying stages of maturity and diverse factors that will influence progress through each stage of digital transformation. The model enables both assessment of status and strategic planning for moving towards maturity. To my mind, the digital reengineering thinking going into a potential Capability Maturity Model is a sure key to digital success.

The book is just timely for India, where the dream of Digital India is taking shape so rapidly. India jumped from 155th position in mobile data consumption to the first position in just a matter of a few months. It jumped to the first position in real-time digital financial transactions when it hit 41 million transactions per day. I am happy that the authors present insightful thoughts on the way forward as also a way upwards for the digital reengineering of this emerging new India.

I have known Ganesh and Uma for decades. I admire them hugely, not only because they are great thought leaders, but also because they are action leaders, having themselves helped many companies in digital transformation, besides leading global technology enterprises themselves. They and the third author Lavanya have written this book, which is a must-read for all stakeholders in digital transformation. It is an invaluable guide, embellished with insightful thoughts and a riveting narrative for digital reengineering, that shows how successfully winning enterprises can emerge in the post-COVID world.

Padma Vibhushan Raghunath Mashelkar
President, Global Research Alliance
November 2020

Acknowledgements

Digital has always been a labour of love for the three of us. The joy of discovering digital as people who were never trained for it but who came to use and embrace digital technologies as a way of life and work has inspired us to write this for the benefit of more people like us. For digital natives, who are born with technology surrounding them, this book will be useful to understand the interfaces that need to be designed, with processes, data flows and people, to ensure the success of any business. But there are digital immigrants still leading organisations and functions, and we believe we owe this book to them to celebrate their willingness to learn, adapt and master the new waves of change that are hitting us every day in every walk of life.

Our own adventures in digital and the voyages we have undertaken have been different but have resulted in similar epiphanies. It would be appropriate to thank many people who have travelled with us part of the way, sharing our thinking and participating in debates that have opened our minds to new opportunities. From her first job in Tata Motors to a wonderful decade and a half in Zensar Technologies, Lavanya has been able to soak in and lead marketing leveraging the power of digital marketing. She has participated in the transformation of the company, a leading service provider in digital transformation. Apart from her work with Ganesh when he was leading the company, her stint with Global Talent Track (GTT) led by Uma and her work with Sandeep Kishore at Zensar, Lavanya has participated in consulting engagements with entrepreneurial firms working in digital. She thanks the CEOs and leaders who have shaped her experiences and thinking.

For Uma, the digital journey started at Zee Telefilms, where the opportunity to use technology to change the way computer education could be brought to tens of thousands of people in India and neighbouring Asian countries inspired her to start one of the leading firms in skills development, GTT. She then integrated into it a category to create AI-based digital learning platforms, Skills Alpha. She has held a leadership role in the Centre for Artificial Intelligence and Advanced Analytics. She has also participated in new initiatives with the Government of India's Ministry of Electronics & Information Technology (MeitY) to bring digital capabilities to healthcare workers in the country. These have sharpened her instincts in the use of digital technology for national development.

Ganesh acknowledges his experience in leading Zensar and then investing in a range of digital entrepreneurs through 5F World and Kalzoom Advisors as the main inspiration for his deep interest in the factors that make digital businesses successful. In brief stints as digital advisor to McKinsey & Company and Bajaj Finserv, he was able to participate in leading-edge thinking and implementation of digital. As a Board Director at State Bank of India, Hinduja Global Services, Fino Payments Bank and Principal Asset Management, Ganesh had the opportunity to lead major digital projects to see the light of day. Today, investee companies such as Live History India Digital, Farm Guru, Studio Coppre and SP Robotics are leading digital changes in traditional as well as new areas that can make a deep impact in India.

The authors would like to thank Rajiv Kumar and Ajai Garg from MeitY, Noshir Kaka, Sanjiv Bajaj, Rajesh Sinha and Krishna Ramaswami from the consulting and corporate sector and digital entrepreneurs Ipsita, Mini, Vikram and Rashmi for their leadership and support, which led to many of the thoughts and ideas that have blossomed through this book. And a big thank you to the high-energy teams at APTECH, Zensar Technologies, The India–US Entrepreneurs (TiE), Global Talent Track, Kalzoom Advisors and the 5F World group of companies for their work, which redefines the frontiers of digital leadership every day for the benefit of the country and the world.

The authors would also like to thank co-voyagers on our life journeys—Somendra, Aruna, Ryan, Tara and Maximus for Lavanya, Mr & Mrs SV Iyer, Karuna, Hugh and Arun for Ganesh and Uma who have encouraged and supported the writing of this book. And finally, a big thank you to Shri Dinesh Khara and Ajay Sawhney for their support and Dr Raghunath Mashelkar, who has been a pillar of strength in so much of our work and who instantly agreed to write the foreword to this book and share with the readers his insights into the topic of the book.

1

Digital Business: Reengineering Imperatives

Digital transformation has been a watchword for all business in the last decade as wave upon wave of digital technologies have buffeted traditional organisations and digital attackers have threatened all businesses. Digital is emerging as the true driver of change in the world—for people, organisations, industries, countries and societies. What used to be a fairly simple business approach of building a product or service, opening an outlet or implementing mechanism which could target a customer and persuade her to buy has transformed into innovative methods for a new world. Pull creation, and not push marketing, drives consumer behaviour—customers embark on myriad journeys, with the decision to buy, often taken from the comfort of their armchairs rather than during a visit to the store. Supply chains have been transformed beyond recognition, and employee skills for digital business evolve every year, with new demands on learning content and methodologies. In the immortal words of the music group Queen, this is 'no time for losers, we are the champions'. The digital champions claim to have become the possessors of the mantra for success in a winner-takes-all world!

These challenges for business have their origins in the evolution of human expectations, from technology, from business and society as a whole. We are moving into uncharted waters, into a time when human relationships will erode, elections to high office will be manipulated by devious social media managers and artificial intelligence will determine who we buy from, who we choose to work with and even who we partner within our lives. Eminent futurologist and academic Yuval Noah Harari, has argued in his seminal book *Homo Deus* that the human species will successfully master the secret to immortality in the not-so-distant future. Lifespans of 150 years will be commonplace, albeit with many metallic body parts embedded in all of us. With traditional career options closing down and many new ones opening up, human beings will have to have back-to-school learning experiences every 15 or so years in their careers. Even more daunting will be the need to find multiple partners as the journey of life becomes longer and longer, as a spouse or companion one partnered with in youth may no longer want to be a lifelong companion! Harari also predicts that the search or quest for happiness will continue to be elusive even as people live longer lives and try new things and have new experiences without ever truly feeling satisfied or complete.

The digital present has been with us for just a couple of decades, spurred by the push of exciting new technologies and the pull of ever-changing customer journeys and demands. After the initial scepticism followed by large-scale adoption of the SMAC (Social, Mobility, Analytics, Cloud) technologies in the corporate sector and the increasing comfort with the ubiquitous smartphone, adoption of multiple waves of technologies has become almost synonymous with progress. New technologies at the front-end of access—user interfaces and user experiences, cognitive and actionable insights emerging from the initial experimentation with artificial intelligence, machine learning and predictive and prescriptive analytics and the inevitable backlash from the data security and personal privacy seekers—have all been phenomena experienced in less than a decade. We are all changing, some willingly, while others are dragged kicking and screaming to the altar of digital technologies.

The sad reality is that less than 20% of the proof of concept efforts at digital transformation have resulted in a transformed business. Many anecdotes recount a significant improvement in customer experience in one place or the development and support of a new multi-client digital transformation in another, but most

CEOs are wondering what happened to the big promises of complete transformation made by consultants and internal staff a few years ago. The CEO supported the concept of three-phase transformation, with the CIO handling mission-critical 'lights on' applications, the chief digital officer developing a digital innovation strategy and getting cloud computing, mobility, big data and edge applications such as augmented reality and internet of things (IoT) into the organisation and the chief marketing officer fighting for and getting her own technology team to pilot new customer delight applications and garner a bigger market share. But at the end of the year, when the board asks 'Have we been able to quantify the benefits and is it more than our investments?', not every CEO has been able to confidently say, 'Yes, of course, and here is the proof'.

ENTER COVID AND LOOK AT THE CHANGE!

It all happened almost imperceptibly as word came out of Wuhan in China in early 2020 that a strange virus had grown bigger than a minor menace and could well cross the borders of a city that had a practice of eating wild animals in their wet market and move beyond China, a country shrouded in secrecy. Sure enough, Singapore and the Koreas started to feel the impact of COVID, and when a group of Chinese workers flew back after Chinese New Year to their workplaces in Italy, all hell broke loose in Europe. India and the US started to feel the might of the coronavirus and soon enough the whole world too. And the rest is history, which continues to unfold in front of our eyes.

The global digital proponents, who were beginning to wonder when the world would wake up to the real transformative power of the myriad digital technologies, rose to the challenge of COVID induced social distancing and recognised the opportunities from lockdowns and long term work from home in organisations, cities and entire countries. Suddenly there was a scramble, first to move equipment and communications technology to enable work from home, then work reallocation and collaboration to maximise productivity and finally a rethinking of managerial tasks to be less input-driven and more focused on output and outcomes. Soon, the challenges and opportunities involved in communicating with other stakeholders—customers, supply and demand chain partners and investors—had to be addressed, and clear differentiation between a choice of technologies for office collaboration, webinars and large events became the norm.

In India, as the technology industry's quarterly results started coming out in April 2020, less than four weeks into the process, industry CEOs preened at the return to 90% plus productivity. One market leader confidently spoke about moving to 70% employees working from home in future as compared to the past percentage of less than 20 and alluded to a significant reduction in input costs and substantial improvement in manpower productivity. While such miracles have naturally not been feasible in industries reliant on contact and machinery operations, there is no doubt that the use of technology in general and digital innovation in particular is uppermost on the mind of industry strategists and CEOs as the world moves from relief to recovery to resilience in the battle against COVID.

The future is going to be a strange place. The futurologists paint strange new pictures of mixed (virtual and augmented) reality, the power of quantum computing and 5G and the hitherto unexplored capabilities of artificial intelligence as well as distributed digital ledgers brought to us by the push towards blockchain. On the one hand, the excitement around new technology products and services is enormous—ABB's new factory near Shanghai with floating shop floors and myriad robots manufacturing a range of industrial robots, Tesla's wonderful new world of automobile intelligence and an artificial intelligence (AI)-enabled food cart meticulously delivering patient's food orders at lunchtime at a hospital on New York City's Upper East Side. Equally, the prophecies of doom have begun, with autonomous AI and robots taking away hundreds of millions of jobs for which people have been trained in the manufacturing and services sectors, personal data becoming available on the internet to unscrupulous marketers and liberal democracy as we know it falling prey to the wiles of social listening and electronic manipulation of sentiment.

The COVID transformation and the inexorable push towards a 'new normal' for all processes and businesses will definitely see a complete reimagination of work. Digital reengineering will be the new imperative as technologies swarm into the extended workplace, processes get reengineered, design thinking enables a complete rearchitecting of the customer and other stakeholder journeys and touchpoints, new skills and cultural change become the new imperative for human resource functions as well as the C-suite of all corporations. We will explore all these fascinating opportunities in this book and build the 'new narrative' as we go along.

THE DIGITAL FIRM: CHANGING PUSHES AND PULLS

The surest way to understand the impact for the firm is to appreciate the context. Research shows that since the year 2000, 52% of the Fortune 500 firms have gone bankrupt, been acquired or ceased to exist in their original form as a result of a digital disruption. The average tenure of S&P 500 companies is predicted to shrink from 20 to 12 years and 50% of the current companies on the list will be replaced in the next 10 years. The World Economic Forum has predicted that while 75 million jobs will be displaced by automation and the fourth industrial revolution, 133 million jobs will be created. No wonder then that half of the ten top valuable companies in the world today are technology companies and the march of the FAANG set (Facebook, Apple, Amazon, Netflix and Google) seems unstoppable.

Industries of every kind have been affected by digital and the pace of change has been accelerating every year. Tourism, hospitality, media and publishing, retail banking and retail distribution have quite naturally seen the most significant changes. High tech, telecoms, automotive and assembly-oriented manufacturing have substantially transformed, and digital has also started making its presence felt in utilities, process manufacturing, oil and gas and even the public sector. Disconcerting for some and appealing to aggressive digital disruptors is the fact that a 'winner takes all' dynamic has begun to emerge, which has resulted in digital missionaries such as Mark Zuckerberg and Elon Musk becoming objects of adulation as well as derision, with anti-trust hackles raised against the perceived mercenaries and digital pirates of the new era.

With over 25% of new revenues in many industries being taken by digital attackers, incumbents are progressively seeing technology as the most significant investment area in present times and most incremental technology investments are digital. But before delving into the fast-changing world of digital technology, let us focus on the principal raison d'être of a business, its customer! With multiple ways of engaging, exploring and purchasing now available, any business will find it extremely difficult to predict the customer journey and their enquiry and buying behaviour at various points of the awareness-consideration-purchase process.

The touchpoints created by any firm are today outnumbered by the touchpoints available to the customer through external sources. The traditional approach to public relations, push advertising through radio, television and print and outdoor media, now needs to be supplemented by a variety of digital or online presence points—email, paid content, third party sites, landing pages and social media. The physical buying location, which used to be the store or an agent, is being supplemented and, in many cases, overshadowed or replaced by mobile apps, recommendation engines and internet communities. The service and loyalty expansion activities of customers are also being transformed, resulting in brands losing customers to another brand by the allure and digital savvy of a competing proposition.

The technologies that are enabling digital transformation today must be examined through the lens of outcomes and benefits rather than the wonder of the technologies themselves. In the world we all inhabit today, with its abundance of choices for customers and hyper-competition between products and service providers, enhancing productivity, improving customer experience and innovating on the business model of the enterprise are the key drivers for digital leverage. From SMAC to connectivity devices such as sensors and beacons, tools such as user experience and user interfaces, mixed reality, blockchain, AI and machine learning and all forms of analytics, the technology stack can be best selected and deployed if it provides measurable benefits in the areas of 'everything as a service', which will maximise productivity, automation of production processes and even knowledge work through robotics, internet of things and AI and integrated cyber and physical experiences to meet the needs of various anticipated customer experiences. Of course, it would be wise to remember that some technologies can be used to create solutions that the customer never really asked for. Digital transformation practitioners would do well to progress on a path of incremental but continuous innovation while keeping an eye open and an ear to the ground for truly disruptive ideas for the business.

GOING DIGITAL: THE STATE OF BUSINESSES

Organisations are understandably at various stages in their digital journeys, though there are hardly any Rip Van Winkles out there who have not yet seized the opportunities and benefits of a digital journey. Research from Dell Technologies has shown that the number of digital laggards—organisations with no plan or very limited initiatives—has come down from 15 to 9% from 2016 to 2018, the number of digital adopters and leaders with comprehensive digital programmes and digital ingrained in their DNA has gone up from 19 to 28%, with the middle set still in digital follower or evaluator mode. There is clearly a case for acceleration across the board.

The research further underlines the maturity of digital adoption in business with digital knowledge being shared across business functions in 44% of the polled organisations against just 19% just two years ago. And investments in skilled talent and a digital culture have shot up to 46% from 27% in the same period. Investments in progressive firms continue to be on integrating digital goals into all departmental activities, agile software development, action taken on intelligence in real time and adoption of artificial intelligence and analytics in decision-making models of the firm. Building data security and privacy into all applications and algorithms is also mainstream, which demonstrates the serious intent of organisations to begin and continue on the digital journey.

The Boston Consulting Group has corroborated these findings on the very deliberate moves being made towards digital success in its 'Factory of the Future' research. It points out the increasing role of robotics and AI in the design of manufacturing systems. With shop floors, warehousing and in-plant transportation systems already nearing full automation, the cyber-physical interfaces are seeing enterprise resource planning and manufacturing execution systems providing dynamic information to men and machines. This enables them to optimise operations based on material availability and process data. AI systems predict demand based on environment and consumption pattern data, develop new products based on generative design principles and completely manage factory operations, from quality defect identification, incident solution recommendations based on earlier failure reports, predictive maintenance needs, dynamic optimisation of warehouse needs and overall factory management.

Jabil, one of the leading design and manufacturing systems solution providers who have set up digital factories in Mexico and Malaysia, have demonstrated that their approach of connecting equipment, sensors and people using real-time predictive analytics has improved the velocity of operations and developed a platform with an 80% accuracy level for predicting early equipment or process failure resulting in 10% energy savings and 17% rework savings and substantial improvement in manufacturing cycle times.

In multiple industry sectors, the availability of advanced digital solutions has enabled companies to reset the parameters for judging performance. Reports from McKinsey, IDC and Accenture suggest that 40% of e-commerce will be enabled by cognitive social shoppers and social networks. Further, usage-based insurance rather than long term 'just-in-case' policies will account for at least 15% of the global vehicle insurance market.

And trade finance companies are exploring the use of blockchain and distributed ledger technologies for over 20% of their global platforms. On a more futuristic basis, 50% of retailers in the next two years are expected to use robots as store greeters or assistants, more than 50% of field service calls will be managed by virtual service technicians and by 2026, over 25% of emergency rooms and paramedics will use 3-D printing to deliver real-time care on the field.

The world is changing for sure, and the question each business and firm must answer is this: are we ready to compete? Competing for the digital future will necessitate a balanced focus on all the four pillars that will hold up future digital businesses—processes, technology, data and culture.

BUSINESS PROCESS REENGINEERING: REIMAGINING DIGITAL FUTURES

Michael Hammer and James Champy, early pioneers of business process reengineering, predicted that organisations would need to move from functional silos meant for an earlier era of top-down hierarchical organisation design to customer-centric business processes. In fact, it was argued in the 1990s that three key business processes—product design and realisation, order fulfilment and supporting logistics—would enable high-response future-focused organisations to break through functional boundaries. And in pathbreaking research in the 1980s, the Massachusetts Institute of Technology (MIT) predicted that corporations would move from the exploitation of information technology for a local departmental benefit and internal integration to truly explorative uses, enabled by business process reengineering, business network redesign and, eventually, business scope redefinition. Even MIT and Hammer may not have imagined how the relentless customer pull for better, faster and cheaper products and services and the accelerating technology push of digital would change the world of business beyond recognition in the new millennium.

What digital has provided in the last decade and more is multiple touchpoints that allow businesses to engage with every stakeholder—the customer, the supply chain partner, demand generators and employees—in hitherto unimaginable ways, tapping into the power of sensing opportunity, predicting behaviour and almost prodding the stakeholder to respond to stimuli provided by the business. Imagining just one customer journey in retail brings this opportunity into sharp focus. Today's customer becomes aware of a product from multiple media and receives information about its availability in a nearby outlet through geo-positioning devices that transmit suggestions for a quick shopping detour while driving to work. The buying decision, as mentioned earlier, can be quite unpredictable and requires processes that make it easy and convenient whenever the sale opportunity occurs. Today's design thinking methodologies can facilitate multiple customer journeys to be imagined.

The same opportunities abound on the employee side. Process reengineering enables career management discussions, skills acquisition and enhancement planning and seeking out of mentors at a time and place convenient to the employee rather than having to wait for organisations to schedule these sessions. Designing new processes to fully exploit technology, engage all stakeholders and continuously learn from every interaction, lies at the core of the new digital businesses and often separates the winners from the also-rans in any industry segment. Infuse digital technology into these reimagined processes, combine the new process ideas with the power of data and analytics and put in place a highly skilled workforce with the culture of 24×7 availability, and a brand-new organisation design seems to be the new imperative.

THE SMORGASBORD OF DIGITAL TECHNOLOGIES

Digital has come a long way from the early days of cloud computing and mobile applications. The exploitation of social media usage for personal use to providing selling opportunities to willing consumers has opened up a whole new range of data flow between people's personal and business worlds. In the early days, business intelligence and dashboards made data more understandable for decision support.

Technology today has invaded every aspect of work. On the shop floor, ubiquitous sensors and beacons are transmitting data about machine performance while maintenance needs are being forecast and messages sent in real time to minimise field breakdowns of capital equipment. In warehouses, picking lists are being facilitated by augmented reality while virtual reality is bringing situations into the training rooms of novices before they enter the work environment.

The old prediction about business network redesign is being brought to life with blockchains and distributed ledgers determining where and when work is done and creating a world of smart contracts. AI and machine learning will soon make every conceivable engagement process a reality and open up new vistas of opportunity.

MANAGING DATA, LEVERAGING AI AND MOVING TO PREDICTION AND PRESCRIPTION

Big data is a term that came up almost synonymously with digital. The awareness that all the exciting technology being deployed for digital transformation would deliver less than optimal results if data was not managed well was lost for almost a decade. Organisations struggled with social networks, built mobile applications as though they were the true holy grail and installed sensors and beacons to grab data. But the ability to analyse this data and draw meaningful conclusions remained elusive for most businesses except the very smart e-commerce technology leaders. However, this capability is what has created the powerhouses called Amazon, Google and Facebook, and this is the ability that practitioners of digital transformation must develop to really be the winner in their industry segment.

The reason for the problem that exists today—we are capturing the data and throwing it into a data mart or warehouse and even generating some reports, but we are not managing it well for the potential it has to transform our businesses. Figure 1.1 explains the stages this will require.

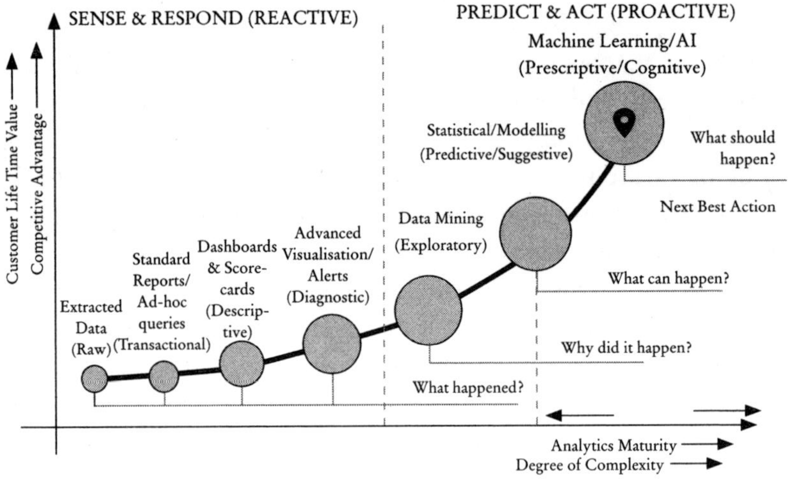

FIGURE 1.1 *Analytics Maturity Journey (Courtesy: Systech Inc., Glendale California)*

The data captured from various sources during the normal operations of the firm is what is being called raw data here. As knowledge management practitioners would know, data becomes information when it is categorised and put in a presentable plan, but information becomes knowledge only when it is contextualised. Many early practitioners of business intelligence and data visualisation attempted to fish in the data pond and developed simple reports that captured the last month's production or sales, compared it with the previous month or year and in some cases even compared it with external data such as industry- or competitor-published information. This is what we call in the chart transactional or descriptive analytics. While in some companies even this was a substantial improvement over the expertise reliant or hunch-based decision-making of the past, it still leaves a lot of the potential untapped. The context in which the data was created and the learnings about customer or equipment behaviour do not figure in the first stage of 'what happened'. At best, some diagnostics provide alerts for the future with some visualisation.

This addition of context is today being made possible with machine learning and AI, which can extract actionable insights from large volumes of data when also given the context and experience related to the creation of that data in the first place. The stages through which analytics can progress—exploratory or 'why did it happen', predictive or 'what can happen next' and finally prescriptive or 'what should happen'—translate knowledge about the context into action that can really add to the wisdom of the firm in dealing with stakeholder expectations of the future.

A strong analytics capability founded on excellent stakeholder experience management and technology to enable multiple touchpoints is the winner's post in digital transformation for most firms today. How many companies are getting there and what do we need to do to increase the win rates? More of that as the book progresses!

EXPLORING AND CREATING NEW CULTURES IN BUSINESS

One of the most attempted changes to 'business as usual' processes of a firm has been the way people learn new skills. It has been 50 years since learning and development managers had their epiphanies and realised that training batches of employees in classrooms, whether in the company or in open programmes, was yielding mediocre results. The much-vaunted MOOCs (massive open online courses) offered by modern universities and the proliferation of content offered up in e-learning formats may have reduced the cost incurred by training departments in mounting and executing training programmes, but they have not substantially changed learning outcomes with course completion rates on e-learning platforms being in single digits or low teen percentages.

Adaptive and personalised learning has addressed the issue in recent times, but the real breakthroughs in learning and digital culture building have been through the introduction of artificial intelligence and machine learning into individual learning processes. Digital platforms of today offer a slow but personalised immersion into need-based learning delivered in a style optimised for career aspirations as well as individual learning styles. A plethora of data on other learners and available mentors encourages enthusiastic learners of the day to embark on a continuum of career management, skills development, peer learning and mentoring, providing real meaning and excitement to a new generation.

In the world of digital business today, service providers as well as business organisations have an imperative to not just reskill and upskill their human resources but also create a culture of experimentation and innovation that will drive change on an ongoing basis.

BETTER BUSINESS TO A NEW BUSINESS

The excitement of digital transformation often begins after the race to optimising the existing business has been won through becoming a truly data-driven organisation. Logically better digital business will lead to more targeted marketing campaigns to existing and new customers, a 360-degree view of customers, supply chain partners and employees, better prediction and management of competition moves, timely new product or service introduction and ongoing customer delight. That should be enough to keep many businesses happy, but in a fast-changing world of digital disruption, it just won't do!

Take just two examples. Discovery Insurance in South Africa realised from its analysis of customer behaviour that nobody was really enthusiastic about health or life insurance but would really appreciate personalised advice on exercise, healthy foods and how to live a happy life. The launch of its wellness chain Vitality as a new business used data about customers to create a new profitable business stream. Of course, it sold more insurance for Discovery as well. Ant Financials is the runaway success story created by Alibaba in China. It monetises the huge data about small merchants who almost exclusively use Alibaba for e-commerce and has built a full suite of products to serve this hitherto underserved market segment. With the single largest stakeholder in Ant being Alibaba, here is one monetisation of data that is positive: it adds value and is useful to all stakeholders.

When data becomes the product and not just the driver of transformation, it drives new business models through the monetisation of the data product. The data of large TELCOs in the form of location information, search data and usage, retail's clickstreams and purchasing pattern data, sensor and consumer usage pattern data in the energy and utilities industry leading to smart metering—all these and more are opportunities arising from data management. Of course, the exemplars of companies built on data rather than asset ownership are Uber, Airbnb and Facebook, which have built valuable companies just by trading information. But the ability of incumbent firms to innovate around their business model and build new businesses is what true digital transformation will deliver in the future for many businesses.

DIGITAL BUSINESS MODELS OF THE FUTURE

Digital has the power to be whatever one wants it to be for an organisation—it can substantially improve productivity, enhance customer experiences and build new businesses. Amazon, the true exemplar of digital business, has transformed from being a simple internet bookseller to one of the most successful e-commerce and related business builders of our generation and has shown the efficacy of the cost model. Others like Alibaba, and to some extent even Google and Facebook, have taken this approach to building hugely successful businesses riding on extremely low costs and free consumption for all consumers. LinkedIn has succeeded more than some others with a free and freemium model, and many others exploiting this cost model have used reverse auctions and buyer aggregation while always retaining price transparency as a key virtue of their business.

Netflix, Disney and to some extent even Apple have chosen the experience model built on extensive automation, personalisation and instant gratification to build a set of empowered and satisfied customers who enjoy the friction-free environment they provide. More and more consumer-oriented models will attempt to emulate them even as human beings increasingly prefer anonymity and reduce human contact.

The truly exciting model of the future will be the platform model, which has been perfected by Amazon for e-commerce but can now lend itself to multiple single-focus as well as multi-stakeholder businesses. Data orchestrators will build digital marketplaces, use crowdsourcing extensively as a means of building millions of participants and thrive in an ecosystem of mutually supportive and complementary users and customers. The rise of digital platforms, the ability to harness technology through superior business processes and the ability to use well-trained people to transform stakeholder experiences are phenomena we will explore through this book as we investigate and understand the new world of digital business and all its connotations and ramifications.

SUCCESS WITH DIGITAL TRANSFORMATION

In this confusing and simultaneously compelling era of new customer pulls and ever-changing technology pushes, it is good to attempt an early definition of digital transformation for every organisation seeking to compete and conquer in the new world.

Digital transformation is the *continuous process* by which enterprises adapt to or *drive disruptive changes in their customers and markets* by leveraging *data*, investing in *technology innovation*, reengineering *processes;* change the *culture* to enable *new business* models; create new products and services to meet the requirements of; and capitalise on the new opportunities of the digital economy.

The five imperatives that are emerging for a successful digital transformation journey are as follows:

1. Reimagine stakeholder journeys. One insurance company in the US has perfected the discipline of mapping every new customer journey by actively polling search processes and 'moments of truth' for buying decisions. Others have transformed career management, skilling and mentoring journeys for all their employees to ensure high levels of engagement and motivation. The process of 'design thinking' and constant reimagining ensures that stakeholders enjoy truly innovative and inspiring interactions with the company at every interaction.
2. Digitise operations by investing in new processes designed to delight stakeholders and plan for digital touchpoints in each process and maximise engagement. One financial services company in India has innovated across their customer ecosystem and given options ranging from cyber-physical to fully digital to meet the expectations of widely varying demographics and preferences in their customer groups.
3. Building a data and analytics culture throughout the organisation with a high emphasis on using data and design thinking to predict stakeholder behaviour, prescribe products and solutions to customers based on likely choices prompted by AI and machine learning. Avoiding hunch-based decision-making and demanding predictive and prescriptive analytics to develop actionable insights is the way of the future.
4. Develop an innovation ecosystem. This is the subject of a more detailed discussion in the book, but it should be mentioned here that this is both internal and external and needs an active engagement with participants from across industry segments, start-up and entrepreneurial partners and external experts who help the firm challenge the status quo and constantly innovate for stakeholder benefit.
5. Focus on skills for the new digital organisation. The biggest cases of failure in the corporate sector despite massive investments in technology, analytics and consultants have occurred because the people who touch the lives of customers in sales or service situations every day are not available when needed or do not have the skills to deal with the omnichannel expectations of new customers, particularly of digital natives.

When does digital transformation really succeed? When it no longer stands out as a new gizmo or idea but integrates seamlessly into the tapestry of processes and technologies in the firm and becomes a part of its cultural DNA. Self-service mechanisms allow the band to be 'always-on' or always available to every stakeholder any place they choose to engage through any device. The context for such perpetual conversations is provided by judicious deployment of technologies that intelligently capture and manage data, predict behaviour and outcomes and recommend better solutions for both the firm and its customers. Seamless interaction with customers and the community enables successful digital firms to deliver the best returns on capital, whether monetary, human or social.

Designed and implemented correctly, the digitally transformed firm will manage customer stakeholders and journeys extremely well, implement technology as a true process and be an experience enabler for all stakeholders, make every employee digitally comfortable, reengineer the old and build brand-new processes and be prepared to innovate fearlessly—with products, processes and the business model of the firm.

This state of transformation and the achievement of all the outcomes envisaged for the digital journey will be a result of this science and art we call digital reengineering. In this book, we will explore all the pillars of digital reengineering—design thinking, stakeholder journeys, technologies, processes, domains, data, analytics, artificial intelligence, skills and culture in their independent capabilities and potential and put them all together to build the premise for digital capability maturity for any organisation serious about digital success.

TOWARDS A DIGITAL CAPABILITY MATURITY MODEL FOR THE ENTERPRISE

The imperative for all incumbents in a business segment or industry is to reimagine the future. How will customers, employees, supply and demand chain partners and every stakeholder of the enterprise respond to the outreach of the firm and place new demands on it and how are we prepared to address these demands and satisfy and delight all stakeholders? In the global technology industry, in which all authors have won their spurs and led enterprises, the climb towards success for most organisations has been by following the famous Capability Maturity Model of the Carnegie Mellon Software Engineering Institute (SEI-CMM). In the digital world, this book presents to you a Digital Capability Maturity Model identifying stages of maturity and factors that will influence progress through each stage. The model enables both assessment of status and strategic planning for moving towards maturity. The same Capability Maturity Model approach got applied to the management of the human resource function and the less famous People Capability Maturity Model (PCMM) emerged, also from Carnegie Mellon. And in his PhD work and dissertation on Knowledge Management at IIT Bombay in India, Ganesh Natarajan has researched many organisations to establish that success in knowledge management also comes through a series of stages that organisations necessarily go through and various factors influence the speed and success of transition through each stage.

In a later chapter in this book on imperatives for business, after we have done the full tour of technologies, processes, domains, customer journeys, data and analytics, skills and culture, we will integrate the digital reengineering thinking into a potential Capability Maturity Model for digital success. We truly believe that digital reengineering will set up new challenges for each business, cause a rethink of what really constitutes maturity in the new post-COVID world that we are all entering, how each of our factors increases the chances of success and what leadership should do to accelerate the company's progress on the digital journey. It is going to be a complex journey, bumpy at times, but we are sure you will enjoy the ride. Onward!

2

The Post-Pandemic World

Amid the worst pandemic our generation has witnessed, we battle the perils of extremely cautious socially distant living, loss of jobs at all levels, economic depression, migrant worker displacement, disease and death. But even in the face of grave losses, wearing a critical lens and gathering our learnings on the way are crucial. It could shine a light on what today seems a dark and dreary path to the future.

Every great catastrophe in history has led to a new way of life. World War II (WW II) gave birth to at least ten revolutionary innovations. The Great Plague in Europe brought jobs at par and enabled a skill-based pay scale changing everything from society to modern medicine. The Boston Smallpox gave rise to the free press as we know it in the modern world. More recently, SARS accelerated internet penetration in China and Hong Kong and also gave birth to e-commerce in the APAC region.

Let's take a closer look at these historic events.

WORLD WAR II SPAWNED INNOVATION FOR THE SURVIVORS

War pushes humanity to its limits. Even though the horrific atrocities of war often overshadow the advancements made, there are indeed those that change the world forever, and for the better. So, while we dream of a world where millions of people aren't swept off the face of the earth so that the rest of us can enjoy the scientific and technical by-products of wars, here's a list of ten revolutionary innovations that WW II generated: the first computer, nuclear power, the V-2 ballistic missile, penicillin, radar, radio and landing navigation, jet engines, synthetic rubber and oil, the pressurised cabin and the jerry can.

THE GREAT PLAGUE AND RISE OF THE PEASANTS

The European economy at the close of the Middle Ages in the 1300s was significantly different from the pre-plague economy. The peasant became freer, earning more from his toil. Fixed rents if not outright ownership of land largely displaced customary dues and services and, despite low grain prices, the peasant more readily fed himself and his family from his own land and produced a surplus for the market. Yields improved as a reduced population permitted a greater focus on fertile lands and more frequent fallowing, which greatly helped the peasants. More pronounced socioeconomic gradations developed among peasants as some, notably the more prosperous ones, exploited the changed circumstances such as the availability of land.

In trade and manufacturing, the relative ease of success during the High Middle Ages gave way to greater competition, which rewarded more efficient business practices. Greater sensitivity to the market and cost-cutting ultimately rewarded the European consumer with a wider range of goods at better prices.

In the long term, the demographic restructuring caused by the Black Death (1346–1353) perhaps fostered the possibility of new economic growth. The Black Death, unlike other catastrophes, destroyed people but not property, and the reduced population had the whole of Europe's resources to exploit. Survivors also benefited from the technological and commercial skills developed during the High Middle Ages, such as the tidal mill or the heavy plough that led to the Agricultural Revolution. The Black Death was a cataclysmic event, but it ultimately diminished economic impediments and opened new opportunities.

Due to the lack of manpower with the numerous lives lost to the Plague, people needed to work, and they needed to work harder and longer—giving rise to today's work style. Wages rose, and the poor became wealthier, equalising society. And as incomes rose, so did literacy, leading to new thinking and freedom of thought. Hierarchies broke down with education and gave way to a society further grounded in parity.

With more people working harder and for higher pay, one of the first things that came into existence were clocks and hourglasses to keep track of the time people worked. The plague also made citizens realise that the medical system they had relied on was rooted in religion and the previous hierarchical society had done little to keep them alive. This spawned modern medicine, which was grounded in science and experimentation. And as labour became more precious, tools were invented to make it easier to do things. The first eyeglasses were introduced to help people become more productive, as were hospitals, guns, modern homes and a host of other innovations.

There were other outbreaks of the plague. In 1592, London faced an outbreak that drew the shutters down on theatres for six months. This led Shakespeare to write poetry to make a living and this is when he wrote 'Venus and Adonis' and 'The Rape of Lucrece'.

Another plague in 1606 also closed the theatres in London, and this time Shakespeare apparently wrote *King Lear*, *Macbeth* and *Antony & Cleopatra*.

A plague from 1665 to 1666 had Isaac Newton flee to the countryside where he emerged with his theories on calculus, optics, laws of motion, and gravity. Yes, that's when the apple chose to fall.

THE BOSTON SMALLPOX EPIDEMIC AND THE FREE PRESS

In 1721, a terrible smallpox epidemic hit Boston. Half of the city's population of 11,000 was infected. The death toll of 850 was significant at the time, but not nearly as deadly as many other epidemics. With so many infected, an extreme response was needed to curtail its spread, especially because smallpox was deadly, having killed millions around the world. The only solution that seemed to work was variolation, which involved taking the pus from the lesion of an infected patient and inoculating a healthy person with it. It caused a mild infection but secured the patient from the full-blown version of smallpox.

The very thought of taking infected matter from a deadly disease and inserting it into a healthy human caused societal rage. While some pushed for inoculating the healthy, most people rejected inoculation on religious and moral grounds. Even though the benefits were apparent (inoculated people had a mortality rate of 2% as compared to 14% for the non-inoculated), this solution was considered repulsive, and the two sides debated incessantly.

As the debate raged on, James Franklin (Benjamin Franklin's brother) decided to share his opinions against inoculation in a newspaper. This became a forum for debate and soon started including other stories about politics, local events along with humour and satire, resulting in the creation of the first independent newspaper in the US. The smallpox epidemic catalysed the development of the newspaper in the US, giving rise to a medium that has shaped how we think for centuries.

Variolation eventually did catch on as the only way to reduce the mortality rate, revolting as the thought may be. Eventually, Edward Jenner found the first smallpox vaccine in 1797.

SARS AND E-COMMERCE IN ASIA PACIFIC

More recently and closer home, we look at the 2003 SARS crisis to understand how the retail industry adapted to worsening market conditions. Many will remember that over 8,000 people were infected by SARS and nearly 800 perished. Schools, factories and shops were closed, and China's bustling cities quickly turned into ghost towns.

But times of crisis also herald several opportunities as is the premise of this chapter. These challenges gave new opportunities to Chinese e-commerce pioneers Alibaba and JD.com in 2003, when China's internet industry was in its nascent stages.

JD.com and SARS

In 2003, e-commerce was just starting to emerge in China, with internet access in the hands of a very few. JD.com was a chain of 12 small electronics shops in Beijing at the time, mostly selling CDs, camcorders and the like. Richard Liu launched an online e-commerce site and planned to expand to more than 500 stores.

But SARS sent the business plummeting, forcing a shutdown of the stores to conserve resources. Goods were being sold on instant messaging service groups and college bulletin board systems forums instead.

E-commerce was relatively primitive at the time. Employees had to manually note orders and send text messages to customers when orders were shipped. Employees personally delivered orders to customers close to the office.

After seeing some interest from users on the internet forum CnBest, Liu set up a revenue-sharing agreement with the company that gave them a cut of each transaction. Sales of CDs, hard disk drives and CD players all went up.

By New Year's Day the following year, Liu officially launched his e-commerce website 360buy with about 100 products and devoted the bulk of his resources to building his online business. The rest is history, as the company quickly became one of the largest online retailers of electronics and, later, for other categories too in China.

Alibaba and SARS

Alibaba was primarily a B2B platform, connecting US buyers with Chinese suppliers—a four-year-old company then focused on matching American procurement teams with Chinese suppliers.

An Alibaba employee caught SARS when she was sent to attend the annual Canton Fair, Guangzhou (one of the largest expos for international B2B trade in China) in May 2003. After she returned to Alibaba's headquarters in Hangzhou and was hospitalised, she became the fourth SARS patient in Hangzhou.

While news of this was suppressed, many within the Hangzhou community suspected Alibaba of spreading SARS in the city, giving the company a bad name. Alibaba's 500+ employees were quarantined at home for 12 days and required to work from home.

Many countries around the world issued travel warnings for businessmen travelling to China, and thus many turned to Alibaba's online business to source Chinese goods. Starting in March 2003, Alibaba's B2B e-commerce business added 4,000 new members and 9,000 listings each day, a 3–5× increase over the pre-SARS rate.

Chinese suppliers, now faced with few options, also invested more in online marketing on Alibaba's platform. Alibaba's business grew 50% that year and saw daily revenues of 10 million RMB. Over half of the 1.4 million suppliers on the B2B platform saw strong sales growth.

Alibaba launched Taobao that year, with Jack Ma commissioning a secret team of six people to work on launching the platform. At the time, the number one e-commerce marketplace in China was eBay, and Alibaba had only been around for four years. Within two years, Taobao took over the market and displaced eBay to become the number one consumer to consumer marketplace in China.

OPPORTUNITIES IN THE COVID CRISIS

All the above examples point to the opportunities in times of crisis. Crisis creates a high-pressure environment for accelerated innovation. Crisis provides a purpose, and a situation like a global pandemic unites the world in a common purpose.

The phenomena unique to the COVID pandemic are as follows:

1. Social distancing: Restaurants, hotels, malls, theatres, entertainment venues and travel industry players, by the sheer nature of their business not being conducive to social distancing, have seen steep declines in demand, severely impacting the small- and medium-sized businesses particularly, who may have thinner margins and smaller cash piles to safeguard

against downturns. The losses are even more severe down the value chain, for example for car rental companies. The brakes have been hit hard on the travel and hospitality industry and will be the last to revive, and when they do, things will have to substantially and tangibly change—vacation pictures in pretty locales will not be a lure enough for the future traveller. She is going to demand more safety, security, hygiene—she is now a more cautious traveller and will want to be sure of contact tracing and minimal human contact. She may prefer closer locations to visit, which she can drive to herself.

2. Remote work: While some industries were brought to a screeching halt, such as manufacturing, some other industries/functions have been fortunate enough to continue with business enabled by technology. Many people quickly transitioned to a work-from-home set-up in these fields. This was not possible in previous epidemics. The accelerated pace of communication and collaboration technologies being adopted in various organisations and the prioritisation of the overall digital agenda is testimony to innovation under pressure.

   The more basic shift is the need for appropriate mobile hardware tools, such as smartphones, laptops and adequate internet access. Many organisations spontaneously ensured that their remote workforce was enabled with the right hardware to continue to work seamlessly from the safety of their homes. While most of the working population already own personal smartphones, laptops were sent over for the workforce. Many organisations also immediately rolled out an internet allowance to ensure the workforce was compensated for the internet bandwidth that remote work in the new scenario now demanded. Companies invested in virtual collaboration and communication tools such as Slack, Skype, MS Teams, etc. File sharing also had to become seamless, so tools such as OneDrive, Google Drive, Dropbox were adopted. Project managers working remotely needed a more systematic and comprehensive project management tool such as Basecamp, Monday.com, Trello, MS Teams. Furthermore, performance evaluation becomes difficult in a remote-working environment when supervisors and employees do not interact in person daily. The best tools today give supervisors, team leaders, and HR professionals on-demand employee feedback and real-time insights that can help them make day-to-day decisions and adjustments on the fly without ever having a face-to-face conversation. Tools such as SAP SuccessFactors and Trakstar are some performance management tools that have risen in importance.

3. Hygiene: Overnight the sanitiser, hand wash and mask industries skyrocketed in their sales figures. Social messages, the autoplay message on calling someone, millions of videos and memes via messaging platforms and social media flooded our media intake to get the world aware on the need to keep ourselves germ-free and stop the spread of the disease. It was no joke how tissue rolls, sanitisers and hand washes went off the retail shelves in minutes. New entrants and local brands now dominate India's sanitiser market that swelled more than fourfold after the COVID outbreak. According to Bloomberg, the size of the category touched ₹43 crores in March 2020 from 10 crores a year ago.

   Last year, Unilever's hand sanitiser business represented an important but small part of their global Beauty and Personal Care portfolio. A popular product was targeted towards hygiene for children, branded to appeal to children with cartoons and clips to hang onto their schoolbags. Sales and market share were stable, and there was clear growth potential, but no one could have foreseen quite what 2020 would bring. In the weeks since COVID took hold, Unilever moved at a pace that was previously unimaginable to help prevent the spread of infections. From 700,000 items a month in January 2020, they went to producing around 100 million items a month and increased production capacity worldwide by more than 600 times in tonnage as hand hygiene became a vital way to fight the virus. The entire value chain had to be transformed, from mobilising people, partners, retailers and resources to scaling up the hand sanitiser production capabilities significantly and to enable distribution to retailers and governments across the globe. They also adapted some existing Unilever sites to produce sanitisers and learnt from existing experts in their deodorants business who knew about working with flammable liquids (like deodorants, hand sanitiser contains alcohol). The company ensured processes and frameworks that enabled agile decision-making and quick deployment of expertise as and where needed. The company sees a high likelihood of consumer sentiment completely changing on this product and the consumption reaching unprecedented heights post-COVID.

4. Essential services: Fresh food supermarkets, convenience stores and online sellers of essential fast-moving consumer goods (FMCG) and over-the-counter (OTC) pharmaceuticals have seen a significant surge in demand as more people stay at home and stock up for emergencies.
5. Cybersecurity: The World Health Organization reported a fivefold increase in cyberattacks in April 2020. The disastrous spread of COVID became an opportunity for cybercriminals to spread malware or to launch cyberattacks—malware, email-based, message-based and phishing attacks, fake mobile applications, Malspam, UPI payment frauds—every form of attack saw a steep rise during the pandemic. In short, while the coronavirus was busy infecting human life, cybercriminals were making hay and infecting computers and phones.

   In such a scenario, cybersecurity shot up in CIO priorities, having to quickly gear up with the must-haves such as multi-factor authentication, virtual private networks (VPN), real-time security monitoring, multi-point network backups and cybersecurity software such as antivirus, anti-malware, firewall and also appropriate employee monitoring software.

While the sheer number of options in tools and technologies is huge, having a comprehensive remote working strategy is vital, and so is having the right IT infrastructure in place. Collaboration and work being limited to the 9 AM to 6 PM office hours is a thing of the past. Teams are connected at all times—checking emails, reading texts and sending messages. Round-the-clock support and a simplified and seamless managed IT solution is crucial for businesses to succeed in this decade and in the ones to come. While this has been a growing trend in the past decade, it has become an imperative now more than ever before.

6. E-commerce and supply chain transformation: With the pandemic came the need for isolation and looming uncertainty, and as a result people hugely changed their shopping behaviours. Bulk buying to online shopping—people literally changed what they were buying, when they were buying and how they were buying, just with one announcement of a lockdown. Non-essential businesses were asked to shut, and customers generally avoided public places. Limiting shopping to plain essentials is becoming a new normal. The retail industry is witnessing a tumultuous turn. No events to attend, no workplace to go to, no social interaction, nowhere to drive to—what then would be the use of the Guccis, the Zaras, the Marks & Spencers or the recently launched Mahindra and Mahindra off-roader, the Thar Stallion?

   Just citing a few examples: in the luxury segment, Vogue Business projects a potential loss as great as $10 billion for this industry in 2020 due to COVID. Department stores such as Macy's and J.C. Penney, large chains such as Abercrombie & Fitch and Nike and DTC brands with some storefronts such as Rothy's and Everlane all closed their physical stores and facing losses. Some stores such as Patagonia planned to halt even their online stores to protect all workers in their supply chain.

   On the flip side is an unimaginably high demand for essentials, with more people staying at home and focusing on basics, such as groceries, medicines, self-care products and hygiene. How can the supply chain adapt to the demand spike? Adding further complexity to the supply chain is how to keep the supply cycle clean, zero-touch (as touch is the worst enemy), efficient, timely and local. A BigCommerce survey reveals that e-commerce sales are not higher across the board, although some industries are seeing significant upticks. This is especially true for online sellers of household goods and groceries. JD.com, China's largest online retailer, has seen sales of common household staples quadruple over the same period last year. A survey by Engine found that people are spending on an average of 10–30% more online.

Market research company Nielsen identified six key consumer behaviour thresholds tied to the COVID pandemic and their results on markets:

- Proactive health-minded buying (purchasing preventative health and wellness products)
- Reactive health management (purchasing protective gear like masks and hand sanitisers)
- Pantry preparation (stockpiling groceries and household essentials)
- Quarantine prep (experiencing shortages in stores, making fewer store visits)
- Restricted living (making much fewer shopping trips, limited online fulfilment)
- A new normal (return to daily routines, permanently altered supply chain)

A WHOLE NEW WORLD POST-COVID

These unique situations arising from the COVID pandemic have created huge waves of change that have swept the world. The pandemic has coerced the world to think differently about everyday situations, about how we work and how we live in general. It has questioned our practices, our perspectives, our priorities. And through these dire circumstances, we are already seeing innovation mushrooming at every level—individuals, families, organisations, economies at large.

There has been a stark redefinition of needs and how they are met. And in that has arisen a demand for drastic change.

Learning from the lessons of past epidemics and the current one that our generation is witnessing first-hand, there is a clear case for rapid innovation across the board. An opportunity now exists for creating lasting sustainable solutions, solutions and innovations that future generations are going to cite as an outcome of COVID. The time is now.

Some of the innovations that we are already witnessing as a result of the coronavirus include the following:

- Using low-cost toaster-size ventilators or scuba diving kits with 3-D printed valve.
- Converting thousands of Indian railways coaches into isolation wards on wheels, making it easier to reach the remotest part of India in the hour of need.
- Developing full-body protection suits in Defence Research and Development Organisation (DRDO) using the adhesive used to build submarines.
- Repurposing sugar mills and distilleries to manufacture hand sanitisers.
- Using robots in countries such as Taiwan and Singapore for collecting samples and dispensing foods and medicines in isolation wards.
- Using geo-location mapped selfies effectively in South Korea along with electronic fencing based on a user's cell phone location to ensure social distancing.
- Showing positive development in workplaces, which will grow once the world gets back to the 'new normal'—teams will be more connected, have more empathy for fellow workers and build a get-things-done attitude, no matter what the situation.

This pandemic will bring a culture of innovation to the forefront of the business of the future. Several companies are openly sharing their patents with competitors to accelerate our response to this pandemic. Such companies will be recognised by society for their empathy, collaboration and activism, and their business is bound to flourish.

We already have smaller manufacturers and larger firms such as the American Inovio Pharmaceuticals Inc. and the German Richter-Helm Biologics working together, as well as larger firms collaborating with each other, such as Sanofi

SA and GlaxoSmithKline Plc, to accelerate COVID-related manufacturing. Private entities and universities have also come together, such as the Pune-based Serum Institute of India and the University of Oxford, who are co-developing a vaccine dubbed ChAdOx1 nCoV-19.

HOW WILL ORGANISATIONS ADAPT TO THE NEW NORMAL? WHAT CAN WE EXPECT? HOW WILL COVID CATALYSE INNOVATION IN YOUR ENTERPRISE? HOW WILL YOU CHANGE AS A CUSTOMER?

The coronavirus will enable innovations that will change our way of life. A few examples we have already seen are mentioned here.

Communication in Remote Working

Humans need to express their emotions to communicate their message. With everyone working remotely, there could be an accelerated acceptance and launch of services around virtual events and online experiences, such as hologram imaging-based meetings enabling people from all parts of the globe to connect remotely but still ensuring the experience of an in-person meeting. Video meetings have already become all-pervasive, from senior citizens connecting with their concerned children in different cities via Zoom to kindergarten students attending online school via MS Teams. These experiences are bound to get richer.

Collaboration platforms such as MS Teams have already launched several new features and offered their service for free to many sectors when earlier they charged a hefty license fee. Zoom, which got instant popularity as the go-to video platform, initially buckled on its security and faced a lot of flak, but they were quick to respond, and the world understood as they requested time to fix the security issues and they did. A host of other platforms already exist in the market, such as Highfive, WebEx, GoToMeeting and some others that are being launched as we speak to capture the virtual collaboration space.

As a response to the pandemic and the resultant work from home, Globant, a digital technology company, emphasised the need to ensure their employees were productive even working remotely, when informal face-to-face interactions are no longer possible. Their belief is that productivity dropped with the initial WFH move, and they needed a platform that would mimic spontaneous dynamics which were a key source of innovation—they called it Augmented Collaboration.

Zensar Technologies, a digital transformation services company launched 'Everywhere Experiences' to render what they call hyper-personalised and immersive experiences for the audience, bringing them together from anywhere virtually and building new interactive digital connections.

Communication-collaboration-interaction-connection-spontaneous-personalised-immersive—are all going to be the operative words to make the remote world productive and effective. And technology is going to enable a meaningful shift in the post-COVID era.

Online Delivery

In the era of social distancing, supply chain and retail have a huge charter of transformation ahead of them. Contactless delivery will be a common requirement in the new phase. Drones that are ubiquitous gimmicks at trade shows may just take centre stage and may see technological advancements that help them fly longer distances, pose less threat to air traffic or less distraction to regular traffic, handle more weight and have advanced real-time traffic management systems.

Food delivery companies quickly adapted to the needs of their consumers, who had grown wary of eating food cooked outside their homes and were turning to them to have groceries brought to their doorstep. Swiggy, a much-used food delivery app, instantly launched the Swiggy Genie service on the same app. This allowed their patrons to have their groceries delivered. They had the supply chain sorted out; they had a captive audience that already associated with them as a food source. This was a master move and worked well for Swiggy, if not in sales, then for the brand for sure: they were seen as a brand that was empathetic and adapted to the needs of the consumer instead of pushing what they had to offer.

Many brands started communicating more and being transparent on their zero-touch supply chain, the body temperature of the delivery person as they left the source of the delivery.

When courier services were put on hold, many companies were quick to adapt and build partnerships with local networks to ensure swift delivery.

How can we address online delivery without a mention of Amazon? Amazon has faced much criticism in recent months along with being accused of not caring for its employees and putting their health and lives at risk. Meanwhile, the e-commerce giant claims that they are doing everything to take care of their employees. They recently announced 'Distance Assistant', a tool to contain the spread of coronavirus in its warehouses. It provides visual overlays on a screen to show how close people are to each other: those maintaining required distance are shown with green circles around them, while those too close are highlighted with red circles.

Robotics

Robotics is no more an element of science fiction. We now see real-life applications in multiple COVID-response scenarios, a few of them being as follows:

1. Robots in the frontline: Robots are being used to clean and disinfect areas where humans are at potential risk. In some cases, robots designed for this function are being deployed, but in others, mobile robots and drones are being refitted, repurposed and redeployed. This is no longer a scene out of a sci-fi movie. Most businesses where human contact is not mandatory or regulatory could well be replaced with robots in the next five years, and this pandemic will only accelerate their adoption. So, the next time you go to a restaurant, you may be placing your order on a tablet on the table and have your food delivered by a robot.
2. Logistics robots: From service robots delivering food and other essentials to drones and mobile robots delivering medicines and consumables such as Personal Protective Equipment (PPE), robots have a clear role to play in the movement of materials

and products. They have, for some time, been deployed in warehouses and logistics facilities and are now finding their way into retail, where they can clean, disinfect and scan and restock shelves. This is particularly relevant in grocery stores and will become increasingly important as other facilities reopen.

3. Companion robots: In times of social distancing, when social interaction is difficult and loneliness a real problem, companion robots are invaluable in care homes and other locations where face-to-face contact just isn't possible. This strategy can also be used for medical practitioners to interact with patients while keeping a safe distance for the protection of both parties.
4. Manufacturing robots: Social distancing guidelines present challenges to manufacturers, who are trying to prioritise their teams' safety while keeping the wheels of industry turning. This isn't just a commercial issue: many factories are producing essential PPE and medical equipment, such as ventilators. This is extremely difficult for manufacturers who rely on manual tasks undertaken by lines of operators. Some have had to add shifts to maintain physical space among operators. Those with more automated facilities are adapting more easily, particularly those with more software-driven automation, which delivers the agility and flexibility manufacturers sorely need right now.

With the increased demand for digital transformation, robotics has an essential role to play in the short term, and it has even more to offer in the future. Demand has been steadily growing for a more automated environment, particularly in the manufacturing and supply chain world. What's more, many expect to see a trend away from overseas manufacturing for critical parts of the supply chain. In fact, governments are encouraging companies to strive for a more resilient supply chain that is less dependent on the $4 trillion manufacturing powerhouse that is China. It is unlikely that brands or consumers will want to pay more for their products in a more regionalised supply chain. The only way to compete in higher labour cost regions, such as Western Europe and the US is via digital transformation and automation. And it is those digitally transformed and automated manufacturing facilities and supply chains that will deliver the agility and resilience needed to withstand the next major disruption.

Healthcare

The pandemic is a double-edged sword for the healthcare sector. The sector is facing the worst in terms of infrastructure insufficiency and staff mortality and is really showing us the warriors of today. However, this very sector is also blossoming with innovation, whether through global vaccine research, pharmaceuticals, testing kits, frugal innovation or even telemedicine. Professionals in the sector are not only battling the perils of today but are globally collaborating to fight the disease and to set up systems and infrastructure to handle the future better if such a pandemic recurs.

COVID has undoubtedly created a severe strain on healthcare resources across the country. From small nursing homes and clinics to large hospital chains, all healthcare institutions are operating at minimal capacity as the focus has starkly shifted to treating COVID, while non-COVID patients are restricted to their homes.

This shift is evident in a few trends in the buying behaviour in the sector. Local searches for 'Doctor near me' have reduced by 30%, while online consultations have gone up by 200% in the same period. Similarly, online pharmaceutical sales have skyrocketed, and there's been a 500% rise in the online sales of immunity-related products such as masks and sanitisers. There's also been a clear shift towards teleconsultations and home sample collections for lab tests.

In many ways, the health-tech sector is finally coming into its own during this time of unprecedented crisis, when offline players are struggling with reduced footfall and service fulfilment issues. However, what's been missing in the health-tech ecosystem so far is a comprehensive player that can bring the entire gamut of health services online. Healthcare institutions, from hospitals to clinics to pharmacies to diagnostic labs, will start seeing the impending need to go digital. Digital would help service not just their existing base of patients (now restricted to their homes) but also help reach an all-new set of consumers looking for digital healthcare options. Digital health services include teleconsultation, e-pharmacy, and e-diagnostics, health product sales, AI-enabled digital prescriptions, clinic apps, health screening, corporate care, community care and so on. This sector will hit a huge transformation after being knocked out by COVID. The healthcare sector in any country, developed or not, was just not prepared enough for what COVID brought to them. Significant shifts will happen in healthcare.

Entertainment

One of the biggest beneficiaries of this pandemic has been the host of content streaming service providers such as Netflix, Amazon Prime, Disney Hotstar and Voot, to name a few. Concerts in empty theatres, Broadway shows, cricket matches on empty grounds all now stream right into our living rooms through the television. The latest movies are witnessing digital over-the-top (OTT) releases. This is going to dramatically change the commerce of the entertainment industry and will also put a compelling force on technological developments to deliver seamlessly over the internet even to countries with low speed, ensuring optimisation of data transfer over the internet. The thousands of people who showed their solidarity at stadiums and theatres with a ticket that they bought will have to be given the same or better experience in newer ways.

Celebrities across the world have shown great acts of solidarity to their worldwide fans and have been collaborating in meaningful ways to continue to bring new innovative content and entertainment to their patrons.

Education

Understandably, the pandemic has had an impact on the education sector too, this impact will most likely stay for a fairly long time. This has given a push towards digitalisation of businesses in the education sector as well.

March is a peak in India for student examinations across various levels. In 2020 though the mood was different—that of uncertainty. To study or not? Will examinations be conducted as per schedule or not? Will the year's education be wasted if I am not able to sit for my examination? Everything came to a halt, and a host of questions troubled the minds of the young and their parents alike. Full marks though to the education sector that took a couple of months to realise that things were not going back to the old normal anytime soon. While decisions were made in favour of the students, giving them benefit of doubt and ensuring the year was not wasted, constructive and swift decisions were made for the upcoming year as well. Teachers, educationists, e-learning companies, collaboration technology companies went on overdrive and came together to build a plan for the young learners, the results of which most parents are witnessing today. Online classes are conducted for students across the board, the content from textbooks has all been streamlined to suit the online medium, teachers have been trained to handle their students online and children have easily adapted to the new ways. The digital medium has achieved nothing short of a miracle to ensure uninterrupted education for children the world over.

There is significant opportunity to enrich learning, whether in terms of content, online experience, engagement, review system, peer-to-peer collaboration for students of all ages and so on. But what is right is that the platform is set.

Of course, there are glitches. Technology and networks don't always hit perfection, children don't get to throw paper planes at each other. However, it wouldn't be farfetched to say that in many ways digital education could play the universal leveller. The platform is here, the purpose is here, and with the right intent, there is huge potential to create equity in the education meted out to students from cities to villages, from the haves to have-nots.

BUSINESS CONTINUITY PLANNING (BCP): REDEFINING THE BASICS

Many organisations that were fence sitters regarding their digital transformation plans have made decisions overnight in the pandemic environment to adopt a digital agenda and have digital as their top priority.

But the COVID blow has driven firms back to the basics and has led them to introspect on existential questions when it comes to the business, on whether they can continue to operate with the status quo and whether they are equipped to survive this pandemic.

The erstwhile lacklustre part of the IT industry service portfolio was business continuity planning—that line item in the proposal that must be there—that everyone knows must be included in their plans for statutory and compliance reasons. But let's say it was a tick in the box at least. A recent study reported that a mere 12% of all global organisations were really prepared for the impact of the coronavirus. Many organisations have adopted BCP in varying measures, but very few BCPs prepared firms for something as sudden and shocking as COVID, which had mighty global firms look like a deer in the headlights. The need for a robust BCP has now become a top priority for firms. And we're only going to see that intensify in the months to come.

Talking of existential introspection, at this trying time, there are a few questions at the top of the minds of leaders who are concerned about business continuity:

1. Does the firm have an empathetic leadership and the right culture to handle employee needs?
2. Does the firm have adequate collaborative technology to enable employees to work from anywhere?
3. Does the firm have a distributed workforce with the availability of right skills from any shore?
4. Does the firm have a combined force of human and machine workers?
5. Does the firm have a distributed global services model?
6. Does the firm have adequate enablement for an agile and elastic model through the right technology, data, security and cloud computing?

WHAT IS IT ABOUT CRISES THAT ACCELERATES INNOVATION IN ORGANISATIONS?

According to a Harvard study, four key shifts occur during a crisis that foster conditions for new thinking and acting. Understanding these can help leaders seize the opportunity to drive useful change.

Uniting Around a Purpose

Inspiring engagement and generating positive energy towards organisational goals is a key leadership challenge. During a crisis, there can be a massive spike in workforce energy to resolve the crisis, finding more than just a wellspring of energy and discretionary effort—they will often experience a wave of new ideas as individuals feel compelled to share insights they normally would keep to themselves. Such was the case on the Apollo 13 mission that was upended by an explosion on board, forcing NASA engineers to improvise to save the crew. The team successfully rallied to design a makeshift device to remove carbon dioxide from the air so the astronauts could survive the trip home using only items available to the crew onboard the lunar module. A crisis can create organisational courage to take actions in support of a purpose that would be unthinkable in times of calm.

Seeing the System Differently

Just as we bring in external consultants for a fresh outside-in perspective to find opportunities to innovate, a crisis can have much the same effect, putting the spotlight on vulnerabilities and problem areas great and small that we've been ignoring or are just plain unaware of. When a crisis hits, we are forced to confront the truth about how our systems work (or don't). The places where things could be done better or more efficiently become glaringly obvious. All of a sudden, opportunities for innovation are staring us in the face.

Unfreezing the Organisation

As organisations grow, they harden their structures to create predictability, efficiency and stability. Crises change all that.

For example, the COVID crisis has upended, globally, the way that grocery chains manage inventory, a process that has been refined over many years to maximise profitability by carrying smaller inventories and turning that inventory more quickly. With the huge spike in demand for products, purchasing managers have bypassed these finely tuned processes in favour of shortcuts that much more quickly source larger quantities of products. The bureaucratic overhead of review and approval for dramatic change has been effectively dropped, allowing fresh thinking to be applied quickly to address the challenge.

Creating a Bias towards Action

Crisis demands movement and change—the pace of ideation, decision-making and implementation all increase dramatically. An organisation that normally gets trapped in 'the intense study of the obvious' must now force itself to quickly experiment, analyse results and experiment some more. This process of experimentation allows the freedom to test different thinking, to fail fast, to learn and to move forward—in short, to innovate rapidly and as a timely response to the problem.

SO, WHAT'S NEXT? HOW SHOULD ORGANISATIONS EQUIP THEMSELVES?

With this backdrop of shocking experiences and learnings that crisis has always brought with it, we have seen how organisations and governments have adapted to changing times. COVID shook supply chains to shrink at a whim and expand exponentially at a whim. The dynamics of the customer journey has been changing radically, both in the B2B and B2C realms. If anything, the pandemic has shown businesses how to reach out to customers and help them in whichever way possible.

How and when we engage with our customers has changed abruptly, leaving us with little time to prepare, react and respond. Omnichannel experiences have been buzzwords for a while now, but the adoption has been an option that some exercised and some didn't, while others did in small measure and yet others led the way to define what omnichannel really meant. However, with this pandemic, there are no prizes for guessing who might have survived, who might have not and who might have led among the above mentioned.

Businesses with a direct-to-customer channel have been able to adapt in an agile manner to their consumers far more than the ones with monolithic infrastructure. Some may have been able to expand to the increased traffic at the switch of a button, and some others may have collapsed with the spike in load.

It might be worthwhile to sit back and think which of the various services we use as a customer rose to the occasion and how in these times.

- Who had an omnichannel experience planned such that regardless of whether you were in the store or the safe confines of your home, it left with you the same smooth experience?
- Who had the data to ensure they were properly tracking, analysing and measuring and had insights on you even while you stayed home and changed your buying pattern in that time?
- Did they see you evolving as a customer with the pandemic and have a 360 view on you?
- Who gave you a new experience as a customer given the shift the pandemic caused everyone?
- Who adapted to give you more interactive content on digital platforms, such as maybe a 3-D graphic of something you wanted to buy but couldn't go to the store to check out like you would have done before?
- Which of your service providers still asked you to give cash on delivery (COD) and didn't have a contactless payment service?
- Who amongst your service providers spontaneously partnered with local providers to ensure you got your delivery in tough times with the same in-app experience as before?

This pandemic has tested organisations on how agile they are, how adaptable they are, how well they understand customer journeys and to what extent they would go to support their customer base on their changing journeys. These customer journeys will continue to evolve in more intense and dramatic ways than we can predict today. COVID has already proven how dramatic that can be, and its effects on consumer behaviour in all likelihood will continue long after the crisis. We can't be sure of how and how much the customer journey will change in the times to come after the quietening of the COVID storm. We can however be sure that change of some sort is imminent, that change is a constant and that a significant amount of innovation is going to be centred around enhanced digital engagement with consumers. Many businesses may have to adopt a drastic digital reengineering strategy that enables them to quickly adapt to change, to build future-proof foundations with modular systems that can be easily replaced or extended to handle any future major disruption or crisis and act with resilience and efficiency to delight their customers.

3

The Evolution of Digital Technologies

In the beginning there was information, and then came an array of information technologies, each seeking to harness the meaning that lay in all the data that firms would generate and classify and store as information. As more and more intelligence crept into data processing and real contexts became important for developing actionable insights from the data, knowledge management became the watchword, and many tools and technologies emerged that made this the area to watch in the 1990s and even into the first decade of the new millennium. And then came the word that would transform everything and rewrite the story of stakeholder journeys, business processes, prediction of performance, prescription of behaviour and transformation of culture. Nothing would quite be the same again after wave upon wave of digital started transforming the social and business landscape.

Viewed from the C-suite, it would appear that the jargon thrown around by CDOs, CTOs and savvy CIOs are just one confusing jumble of new words and is best left to them to put the jigsaw puzzle together and bring an unwilling organisation to digital transformation. However, if one understands the phases through which organisations have welcomed and then incorporated digital, the whole array will begin to make sense, and incorporation will also become easier and business-led rather than technology-driven.

Let us first make a simple distinction that will help us articulate the technologies in this chapter in a simple, succinct and understandable manner for the benefit of the CXO community who are the target audience. In our experience, most members of this community are digital immigrants who started their careers in the fine era of paper reports and electronic data processing. It was only in the 1970s and even the 1980s when minicomputers appeared in organisations and brought computing power out of the glass-walled temples of data to the factory and office flow. Personal computers brought the same technologies to our desktops, and with our computers getting connected with local and wide area networks, the power of computing and communication was suddenly at our fingertips.

Contrast this with people born after 1980, the millennials, and the Gen Z, born after 1995. Being 'digital natives', they cannot even understand the world before the personal computer and the mobile phone. They take all new technologies for granted, and they are the new employees and customers of most organisations. It is essential to understand their language and their expectations for any business to be successful today and definitely in the future. The waves of digital that started hitting us in the 1990s and have transformed the world of work must be understood in that context.

FIRST WAVE OF DIGITAL: THE SMAC STACK

Digital became a serious concern when the opportunity came up to convert CAPEX to OPEX and delayer the large computing departments and functions that seemed to be adding significant overheads to business organisations.

When IT spending was focused on onboarding, maintenance and upgrade of physical machines and servers, the spend came under capital expenditure (CAPEX). With new areas such as cloud and on-demand IT services, from computing power to storage, there has been a significant shift in the nature of the expenditure. Organisations are increasingly moving their data and applications away from the data centre and into the cloud. They favour the flexibility it gives them to scale dynamically with demand and offloads the risks associated with investing in their own infrastructure. As businesses now pay for the computing services they need when they need them, IT spending is transitioning into operational expenditure (OPEX). Yet this transition from a well-governed CAPEX model to a fluid OPEX model can be challenging for any finance team in organisations.

The SMAC stack started the technology adoption processes for organisations—Social, Mobility, Analytics and Cloud. In terms of availability and adoption, Cloud and Mobility probably came first, followed by the spread of the business use of social media and the capture of data from multiple sources that made its use and dissemination, after suitable analytics, a key differentiator of successful digital organisations.

Cloud

Cloud computing became a topic of interest for IT organisations over a decade ago as the internet started moving from a medium for email to serious business applications. With early movers and cost aggregators in the internet era, Google and Amazon building massive infrastructure and taking over the hosting of software applications, infrastructure and even multi-company platforms on their industry strength server farms, it seemed possible that the much-awaited commoditisation of IT would begin. If we need electricity, we just get a connection, we don't install a power plant. Why then would we have data centres and servers installed in our organisations when the plant equivalent was being set up by well-funded aggressive companies? Why indeed would we not trade CAPEX for OPEX and eliminate one large infrastructure item from our balance sheets?

Cloud computing took longer than anticipated to become mainstream, primarily because the bogey of data and information security got raised by sceptical security and risk management groups who painted a sordid picture of market-sensitive company data leaking out of shared data centres. It took time for the believers to point out the investment in security made by large vendors was substantially higher than any one corporation could ever afford, and in that sense, it was safe as Fort Knox to keep your data with trusted vendors, much safer than inside your own organisation, where it would be subject to hackers and data pirates penetrating weak firewalls at will.

The nomenclature 'cloud' originated from the concept of a bubble that contains non-critical stuff that the user does not have to worry about. While this may not strictly be true, cloud computing has indeed taken much of the storage, processing and usage of data, software and hardware from the realm of the business user and the IT function to a third-party service provider.

The precursor to cloud computing was data processing bureaus, which rented out large computer time to clients who did not need to buy such a computer for their limited data processing needs. The advent of minicomputers and personal computing and later corporate data centres made these bureaus obsolete, and almost the entire capital and operating expenditure on IT in large corporations moved to in-house facilities. Towards the end of the dot-com boom in the late 1990s, utility computing and application service providers began questioning the validity of keeping all this capability in-house, and the move to cloud computing followed early in this millennium with software as a service catching the fancy of early adopters and becoming mainstream, particularly in the last decade.

With the rapid rise in capabilities, investment power and security of large external data centres of Amazon, Google, Microsoft and other lesser-known third-party entities, it was only a matter of time before corporations would realise the futility of creating large on-site computer architectures and decide to move everything possible to the cloud. Commercially, the advantage of only paying for what is used rather than incurring large capital expenditure on software, platforms and infrastructure has made the option of cloud computing even more compulsive.

Today the range of cloud services is truly extensive. Apart from email services and simple back-up and storage services, organisations are using the cloud for core business systems as well as all support functions. Available cloud computing services range from simple storage and processing to artificial intelligence and natural language processing. Hardly any form of computing needs physical proximity, so there almost everything can be safely and profitably moved to the cloud.

Companies are accessing cloud computing through three modes:

1. Private clouds, where security obsession prompts companies to set up a fully gated facility for their own infrastructure, data and applications and keeps business functions and stakeholder interactions away from any potential privacy concerns;
2. Public clouds of the type provided by the major players through their high-investment high-security server farms, where all the hardware and software infrastructure are taken out of the company into the third-party facilities;
3. Hybrid cloud, where organisations retain mission-critical or sensitive applications on their own servers and move non-critical work to the public cloud.

Community clouds also exist, where applications are shared across multiple companies serving a similar category of customer or even sharing a processing software that serves a cluster of small companies on a shared-platform basis.

Services used via the cloud largely includes simple software as a service, where software can be used on a subscription or pay-per-use basis and the customer always has access to the latest version with security and maintenance, including upgrades becoming the responsibility of the service provider. The next to move to the cloud has been infrastructure. Most major servers and data centres have moved to the cloud with access given to every user from as thin a client as possible, including the ubiquitous mobile phone. Platform-as-a-service has been a natural evolution from this with the creation of an on-demand environment for developing, testing and managing software applications and in some cases, shared platforms across organisations using the same service provider.

Finally, a natural level of abstraction from platforms has been functions as a service, where functions are created and pre-loaded in a repository to be called and used by application developers when triggered by certain events. In recent times, both microservices and application programme interfaces are an essential feature of large packages delivered to clients, which enable interoperability between service providers. For example, a large production scheduling application for discrete manufacturing industries may only have product-specific features written, functions such as a bill of materials explosion could be a microservice and access to pricing data could be from other third-party applications accessed through APIs, for application programming interfaces, a software intermediary that allows two applications to talk to each other.

Cloud computing has now become mainstream. The analyst firm Gartner predicts that global spending on cloud services will soon be over 300 billion US dollars. A large portion of this is by vendors, including the very large software firms that now offer only cloud versions of their products, since the selling and servicing of one-off on-premise licenses are very cumbersome in comparison to more predictable and scalable cloud subscriptions.

Why has cloud computing taken nearly two decades to reach this level of universal applicability and acceptance? After the initial security concerns were addressed, the lack of a visible investment proposition made cloud computing drop from the attention of top management of companies. It is only in recent years, with cloud computing becoming the only game in town and the aggressive visibility of Amazon Web Services, Microsoft Azure and Google Cloud that leadership has begun to take note of platform use rather than projects to be sanctioned. Platform ownership is now assigned, particularly for those platforms that impact customers, supply chain partners and employees and ongoing funding is being reviewed consistently. The CXO suite needs to continually assess the business domains that can benefit most from the scalability and innovation that cloud platforms can provide and ensure the benefits are delivered.

Mobility

The next technology to go mainstream was mobility as the proliferation of smartphones and their increasing capability of acting as a telephone, camera, music and movie player and data manager rolled into one made all the legacy equipment go increasingly out of fashion. Most importantly, the Mobility phone provided convenient and easy access to customers of the business to engage and transact commercially with merchandise providers and also provided ease of access and interaction for every stakeholder, internal and external, with internal service providers.

At the risk of sounding simplistic, it would be good to trace the evolution of the mobile phone from a simple adaptation of the telephone with the ability to make and receive voice messages to what it is today—a device for communication, information, entertainment, education and even enlightenment. The popularity of the mobile phone can be evidenced by its spread: from its inception in the 1980s to reaching 20% of the world population in the 1990s to proliferating with over four billion mobile telephone subscribers by the year 2008. Soon the number of phones will surpass the population of the world, although every individual may not possess one.

Today mobile phones are ubiquitous because of the efforts of mobile network operators in a highly competitive environment to divide the geographical coverage area into cells, with multiple smaller cells in high-density areas to ensure minimum drops as phones move from one cell to another with relatively seamless handovers. The transceiver base stations in each cell that establish and maintain the wireless connection to every mobile phone in the network are what currently make this form of communication the most sought-after medium of communication.

The reason for its popularity is not just price or size, though those are very important considerations in poor countries such as Kenya or Columbia or India, but also the ease of use and convenience as a connected device. From the world of PCs and modems and connections to the internet, we have moved to a seamless internet connection, albeit at some cost. While this cost can be fairly significant in the case of travellers, the sheer joy of being 'always on' and being accessible and have access to every aspect of life and work is great. The most obvious manifestation of the power of the mobile phone is the central role it has played in India in the famous JAM trinity—Jan Dhan, which was the promise of a bank account for every citizen; Aadhaar, or a unique identity for each individual and the access device, the Mobility. In every way, this positioning epitomises the value of the mobile phone in every aspect of life and work in our times.

Mobility has changed India in four ways. First, connectivity has become affordable. As a result, it ceased to be a rich man's monopoly long ago. With cell phones now becoming multifunctional with mobile internet, the floodgates of human creativity have opened. Lastly, it has become a catalyst for enrichment and empowerment of common Indians in ways unthinkable 25 years ago. In COVID times, it was telecom services that kept the wheels of the economy and communications between individuals going.

Taking inspiration from this memorable journey and the position that mobility has acquired, digital success in the industry will be built on the bedrock of a world-class connected digital ecosystem of the future with the help of every player ecosystem of an organisation, a community or even a country and the world.

Social

Social media came along initially as a medium for people to exchange messages, jokes and pictures with friends. But with applications such as WhatsApp and facilities for telephonic audio and video conferencing, serious business started getting transacted on the mobile phone. Paper exchange first gave way to email, then email was slowly relegated to just another option by WhatsApp and video conferencing. It would be hard to imagine a world today without Google Hangouts or Microsoft Teams or Zoom, with early movers like WebEx and Telepresence being upstaged by more nimble and aggressive entrants to the collaboration space.

Investing in social media is now an imperative for reaching out to customers, listening to all stakeholders and being available to them around the clock, from selling ideas, products and services to providing service on demand. From the days of the humble website, which was a somewhat static mode of delivering the core message of the brand, the opportunity and the imperative to get closer to present and future stakeholders, whether shareholders, customers, supply chain partners or employees, to the modern-day proliferation of digital marketing, there are four core reasons why social is an essential part of every firm's business strategy: creating a market entry strategy for a new business or presence, differentiating from the competition, providing a capability for customers and stakeholders to interact with and make demands on the company and finally, the ability for the company to evolve and rise beyond its own self-limited boundaries. Let us look deeper into each of these areas.

Awareness and brand building are undoubtedly the core objectives of any business activity, and communicating the brand promise and personality without ambiguity is the first principle in modern business. This is especially true as every customer or prospect has a thousand distractions and is more and more inclined to pull what they need from the internet while shutting off all attempts to push selling messages on them. One of the old truisms of marketing was that you should never expect the customer to automatically beat a path of gold to the man who makes a better mousetrap. Creating an outreach mechanism that ensures targeted, attractive and faster communication and evokes the desired response should be the prime focus. Brands will have to be very clear on what makes buying decisions happen in a customer journey because having a large number of likes for a brand advertisement on a social media platform does not imply higher revenue. The connection of social success with search engine optimisation, giving more opportunities for the brand to pop up in front of a customer, is of course the subject of ongoing research.

Telling the brand's story is a critical success factor in good marketing and creates legends around a brand that demonstrates its passion and brings to life the people and incidents behind its success. A good story makes a brand and a business stand out more than multiple clever marketing lines or brand pushes.

Differentiating from the competition and presenting a distinctive 'point of view' to discerning customers is also one of the key attributes of successful social media marketers. Building networks with frequently visited sites and engaging with social influencers is an expensive but proven method of using social media for measurable benefits. In these days when all information is just a Google search away, being perceived in searches as superior to the competition is important, as is ensuring that reviews of a product or service are better than the competition, ideally in as ethical a manner as possible without being accused of having planted anything. Customers must believe that the business is innovative, responsive and will truly care for them during and after a purchase.

Tracking the activities of competition meticulously and learning as well as reacting to their tactics are essential. The ability to understand the competitor's positioning and to use clever social media messaging and influencers to reposition them such that they are less appealing to customers are what good advertising was about, and with the interactive power of social media, this becomes a total imperative.

Evoking a response from consumers in this world of excessive social media messaging is not just a function of the message itself but of deep research into preferences across demographic and geographic differences. A case in point is the great work done by campaign strategist David Axelrod in the first Obama presidential campaign, where research equipped them to send out specific messages to people in Southern states just a couple of hours before the closing of voting booths to give the final push to people who were sitting on the fence on whether to vote and who to vote for. For B2B marketing, the science of inbound marketing to persons within a target organisation who would be most likely to be key influences or decision-makers has become more important than outbound marketing, which can often be an expensive hit-and-miss game. Backlinks, shout-outs, increased referral visits and word-of-mouth measurement are ways to maximise customer response to the brand.

Responding to customers with speed and authenticity both for good and bad feedback builds a company's success over the long term. A 24×7 culture instilled in all customer-facing activity, for sales or service, will help in creating and maintaining a two-way relationship. Social listening technologies that we will cover later are also an excellent addition to customer service capability. This also means training employees to be able to respond to live feeds of data and information and not wait for pretty analytical dashboards that may come too late. The science of digital data engineering comes into play here, and new practitioners are making this come alive for customers.

Evolving to new services based on interactions with customers is the ultimate goal of using social media to build a relationship with customers and other stakeholders. As we go through this book, we will see how artificial intelligence and predictive analytics can play a major role in this. Increasingly, the linkage between physical visits to a display area and price discovery or purchasing decisions is evolving all the time. Predicting and even facilitating different customer journeys will be the key to future success. Many businesses are moving towards user-generated content and crowdsourcing ideas to ensure that they widen audience participation and offer credibility as a key brand value. Getting users to send in comments, videos and their own content is what made TikTok such a favourite brand in India and the US, and in any consumer-oriented business, getting more and more participation is emerging as a key to success.

Maximising the use of social media to build and promote the brand and building favourable consumer opinion in both B2B and B2C formats will prove to be a key differentiator in the times to come. Of course, marketers should remember that one bad experience can be devastating for a highly visible brand and should ensure that the brand promise is always backed up by impeccable service delivery and superior products. And since nothing happens in isolation, the brand must ensure that the messaging on social media mirrors the perception created by all other channels for two-way communication with customers and thus build and sustain a beneficial relationship with markets and customers.

Analytics

One of the early entrants is the 'A' in SMAC, which stands for analytics, and it is still evolving. Data was always seen as important, but in the early days of treating data as a commodity and relying on information and knowledge, organisations lost the ability to garner intelligence and actionable insights from the data itself. It is only after the term 'big data' was coined and data locked in myriad databases started flowing into more accessible data marts and warehouses did we see phrases such as 'Data is the new oil' entering the corporate lexicon. Corporate strategists could fish into these data lakes using business intelligence tools, and dashboards and other visual forms could be created with presentation software, firmly establishing the era of descriptive analytics. Both data and analytics for sales, production, finance and any other area were always available with a single click.

In the early days of information systems development, and later in the realm of knowledge management, researchers and practitioners were very clear about the progression through what was called 'the D-I-K-W quartet'. Data, when classified, became information, and when context was added to the information, it became knowledge. In our own work in research and writing on knowledge management (*Knowledge Management*, McGraw Hill, 2005), we developed two hypotheses that became the subject of PhDs in one of India's reputed technology and management institution, IIT Bombay. The first hypothesis was very similar to the five-stage Capability Maturity Model for processes developed by the Software Engineering Institute of Carnegie Mellon (popularly known as SEI-CMM). There could be four identified levels—initiation, assimilation, expansion and maturity for knowledge management. And the second hypotheses suggested key factors such as technology, processes, leadership and culture, which could provide the needed push from one level of maturity to the next.

Organisations starting focusing on big data, and traditional databases naturally evolved into data marts and data warehouses for large organisations. And the fishing rods that were needed to capture the data from these huge lakes and oceans were the business intelligence tools of the 1980s and 1990s. To put it simply, the multi-billion-dollar market for master data management (MDM) emerged from the need to eliminate redundancy and provide a 'single source of truth' and the imperative to develop a single master reference source for all critical data in the organisation.

Initially developed for large organisations, the operational efficiencies in managing, storing, analysing and disseminating data and information quickly made this a prerequisite for any organisation seeking to use 'data as the new oil' for business.

To ensure that data was made more meaningful for the user, business intelligence (BI) evolved as a method of generating actionable insights from raw data. BI is a set of architectures, technologies and processes that provides actionable insights and enables fact-based decision-making. It has become much more graphical in recent times with easy-to-understand dashboards, maps and graphs that provide a descriptive analysis of performance and insights into the business.

The limitations of master data management and descriptive analytics were exposed as the next array of technologies entered the corporate arena. Today, data gathering, storage, conversion to business intelligence and eventual transformation through artificial intelligence and machine learning to obtain actionable insights has become extremely important, and a deeper discussion follows in a later chapter of this book. At this stage, let us just assume that it is the ability to create predictive and prescriptive ideas for users that truly facilitates transformation in terms of stakeholder delight and operating efficiencies of any firm.

THE SECOND WAVE OF DIGITAL

The second wave of digital can be said to have truly begun after 2012, when many of the large software product vendors started moving their products to the cloud, resulting in lower license prices for customers and substantially reduced implementation support fees. This was also around the time when the early cost models of digital, pioneered by Amazon, Google, Facebook and LinkedIn and further exploited by aggregators such as Uber and Airbnb gave way to a more experience-driven model, led inside homes by Netflix and Amazon Prime services and brought into the homes by online shopping and all forms of e-commerce and mobile commerce. Easy-to-navigate user interfaces and user experience software became integral to the digital transformation experience. With more and more digital touchpoints making business processes increasingly digitally enabled, the proliferation of data made it possible for users to seek actionable insights. Two older innovations in the area of management—business process reengineering and knowledge management—emerged from the woodwork and became increasingly relevant in successful digital transformation.

Four significant technologies could be flagged as the creators and enablers of this second wave—the internet of things, UI-UX, blockchains and artificial intelligence.

IoT

One of the technologies that has been most talked about in the digital domain is the internet of things (IoT). IoT has been accurately named because it literally means the ability of everyday objects in our life and work to communicate and exchange information and data on the internet. Just two examples will bring home the value of IoT, both applications that we have conceptualised with large organisations in Asia and Africa.

The first and the expected example is the attempt of an organisation in India to become totally digital and embrace all smart manufacturing and Industry 4.0 principles. With computer-aided design and manufacturing systems already in place and early investments done in fully automated manufacturing execution systems, the company needed a method of capturing data from every machine and material handling equipment on the shop floor, integrating that with production planning and scheduling systems and creating an optimum machine loading plan for the day. As the equipment it produced was large capital items installed in every part of the country, it also needed performance data to be monitored and analysed in a control tower at the central facility and the ability to send back preventive maintenance suggestions and minimise downtime. IoT sensors everywhere on the shop floor, on every productive resource, all material handling equipment, in the warehouse and on the products before they were dispatched created a comprehensive information interchange system that addressed all these issues.

The second example is in Africa, where a company running a chain of wellness centres wanted to steal a march over competitors and demonstrate that it was much more customer-focused than them. The strategy developed was to spread beacons across every parking lot in the vicinity of each of their health clubs and collaborate with the leading telecommunications provider to access the location of every client and prospect who had shown an interest on any channel in their services. From the time the person drove into the car park, the beacon would pick up her presence and start giving special deal promotions on her phone. And when she walked in, the receptionist would give her a customised plan that showed research into previously reported health problems and a social understanding of the kind of health regime that was most likely to excite her.

What are sensors and beacons? Very cheap data gathering systems that are the front end of a verge marketing or operations management activity. For the data to be truly productive, it needs to be transmitted accurately and in time, processed with algorithms designed to provide the desired insight and presented through suitable user interfaces to make it easy to use. Data gathered by the IoT sensors and beacons can be transmitted to the cloud in many ways: Wi-Fi, optical networks, local and wide area networks and high-speed Ethernet. While the processing of data is quite obvious, the choice of what level of information versus interactivity to provide to users is a critical element of the IoT decision-making or decision support process.

Global examples of success abound. The Shell company in the Netherlands has reported a ten times (10×) return on investment in using IoT for remotely tracking oilfields and the smart asset monitoring application has reported substantial savings and information access for the company. Motorcycle leader Harley-Davidson has used industrial IoT extensively on their assembly lines for both standard and customised motorcycles. They have reported a reduction in operating cost to the tune of over 200 million dollars through data retrieval and usage on the shop floor.

And even chocolate maker Hershey has reported half a million dollars of savings from every chocolate with IoT monitoring over 60 million data points in the chocolate production processes.

UI/UX

With the world of digital moving from cost and productivity improvement to outstanding user experiences, one of the areas which has received maximum attention is designing for superior user experience. This calls for a deep understanding of customer preference and consequent behaviour and also mastery of the science of user interface design.

Designing for user experience starts with a process of determination and prediction of the nature, time and desirable outcome of every user interaction with a product, service or even website or sales outreach that presents the product or service. This also implies that it's a new field of work. But, on the contrary, designing for users has always been intuitively done by trying to invoke the desired response from any stakeholder, whether customer, employee or business partner. Making conscious designs armed with deep knowledge about the impact of sound, sight and colour on various categories of audience is what converts this art into a science.

There are many ways of achieving the perfect user experience, and one known practice is to co-create with the customer so that she is invested in the final outcome. User experience design needs to focus not just on aesthetics, usability, accessibility and other functionality, it should also evoke emotions such as joy and delight. A case in point is a statement by Eric Yuan, CEO of Zoom at the India Internet Forum in August 2020, when he spoke about leaving his employment at a Fortune 100 technology firm because the product he had designed did not make customers happy. Instead, he created Zoom with the promise that everybody would love it for its user interface.

User experience is not just about the user interface, it also involves compelling content in the form of information or education, which can be delivered to the delight of the consumer. A case in point is a learning platform for students in universities and corporate employees called Skills Alpha, which is featured in the skills section of this book. Interaction designers and product managers have collaborated to provide a seamless user experience to the learner from the time an AI bot welcomes them to the platform through a process of motivation, understanding and assistance on the skills journey and enabling peer-group interaction as well as the choice of a mentor. The entire journey and ongoing usage over months or even years is made really engaging by attention to detail in all aspects of the time spent on the platform. The same is true of many social media platforms that people, particularly the young, are spending many minutes or even hours of their day and night on—WhatsApp, Instagram, Facebook.

Effective UX must be created through empathy directed towards solving real engagement problems of customers and community and remove friction in interaction, in turn leading to satisfaction and delight. Well-crafted human–computer interaction is a result of the combined principles of ergonomics, user-centred design and usability principles and ideally generates positive emotions to transform the quality of experience. Logically, good UX can extend to communications even emails and not just entertainment or education experiences. Hence the ambit of user experience is truly vast.

User interfaces can be through graphics, audio and visual input, including gestures, and succeed when they allow a user to get their task done with the least stress. Every element that can make the interface more fun, including gamification, pop-up hints and assistance, can help make user interfaces fun and addictive for the customer.

AI and ML

As already mentioned, artificial intelligence (AI) is the ability to mimic the intelligence and responses of humans to the maximum extent possible. The applications and benefits of AI will be examined in detail in the analytics chapter later in this book. At this stage, it suffices to state that AI is truly a transformative force for business processes, learning and performance management in every field of human endeavour. Machine learning (ML) is a computer's ability to improve with transactions and learn from interactions, responses from consumers and even sentiments expressed in emails and voice transactions.

The reason for the huge fear and expectation surrounding AI and ML whenever they are considered by a function, an organisation or even a country is the dual emotions of the humans being replaced and the increased human intelligence in every field of economic endeavour. As we will discuss later in this book, the push from AI and ML technology will continue to grow. It is the choices we make to use them in an autonomous, augmentative or just assistive manner that will determine the extent of transformation we aim for and achieve.

Historians of AI will certainly record the fact that IBM's Watson, which was the great white hope, launched with much fanfare and initial success. Sadly, it failed to live up to its promise. Today Watson is nothing but a set of disassembled APIs (application programming interfaces) that can find its way into chosen domains, while other hype creators who have promised everything from self-driven cars to fully robotised stores have still to deliver them commercially. However, a number of start-ups have emerged that are demonstrating that AI used to specifically transform functions such as recruiting, customer service and production on shop floors can be truly cost and value optimising.

Machine learning and deep learning have both demonstrated the ability, one with computer data and one with additional inputs from other artefacts to learn and optimise processes. We are just some time away from where computers will not even need to experience a process to learn enough about it and will use judgement to find solutions through some trial and error and some intuition. Machine intuition, now that's a scary thought, isn't it?

Blockchains

Blockchains have for long been the most enigmatic of ideas in the entire stack of digital technologies, but they are actually quite simple to understand. When security or even secrecy maintains that ledgers of information are better kept separate from each other, the technology of storing blocks of information as smart ledgers connected with each other is what makes blockchains so effective for contract management and many other applications in the finance environment.

How do blocks get stored and identified? Digital information is stored in each block, cryptographically connected by hashes that identify the data and provide a timestamp of when it was created. This information gets connected to the chain that creates complete and usable information. Transactions between two parties can hence get recorded in a permanent way that is totally secure and fully verifiable.

Blockchains were originally used interchangeably with an alternative currency called bitcoins, which were frowned upon by monetary regulators. But blockchains themselves will become one of the most efficient ways of storing transactions and ensuring traceability for the future.

THIRD WAVE OF DIGITAL

The third wave of digital started when innovators around the world realised that digital was going to embrace audio visual and other sensory technologies in ways that were never imaginable in the staid days of data processing and office computing. Computer vision made it possible for every shop floor to be equipped with eyes. Once that happened, augmented and virtual reality soon enabled operators and even product designers to look beyond the obvious and create an enhanced and often mixed version of reality. All these capabilities also allowed robotics to automate large segments of manufacturing and even healthcare. Household work, along with the services sector, managed to adopt the same principles to embrace robotic process automation and substantially enhance the productivity of every field of human endeavour. And finally, 3-D printing has emerged, which enables the digital concept of the world to be manifested as physical.

Computer Vision

Computer vision, as the name suggests, is the ability for computers or robots to have the visual acuity of human beings. From the early days in the 1960s, when computers could discern the edges of objects, to the ability developed in the 1970s to use optical character recognition to interpret text, the maturing of the internet over the last 50 years has made rapid image processing a reality, and computer vision has moved to facial recognition and beyond.

The affordability of computing power, the ability to analyse artefacts of all types through deep learning and the ubiquitous mobile cameras and videos have been inputs into processing evolutions in algorithms such as convolutional neural networks to create discernible patterns and images that make sense to analysts on a real-time basis. Today's intelligent computer systems have the ability to 'see' and process images with much more alacrity and accuracy than human beings, and artificial intelligence can also enable almost instantaneous responses and reactions to what is analysed.

The working processes of computer vision are not dissimilar to the way humans approach a jigsaw puzzle. A computer spots images by identifying different pieces and edges, creating sub-components and finally piecing together all the parts of the image. And because computer vision operates on images, it does not need to know each constituent part of the image, human or otherwise, to develop a reasonable hypothesis on the identity. Today, massive increases in computer speeds have further enabled moving images such as a high-speed basketball game to be processed. The day is not far when it will be able to feed new moves or football plays in real time to the players on the field, if allowed of course.

AR, VR and Mixed Reality

We have all heard examples of augmented reality (AR) in training workmen on the internal workings of a compressor or assisting robots to do 'lift and shift' operations in automated warehouses and virtual reality (VR) bringing the Northern Lights to life in the studio in the city of Reykjavik. But the most useful application of VR has been in the city skills lighthouses that the Lighthouse Communities Foundation runs for youth from the slum areas of Indian cities. Designed to overcome the natural fear of a person who has grown up in a small home and has a weak economic background and low self-confidence, this application uses virtual reality to transport the young person into the operating theatre of a large hospital. As the operation proceeds, the youth watches someone who looks like her confidently assist the doctor, take the blood pressure and perform collaborative functions. Without anything being said, the fear vanishes, and the desire to take up a career as a paramedic and eventually a nurse is created. As digital pervades the world, we will see more and more such examples where mixed reality creates a better reality in the real world for all.

In its very elementary sense, augmented reality is just that: an augmentation of reality, where any object can be captured on a camera and any part of the object expanded so as to see and learn from a more minute analysis. AR enables the overlay of enhanced images on real environments, allowing detailed inspection, analysis and decision-making. The benefit so far has been in automated picking in warehouses, teaching and learning in areas ranging from automotive engineering to laser surgery and potentially any area where visual impact is important. Virtual reality can transport a slum-dweller in the city of Pune into the operating theatre of a hospital to watch a patient being prepared for a procedure through her VR headset and effectively simulate experiences that are not otherwise accessible. VR provides an immersive experience, in an operating theatre, in a field from which a nearly 360-degree view of the northern lights becomes feasible and science fiction terms such as 'think gaming' and 'avatars' become part of the daily lexicon of customer experience.

Real estate developers are able to provide a near-real walkthrough of potentially new dwellings, first through VR and then a deeper inspection of bathroom facilities etc. through AR, potentially a marketer's dream. In the current COVID situation and after the COVID pandemic and with disruptions, social distancing and the low likelihood of physical site visits, mixed reality experiences are gaining momentum as an indispensable tool for better marketing. The day is not far when a press release will be in the form of a holographic projection of the company's chairman or CEO presenting a full visual analysis of the company's quarterly results. Brands can also create virtual beings who can represent them and interact on behalf of them, which are a superior version of today's Alexa or Siri or Cortana experience.

Experiencing products without entering a store is likely to be the best example of AR/VR use today and in the future. Busy commuters walking through the myriad Tokyo subways can just scan the QR code of a product or the promotional shop code and access to all the products later from the comfort of their homes, turn the products around, see how they look wearing them and make purchasing decisions. Why would you ever go into a store again? Well, that is a subject for a later chapter in this book.

Robotics

The field of robotics is one that has probably received the maximum attention, prompted partly by science fiction and partly by the very real integration of robots into manufacturing shop floors in every country. A personal experience we have had is a company in Shenzhen China engaged in electronics manufacturing. When we first interacted with this company five years ago, the company employed 5,000 workers, mainly women. They worked assiduously each day with barely a half-hour lunch and nap break. Three years later, the same factory reported that their productivity had more than doubled with the deployment of 1,200 low-cost robots and the number of employees reduced to less than 400. Each woman who remained in employment had been trained to simultaneously manage two to five of the robots and the person–machine interface had been designed beautifully to optimise output while reducing fatigue levels.

So, what is robotics? As the example illustrates, robotics applies engineering and operations management principles to replace human activities in any manufacturing environment. Deep studies conducted on any physically operated process throw up opportunities for robotics deployment, and the design of appropriate human–machine interfaces make a robotics system truly effective. Today, robotics ranges from simple operator-interfaced robots, where the robot plays a purely assistive function for repetitive tasks as instructed by the human, to AI-enabled robots capable of nearly independent operations movement and self-adjustment in the operating situation.

Modern robots are capable of locomotion using wheels, metal legs or even propellers. Some also have mechanised arms, fingers and even claws. Add to this computer vision and robotic eyes and sensory tactile capabilities, and you can have a robot that can mimic a human to a very large extent. Smells is still one area yet to be mastered, but surely that day is not far away with experiments already in progress.

One-way communication with robots typically occurs using programming languages and sensory robots are now able to make simple course corrections when required. Machine learning algorithms are already being used to enable dynamic interaction and robotic learning through previous incidents, which will greatly facilitate their operations in crowded workspaces and unpredictable traffic.

Like any form of automation, robotics has both negative and positive connotations. The obvious negative consequence could be the potential loss of human jobs, but the positive that can and will be considered is the ability to upgrade the quality of human livelihoods by having mundane activities done by robots.

Robotic Process Automation

For people in the services sector or in-service functions anywhere in the world in any industry, the benefits of robotics on the shop floor in manufacturing would have been an inspiration to experiment with the same principles applied to business processes. Robotic process automation (RPA) has truly taken off in a big way. Applied to any repetitive process, RPA streamlines workflows with software robots easily trained and integrated seamlessly into the process with greater accuracy and measurable cost savings. Not only do processes become more compliant and highly scalable, but RPA also frees up innovative thinkers to focus on value-adding work and leave the repetitive activities to RPA.

As the RPA industry has evolved, process robots have demonstrated their ability to learn and mimic even relatively complex processes, involving multiple forms, files and folders. They can deal with both structured and semi-structured data and scraping of browsers to find more reinforcement information. With the addition of AI technologies such as text analytics, optical character recognition and machine learning, cognitive RPA is becoming a reality.

The real success of cognitive RPA is its ability to automate processes that include artefacts such as unstructured data sources, documents, emails and voice and video recordings. Cognitive RPA learns from multiple transactions and interactions, as well as by analysing specific words used in the context of customer service that may sound like a complaint and starts to mimic the response of an intelligent human.

Till very recently, there was always the possibility of an RPA handing off to a human operator in case of critical data missing or even sentiments that seem to go beyond the normal limits. But cognitive RPA has the ability to improve data and automatically convert it from unstructured to structured data using text analytics, natural language processing and machine learning. More evolved RPAs can also make automated decisions, with their decision-making qualities continually improving over time. RPA can also manage omnichannel communications, switching seamlessly between interactive voice response, instant messaging and standard emails and using AI triggers to send the right communication at the right time. When voice is integrated into these communications, one can theoretically eliminate the human interface altogether. This can lead to cognitive automation as well, which will again be a paradigm shift.

RPA is working today in a variety of functional processes, from accounting, legal responses to HR to customer service and myriad industries—retail to banking, insurance and even healthcare. Between robotics and RPA, between processing speeds and AI, there will be almost no function or process that cannot be automated. What will humans do then? We will answer that question, but later!

3-D Printing

The easiest way to understand 3-D printing is to examine normal manufacturing processes. Bars or rods of metal are transformed into objects of use by eliminating unnecessary material with lathes, milling machines, grinders, etc., creating material waste, scrap and pollution. The contrarian approach to creating objects would be to avoid metal reduction methods or subtractive manufacturing and instead turn to additive manufacturing. This is 3-D printing, which can add materials in layers using biomaterials, composites and even plastics to create objects that have the desired size, shape, colour and material properties.

The use cases for 3-D printing are unlimited. In many cities, waste disposal bags are 3-D printed, and applications are being envisaged where materials required for field hospitals can be printed on-site rather than waiting for them to be shipped from the nearest big city. 3-D printing was originally used for prototype development, but it will soon be a mainstream alternative to designing, manufacturing and distributing materials in the traditional way.

FUTURE TECHNOLOGIES: ENABLING NEW WAVES OF DIGITAL

In the last two years and more, an increasing number of organisations have reported real benefits from digital transformation. It would have been futile to expect ongoing investments in digital technologies and indeed to let digital take the lion's share of all technology purchasing if this stage were not realised. This has also led many organisations to start pushing the boundaries of digital capabilities to include, and in many cases accelerate, the power of human learning and adaptation. Social listening, cognitive automation and augmented collaboration are three such areas that are leading organisations to quickly adapt to what they sense from customers, collaborators and employees and respond optimally. And this ability to sense and respond and engage in quick, personalised and adaptive conversations is what the future is going to be about.

Social Listening

An important tool that can guide every product or services company to respond to customer perceptions about your brand or your competitors is social listening. Put simply, this is a capability that has been around for nearly a decade and has become a part of mainstream communications mix in recent years. One social listening initiative we have been involved in was for a large telecommunications and networking equipment company that used multiple social solutions to track all chatter on the internet about their products. The company also proactively used brand ambassadors and influencers who were well-known thought leaders to counter negative brand noises by positive voices put out to mitigate the negative impact and start a positive thread of conversation.

A number of tools have emerged in the social landscape. Hootsuite is a very popular dashboard that integrates streams from various social channels and allows response from one point rather than having to move across multiple platforms. It also provides capabilities to reach out to social influencers and has an insights package that using Boolean strings and keywords to do a pattern or trend analysis and deliver actionable insights to brand managers. Talkwalker, AdView, Review Trackers, Reddit and a host of other tracking and analysis tools make social listening an imperative and easy to implement in an organisation.

Cognitive Automation

Automation, at factory shop floors or in-service processes, has been around for some time and with the lasting effects of COVID, the need for social distancing will be very well served with automation. However, cognitive elements have to be integrated into the automation blueprint of any organisation to ensure that the sensitivity to stakeholders is not lost in the chase for automation. Cognitive automation applies artificial intelligence, natural language processing and machine and deep learning to emulate human intelligence in acknowledging differences in tone of voice, sentiments and emotions and identifies and solves sensitive relationship problems.

Customer service offers the most obvious use case for the application of cognitive automation. By tracking responses coming in through social listening from myriad sources, cognitive automation can divert resources to tackle critical problem areas and can rejig production schedules in manufacturing and supply chain priorities as needed. A McKinsey article has suggested that with the post-COVID disruption of global supply chains, cognitive automation may understand geopolitical sensitivities and transfer a contract to another part of Asia to Malaysia if it senses delays at the port or restrictions to shipping from a specific country.

The power of cognitive automation lies in the fact that it combines the capabilities of two extremely powerful technologies—robotic process automation, whose market size is expected to cross 3 billion US dollars by 2025, and artificial intelligence, which is set to reach a 200-billion-dollar market level by the same time. Bringing near-human intelligence to information-intensive processes will change the world in ways difficult to conceptualise today. To paraphrase a famous Steve Jobs assertion that you can never trust the customer to know what she wants, the digital folks may be justified in believing that you can never trust the C-suite to lay down exactly what miracles they expect from digital, so we should give it to them anyway! With fast-changing demand patterns, it also becomes easier for cognitive automation to trigger proactive measures for supply chain inventory optimisation to ensure high availability and least cost of operations. And what about the people? Handing over automatable tasks and decisions to cognitive technologies will give leaders and managers more time to focus on people anyway!

Augmented Collaboration

In the great move towards work from home (WFH) and the initial euphoria that productivity had not suffered and even improved instead in many services industries a couple of weeks after cities locked down because of COVID, it was forgotten that isolation issues would soon emerge, particularly in crowded cities where WFH intruded into the private spaces of families and lack of contact with colleagues began to affect the quality of output.

Companies such as Globant Inc., a global digital innovations leader, have done pioneering work in augmented collaboration, almost recreating the warm experiences of grabbing a quick lunch together with colleagues or being in an impromptu group around the coffee machine. This is recreated in the online environment with an opportunity to do a 10-minute conversation on non-work-related agendas with a person from the organisation who does not work directly with the individual. The osmosis of ideas is seemingly generated at random, but in reality, there is a lot of behavioural analysis and AI that goes into the picking of these chat partnerships.

One technology that enables such collaborations and the simulation of a real-life workplace is augmented reality. More than a decade ago, CISCO pioneered an amazing video-conferencing technology called Telepresence where it was possible to have five people sitting around a meeting table from five different locations. The experience was so real that after an hour of engaged conversation, people would actually reach out a hand to shake another, only to realise they were actually in different countries. Because of the huge capital expenditure and communications costs, TP rooms were replaced by multiple collaboration tools on the desktop mostly free, but it is important to replicate some of the learnings from that era so that human collaboration truly becomes engaging again.

Quantum Computing

Readers of this book who are interested in particle theory and quantum physics may recall the extraordinary rivalry between two greats Albert Einstein and Niels Bohr when the theory of relativity came head-on with the duality between waves and particles in the first half of the last century. Even though multiple experiments were conducted and schools of thought emerged, that one controversy has never truly been settled. Interestingly, the evolution of quantum computing, while advancing the frontiers of science and enabling digital activity at a frenetic pace, could unravel this mystery of the universe or fall prey to it.

Let us understand the concept first. Quantum computing is built on quantum theory and the assumed behaviour of energy and materials at atomic and subatomic levels. This takes the ability of computers far out of the traditional realm of bits and bytes and the unique values of 0 and 1 encoded in them. The bits in quantum computing have been appropriately named qubits and instead of being in a 0 or 1 state, they have the capability of superposition, by which they can be in both states at the same time. And not only does this capability exist, but qubits can also get connected to other qubits. This 'entanglement' opens up possibilities to solve problems at a speed and at a level of complexity that can only be imagined at this stage.

How does this capability, if fully developed and mastered, help businesses and society to leverage the other digital technologies mentioned in this chapter? The most obvious one is drug research in the pharmaceutical industry. At the end of Phase 3 human trials of a COVID vaccine, it could take companies and countries only a minuscule period of time to analyse the results, draw conclusions and develop a way forward. The same applies to the constantly evolving strategies of hedge funds, advances in material sciences and alternate forms of energy and myriad other industries where multiple data points have to be dynamically accessed, analysed and fed into decision-making processes.

If taken to its logical conclusion, quantum computing techniques can generate as much controversy as the famous experiment in quantum physics where an electron passes through two slits as a wave form and recombines into a particle upon hitting a screen. This seemingly magical method of changing states and embracing alternate forms at will could enable applications of AI that defy current imagination. Potentially the capabilities of quantum computers could far exceed those of normal human beings and call for great care in analysis and a thoughtful approach to deployment when they do get commercialised.

5G

If two technology twins seem to hold the keys to a promised land of computer- and digital-run companies, economies and even lives, they surely are quantum computing and 5G. In the post-IoT world, we will need the capability to seamlessly connect everything and everyone in a global network. That is the fifth-generation mobile network or 5G.

To understand the power and inclusive nature of 5G networks, it is important to understand the evolution that occurred with each generation. The very first generation 1G network in 1979 enabled simple voice communications and mobility, while 1991 saw the advent of 2G digital networks with messaging and roaming coverage. Incremental improvements to data services followed, and 3G in 1998 promised a better internet experience. The mobile apps ecosystem then came to life, creating real value for both mobile phones and high capability networks till we got 4G. This started as a long-term evolution in 1979, when data speeds doubled and serious work moving from the desktop and laptop computers to the now-ubiquitous phone.

5G networks will expand broadband wireless services beyond the mobile phone to other communication modes while still using cell sites and territorial sectors with data coded and transmitted as radio waves and enabling connections through either a wired or wireless connection across the network. Even to the layperson, it would be obvious that to take on a majority of data and business transactions, real-time interactivity and cloud services must be delivered with very low delays or latency. They must also consume low power so that all devices can operate on the network with minimum human intervention. The simple imperative is no performance drops under any circumstances and a fully connected world where every user, whether from home or business or government, should be able to get the power and cost that satisfies them. Applications may require near-zero latency such as fast-driving driverless cars, while some may need massive data analysis such as drug research. It is expected that 5G will cater to both.

If some readers feel that like quantum computing, 5G is also just a concept, some data will be reassuring. Commercial 5G services have already been launched across all continents and were even used by South Korea in the PyeongChang Winter Olympics of 2018. AT&T in the USA, Vodafone in the UK, China Unicom in China and soon Jio in India are planning large launches that may have got delayed by COVID, but we can expect the roll-out to be more standardised and uniform in every country when it does happen.

GETTING IT ALL TOGETHER

If there is one realisation that we hope our CXO reader would have got from this technology landscape, it is that for every problem, stated or yet to be manifested, there is a technology solution. The rapid changes we expect to see in future in terms of sheer data capture, information processing and storage and transmission power will make information travel at the speed of thought. In fact, there is an unproven allegation that many of the telecom companies are 'doing a Tesla' and creating solutions that might take away the power of choice. Imagine a digital moment when you just think of a person and your thought waves are automatically connected for sharing of ideas. Of course, that would need great disciplining of the mind to control what you think. If that happens, the mobile handsets that proliferate in every part of the world could be put out of business by neural networks.

Real and meaningful applications emerge when the smorgasbord of technologies we have discussed in this chapter come together for end outcomes. New product designs can be experimented with through virtual twins, and an actual walkaround may happen around a holographically projected product. A new store could also be simulated for customer experience during a future potential journey to be charted out. New tools are available to make remote training much more engaging with collaborative whiteboarding of ideas and changes made interactively to new designs. But are just newer and newer tools enough?

In the early days of business process reengineering in the early 1990s, when thought pioneers such as Michael Hammer and James Champy shocked organisations who were happy with their incremental innovation efforts, it became evident that in many traditional organisations, decision-making loops were orthogonal to the flow of work, causing delays when managers waited for approvals before getting on with customer-oriented order fulfilment imperatives. The MIT in the 1990s had already predicted that the world would go through five stages in the management of technology—localised exploitation, internal integration, business process reengineering, business network redesign and business scope redefinition.

THE IMPORTANCE OF GOVERNANCE: CYBERSECURITY

Cybersecurity

In this chapter, we have been through the exciting showcase of digital technologies. Many more are to come as the pulls of environment and customer demand call more for more and more product innovation. However, there is one cloud that already hangs over the open methods of running organisations and societies. That cloud will get darker before the digital light can fully shine through. It is the cloud of data and applications being compromised and confidential information leaked to the wrong hands. As the years have passed, cybersecurity has gained in importance and will be a key imperative for the arsenal of tools and techniques deployed by leaders in digital in the years to come.

At the simplest level, cybersecurity encompasses the entire body of processes, practices and technologies that can protect critical hardware, software and data employed by the enterprise from being attacked by hackers or data thieves through unauthorised access and damage. The security envelope needs to encompass internal databases and warehouses, all software applications, infrastructure and platforms, whether hosted on-premise or on the cloud, networks, the private or hybrid cloud being used and even the internet of things that connects various devices of the organisation.

With the rapid proliferation of the internet, various kinds of malware have recently wreaked havoc, ranging from simple viruses to ransomware, spyware and Trojan horses. While firewalls and other protection devices are deployed in all large establishments today, often the best way to completely protect from malware is malware isolation, which prevents any access to critical applications or data till a thorough check has been done on incoming communications. This ensures that nothing unauthorised can enter and remain on institutional or personal devices. One reason for the acceptance of cloud computing in recent years and the use of public clouds such as those hosted by Amazon, Google and Microsoft is that organisations have realised that the investment needed to completely protect digital crown jewels is likely to be more robust from these companies who have their reputation to protect rather than it will be in-house.

Truly, digital is a wonderful journey. But like all journeys, the knowledgeable and well-prepared are likely to be more successful and reap the maximum benefits. For that, technology must be selected carefully, deployed well and used in conjunction with stakeholder needs, data requirements and the careful management of processes and culture to ensure it is best utilised. More of that as we progress!

As we progress through this book, we will demonstrate with examples from implementers and service providers how real change can happen in processes, networks and business through the intelligent use of digital technologies. Any set of technologies needs to be responsive to the changing needs of all stakeholders—employees, supply and demand chain partners and collaborators. Multiple new methods are available that we will explore here.

It has been said that digital technologies today can enable us to be limited only by the power of our imagination. As you continue reading this book, let your imagination run free and dream on!

4

Design Thinking and Customer Journeys

So ok, you have an idea! You come up with a brilliant and original application that you think will solve your business problems. There are currently no identical solutions on the market, and the one which comes close is not really working the way that customers expect it to.

While the idea is still sizzling in your mind, you start to think, 'In how much time will I be able to launch this idea?'

And since budget and time are always finite resources, the second thing that comes to mind is, 'How much will it cost me to put this idea to action?'

Both are fundamental questions in the making of an application, but they only come after another very crucial question,

'What value can my idea create for the users?'

And this is the only question that stays through the business lifecycle, every step of the way. Not just at inception but every step of the way—every idea's continual endeavour is to look to add value and improve the experience for the customer.

Digital reengineering is reinventing business practices to continue to add customer value. In today's world, technology is constantly changing and improving. To keep up, organisations must be agile and innovative as they integrate these digital technologies into their business practices to stay relevant and competitive. Once the digital reengineering choice is made, the transition from business as usual to digital-first is an uphill task. The digital world shifts rapidly and unpredictably, much more than other worlds. Keeping up can be a challenge, leaving many organisations unsure of how to proceed. This is where design thinking features prominently.

Design thinking is a five-step, user-centric design methodology that does not present a solution upfront but instead examines both present and future details of a problem or need, exploring alternate solutions. It is a methodology that provides a solution-based approach to solve problems. It focuses on understanding the user perspective, with a human-centred point of view. The power of this methodology is the possibility to test quickly if an idea, solution or enhancement can bring our customers real results. Integrating different methodologies, tools, and techniques from different fields (marketing, psychology, design, business), the purpose of design thinking is to put the user at the very centre of the problem we have to solve.

Digital reengineering presents complex and undefined problems. So, using design thinking to embrace your organisation's digital reengineering helps tackle these problems through a fluid, flexible and hands-on approach to interact with customers and come up with solutions.

Design thinking comprises five steps: empathise, define, ideate, prototype and test.

EMPATHISE

The digital reengineering agenda is based on creating a superior customer experience. And this experience cannot be visualised in a box. It needs stepping into the customer's shoes, to empathise with them to understand their drivers—the motivation, need and pain points. The problems we are solving through our enterprise are seldom our own, and hence we should not risk presuming how the customer will act.

Instead, observe as they interact with your product or service. Take note of every move—what they search for on Google or on the site; study clickstream data to see how they are engaging with your site or app; mine chat logs to see what they are asking your customer service agents and even directly interview customers to ask what experience they are looking for. See the problem in context to identify patterns, ask questions and challenge assumptions. The key is to get up close and personal.

Gaining an authentic and deep understanding of where the customer's friction points are along the digital journey will get you the information you need to successfully solve their issues.

A.G. Lafley, a past CEO of P&G and the person responsible for bringing design into the organisation, shared a powerful insight in an interview many years ago which is still relevant. His design thinking manifested in his store visits to see how P&G was looking on the store shelves. He would often take designers along with him. He said that they would observe the shelf in a very different way and helped him see how the customers see the products as opposed to how he saw the shelves as a businessman. This convinced him that design had a lot to offer the company, that marketing may not supply. Once convinced, he set about creating the internal conditions for design to thrive within P&G.

Lafley almost literally stepped into the customer's shoes. Through his design team, he got a professional perspective to help design solutions for his customers.

DEFINE THE PROBLEMS

Defining any problem brings clarity to the problem and hence sharpens the solution. The insight gained from the 'empathise' stage will help you pinpoint where to focus your time and energy. This information can be analysed to formulate the problem statement in an accurate and comprehensive way. This problem statement should be focused on a specific issue and geared towards the user. The key is to be specific. This stage can be overwhelming, as you will discover a multitude of problems that need attention. However, the aim of this phase is not to overwhelm you, but to find and prioritise all the problems discovered into individual, manageable bite-sized opportunities.

IDEATE

Half the battle is won with a well-articulated unambiguous problem. The next step is to generate ideas on how to fix it. The ideation phase must necessarily involve collective thinking to develop a diverse set of creative ideas. The ideas should be sought not just from the team responsible for them, but cross-functional teams, and in a collaborative atmosphere. This phase is not for overthinking nor to limit yourself to one solution. The ideate phase should be quick, creative and, most importantly, collaborative.

One must not belittle the huge intangible cultural value gained through the process of ideating collaboratively. There is a singularity of purpose, richness of diversity in ideas and thought, sense of involvement, pride of ownership and several other intangibles that benefit from this step of collective ideation. Through this stage, you are also building a culture conducive to creativity.

PROTOTYPE

Problem defined. Ideas generated and shortlisted. Time to hit the lab for a proof of concept or what is called the minimum viable product (MVP). In this stage, the team will experiment with various simple and inexpensive models aimed to quickly test and validate your solution ideas. Prototypes should be tested on a small set of users, either with usability testing or on a narrow selection of your site visitors.

Observe the way people interact with the prototype, then collect feedback and use this information to adjust and optimise the next model. This phase is ideally very fast-paced, with quick and efficient improvements. It is critical that these prototypes be built in a safe environment, where it is acceptable to fail and learn from those failures and continually progress in the search for the ideal solution.

At the end of this phase, you should have a good idea of what works and doesn't work and how the actual customer will think and feel when interacting with your service.

While here, picture a warm cookie sample being distributed at the bakery—they want us coming back for more. And we go back with the feeling that they care about their customers.

TEST

Continuously testing your various prototypes is an opportunity to improve each time. Every interaction with a customer is a learning opportunity to enhance the customer experience. In the testing phase, you capture the information needed to revisit previous stages in the design thinking process.

In today's world, adopting digital reengineering for all business practices is a must, and design thinking methodology is an effective way to tackle the problems this phase presents. Adopting this customer-centric method will effectively aid you as you incorporate digital technologies into your organisation. You can't take shortcuts in achieving this, however, as it is one of those things that is the simple to understand but most complex to implement.

DESIGN THINKING: LEAD FROM THE TOP

Solving a problem for a customer or meeting a customer's stated or unstated need is the first step to any business, and design thinking is a creative approach to problem-solving. Questioning whether design thinking is essential to the business is equivalent to asking whether creativity is needed in solving a problem. And that's the difference between enterprises that adopt design thinking and those that don't—creative problem-solving keeping the customer in the centre.

A growing body of evidence suggests that CEOs need design thinking and solutions in their organisations to become successful and that it is the most important factor for success as times become more complex, ambiguous and the solutions to problems less certain.

Many studies have reiterated that creativity ranks amongst the top crucial factors for business success, even above popular choices of management, discipline, integrity and even vision. A big reason pointing to that choice is that creative leaders are more comfortable with ambiguity and uncertainty than their counterparts.

A study over a 10-year period observed that the success of design-led companies is 200% greater than non-design-led enterprises.

Even with so much evidence pointing to the design thinking imperative, it is still not ubiquitous across organisations and industries. The answer to that enigma is that design thinking is not as simple as it sounds. It needs unique conditions to thrive in. Many organisations pay lip service to design thinking when in reality they are not fostering the right culture for innovation and instead focus largely on efficiency at its cost. Innovation means something new happening across the organisation and making space for creativity. Sometimes, it literally is a space, an atmosphere to experiment, fail if one must and continuously learn. It also means to have the right enabling structures, availability of the right skills and the way teams are brought together.

The leadership needs to buy into design thinking and the value it brings. The attitude that goes with a focus on business success, efficiency and results is to also reduce risk, which is a barrier to creative thinking. Creativity is long-horizon thinking, which also means sometimes compromising on immediate results, which most leadership easily shies away from. Successful companies figure this out and make the right space and conditions for creativity, setting their eyes on the results that it can deliver over that long horizon.

The answer lies in controlled risk-taking in order to take bigger steps forward in creating value while not risking the entire enterprise. The culture of the organisation needs to be design-friendly. All levels of the company need to be empowered and given autonomy—the permission to act when they see opportunities that you probably don't. There is a need for a completely safe environment to fail without fear, a need for the entire team to be aligned to the customer, and that must be the sole purpose that drives the organisation as a whole.

To manage this fine balance is where the involvement and commitment of the CEO is critical. Design thinking/innovation/creativity needs to have a champion supporting it from the top. This is often absent, which is why so few companies succeed in creating a design-led culture.

Creativity is what most often drives the differentiator in the organisation. Take Apple, oft-quoted amongst top innovators. Creativity has given Apple its competitive edge over decades and inspired an unparalleled and consistent end-to-end user experience; even its brick-and-mortar stores are as clean and modern as the products it sells. But one can't become an Apple by imitating Apple. Design thinking culture has to be built and nurtured organically, and the journey is unique to each enterprise.

How Apple CEO Steve Jobs led this creative thinking from the top is no secret. He famously said, 'Design is not just what it looks like and feels like. Design is how it works.' And how it works for the people it was made for—not technologists, product managers, sales, marketing, engineering development, production or any other internal stakeholder.

Design is important, only and only because it is vital to the customer experience, to solve the customer's problem or meet the customer's need.

DESIGN CAPABILITIES: BUILD OR BUY, BUT NURTURE!

The principles of design thinking when applied to strategy have shown to drastically improve innovation and organisational success. Design-led companies have reported over 200% higher returns than their counterparts, thus indicating a high correlation between design thinking and successful business execution. With an increasing demand for digital services, IT service providers and consulting companies are building design thinking capabilities to support their clients with more design-oriented solutions. A large number of award-winning creative agencies and design start-ups have been acquired by them. Most of the acquisitions are focused on growing their digital services portfolio.

Given the digital reengineering imperative and the key role that we have seen design thinking play in managing digital reengineering, a significant trend has emerged to create a potent force combining technology, design and business. Towards this, most large companies have either acquired design consultancies or developed in-house design teams. This trend complements their current service offering with a service that will make it more valuable for clients or open new revenue streams.

There are many ways to skin a cat—companies such as Johnson & Johnson, Capital One, Facebook and Google have built their own in-house design units. Other IT and management consulting firms have acquired design shops such as Google (Mike and Maaike), Facebook (Hot Studio), Flextronics (Frog Design), Global Logic (Method), Wipro (Designit), Accenture Interactive (Fjord and Insitum), Cap Gemini (Idean), McKinsey (Lunar), BCG (AllofUs), Accenture (Karmarama), Salesforce (Sequence). The third category is of advertising and marketing firms such as WPP (Centrale Holding).

Whether built or bought, a very real dilemma is how these design capabilities are to be integrated and nurtured within the organisation. To successfully integrate design studios/teams, acquirers need to be mindful of retaining that elusive 'culture of design'. Some companies let the design studio operate autonomously without shaking up the creative culture. This is a service that cannot be commoditised and must not be commoditised as a rule. Accenture, for example, is credited for leaving Fjord's carefully nurtured culture alone. Other integration strategies include giving design a seat at the table and empowering them with autonomy. For instance, big organisations may be tempted to integrate their technology and design teams and may be compelled to push technology partners onto their new design teams. This can be an option, but the designers need to retain their freedom to recommend what they think is the best fit for a specific problem.

Big companies also need to ensure design is embedded into the company's entire culture. Bringing in a design team is not a quick-fix solution; design needs to influence everything from product and service creation to launch and delivery to the customer. It cannot be a retro-fit but instead needs to be integral to the entire process right from inception.

SUCCESSFUL APPLICATIONS OF DESIGN THINKING

Digital reengineering redefines ways of doing business today in a manner that helps the organisation stay relevant, create value by saving time, improve decision-making through data and insights and to primarily enhance customer experience. With the plethora of technology solutions available today that are radically transforming business, it is no wonder that digital reengineering sits high on all business leaders' agenda.

Pursuing a digital reengineering strategy comes with several challenges, which may include resistance to change, lack of a clear vision, data overload, inflexible development processes and constantly re-evaluated business models.

Design thinking has emerged as a key forward-thinking tool and mindset to help overcome these challenges and accelerate the timeline for transformational work. It is a human-centric, collaborative, action-oriented process with a set of techniques and tools that helps an organisation drive change, and all this as a continual process and not just as a flash in the pan.

It would be interesting to study a few organisations that successfully implemented design thinking as a core business strategy.

Daimler

Very recently, when Daimler embarked on a transformation exercise, it underwent several paradigm shifts and one significant shift was from 'requirements analysis' to 'design thinking'. They worked on the 'One Touch Retail' project, a multiyear digital transformation exercise intending to develop an innovative and intuitive digital assistant for salespersons to replace the legacy system, making the sales process more effective, and allow salespersons to work closely with their customers. The one touch retail (OTR) platform was to also give them far more flexibility and agility to changing automobile market requirements. It required the whole firm to stop thinking 'we know our customers' needs intimately—we have been doing this for 20 years', and instead build a new openness and come to the realisation of, 'we simply cannot know every requirement'. They leveraged design thinking principles to build that openness in culture and a platform that was technologically agile enough to incorporate any learnings on the customer and deliver a superior experience.

This paradigm shift towards design thinking was supported by the application of four catalysts:

1. A radical process simplification, reducing complexity and duplication of tasks, allowing greater automation of simpler processes;
2. A shift of focus from the project and towards the product itself;
3. Using speed as a strategic advantage, e.g., to implement customer requirements promptly in products through continuous delivery;
4. The willingness to fearlessly question existing rules and processes and to learn from mistakes and feedback.

Ulbrich

For nearly a century, precision metals manufacturer Ulbrich Stainless Steels & Special Metals, Inc. has embraced innovation, growing from a small-town supplier of military cutlery into a global development and supply chain partner with 12 locations in five countries, spanning the metallurgic aerospace, automotive, consumer electronics, industrial and medical industries. Now looking to take their next step in innovation, they partnered with design consultancy Digital Surgeons to make their business evolve and digitally transform it to better meet the needs of their customers and employees.

Despite being experts in manufacturing, Ulbrich was struggling to deliver a cohesive digital experience that supported the needs of their various sales teams and industry partners. This meant multiple platforms, fragmented domains and a practically non-existent conversion funnel. Ulbrich needed a connected digital experience that could foster better lead generation, enable their sales force and share their history-rich products and services portfolio so they could continue to shape the world for years to come.

With a design thinking approach to customer immersion and stakeholder identification, Ulbrich was able to define and prioritise the business objectives, allowing the design of a brand and marketing roadmap that culminated in a fully refreshed CMS-powered digital experience. The new Ulbirch.com became a connected CRM-led 24/7 sales vehicle built to help them reach and engage with customers and prospects all over the world at any time of the day.

- Their visual language was inspired by physical manufacturing.
- A scalable, product-powered digital experience was crafted.
- New revenue streams were unlocked through business model innovation by tapping into their expertise, which was their key strength (and not just the metals).
- The new experience was to put to test.

Starbucks

If Starbucks believed that introducing a mobile app was equal to digital enablement towards better customer experience, they would have done it. COO Kevin Johnson sums up what they did best: 'Where others are attempting to build a mobile app, Starbucks has built an end-to-end consumer platform anchored around loyalty.' The company's main innovation is their mobile order and pay app. This is fundamentally a customer-first strategy, as it addresses the basic wants of the consumer: convenience, line avoidance and so forth. Coupled with their extensive loyalty programme, the app gives Starbucks the perfect platform to upsell and market to consumers. Furthermore, the app funnels back massive amounts of user data to the company, allowing them to better understand their customers' habits and desires. Starbucks believes customer convenience will be a key driver of revenues for Starbucks in the future. With a voice-based ordering system, the company is looking to make this option more personalised, just like talking to a barista. This is a sign that Starbucks is committed to innovation, both at its stores and in technology to enhance the customer experience. This should drive growth for the company in the long term. Design thinking is uniformly applied across their store plan as also their online platform. Hence the same superior and seamless customer experience across channels.

Tata Trusts

Design agency Tinker Labs worked with Tata Trust on its Project DRUV to get rural India on the web. The challenge was to increase adoption and sustained usage of an internet device in rural Rajasthan, India. Through an intensive business process redesign, social impact programme design and customer experience design, Tinker Labs and Tata Trusts were able to craft strategic solutions for different time horizons. These were aimed at bolstering installation of the device and the early exploration phase and strategically re-examining partnerships and future technology transformation.

They conducted an on-ground culturally immersive research, user journey mapping, and found some clear opportunity areas: (a) giving women safe spaces to learn and not feel judged; (b) enabling exploration of content in a group setting to create shared learning and (c) creating a DIY hack for troubleshooting.

Through a focused endeavour on these opportunity areas, detailed solutions were found for an improved customer onboarding experience, content curation and user interface. The team overhauled the organisation partnerships with the telecom sector, with the content partners, NGO partners, etc. Finally, they had a roadmap for core technology alternatives as well.

MassMutual

The insurance company MassMutual was looking for a way to convince young adults to buy life insurance. Determined to design for action, MassMutual teamed up with the design firm IDEO to create a programme to persuade people under 40 to purchase life insurance. The result of the partnership is a programme called the 'Society of Grownups', which was conceived as a master's programme for adults. It resembles an online class with digital budgeting and financial tools plus a curriculum for investing.

Fidelity Labs

Fidelity Labs, the innovation lab of Fidelity, has eight global locations, 150 people, and over 200 patents. The three foundations of Fidelity Labs' design thinking methodology are 'scan', 'try', and 'scale'. They first 'scan' across industries to find opportunities for innovation, then 'try' to quickly prototype and test products with customers and finally 'scale' by identifying opportunities and delivering them to their 22 million customers and partners. From their work with bitcoin to helping to lift the burden of student debt, design thinking plays an important role in informing the output of Fidelity Labs.

PepsiCo

In her 12-year tenure, PepsiCo CEO Indra Nooyi grew the company's sales by 80%. Design thinking was at the core of Nooyi's tremendously successful run, with design having a voice in almost every crucial decision the company made. When she originally decided that the company needed to rethink its innovation process and design experience, she started out by giving each of her direct reports an empty photo album and a camera and asked them to take pictures of anything that represented good design. When she saw the uninspiring results and when she realised that every time she tried to talk to her employees about design, they would want to talk only about packaging, she realised it was time to hire a designer. 'It's much more than packaging. We had to rethink the entire experience, from conception to what's on the shelf to the post-product experience.'

As an example, she pointed to the Pepsi Spire, a touchscreen fountain machine the company developed. Other companies focused on adding a few new flavours or buttons, she noted, but 'our design guys essentially said that we're talking about a fundamentally different interaction between consumer and machine'. 'Now, our teams are pushing design through the entire system, from product creation to packaging and labelling, to how a product looks on the shelf, to how consumers interact with it', she said.

Salesforce

Salesforce.com, a market leader in the cloud-based customer relationship management (CRM) industry, is constantly threatened by new, value-based start-ups across the globe. To maintain its leadership position and increase consumer loyalty, Salesforce uses a human-centric approach to help clients solve some of their most challenging problems. The company develops customised solutions and innovative products that allow their customers to get closer to the end consumers. For example, Salesforce helped transform the online consumer engagement for Adidas by combining data and technology to personalise content at scale.

SAP

Enterprise software company SAP is a pioneer in applying a human-centric approach to drive innovation. In 2003, Hasso Plattner, the co-founder of SAP, helped launch the Hasso Plattner Institute of Design at Stanford University. He then sent his leadership team to train there in order to diffuse a design thinking mindset throughout the organisation. SAP's design journey led it to become early adopters of Agile, which later became a revolutionary software development framework for the world.

Coca-Cola

Coca-Cola is one of the most recognised global brands in the world. With that status come many challenges, including how to execute a vision across 200 countries while simultaneously developing localised products. In the early 2000s, Coca-Cola made the strategic decision to use design thinking principles to become a nimble organisation with a seamless brand experience throughout a global portfolio. One solution that emerged is a digital visual identity system that transformed the creation and marketing of products. This digital transformation of internal systems has led to localised products that also communicate a single global brand.

DBS Bank

DBS Bank redefined the consumer banking experience in Southeast Asia and is now considered one of the most innovative banks in the world. DBS realised in 2010 that the digital revolution will inevitably impact the banking industry. The company's leadership embraced this challenge and reconfigured the organisation end-to-end, including internal systems, consumer experience and data use. From co-creation to journey mapping to design spaces, the company has incorporated design toolkits throughout its value chain to transform consumer interaction.

L'Oréal

L'Oréal partnered with Valtech to effectuate just such a digital transformation. They wanted to become the No. 1 digital beauty brand in the world and deepen brand loyalty and improve the online experience for their billion-plus consumers. L'Oréal wanted to move from 'business as usual' to 'digital first'. It was an ambitious plan that meant refreshing and relaunching 600 websites for 15 brands in 60 countries in three years. The project started with partnering with Sitecore to develop a 'website factory' that would serve as a marketplace of reusable web templates and functionality. Individual L'Oréal brands across 60 countries, each with widely varying needs, would use the website factory to create and deploy websites quickly and easily. In other words, the website factory, in itself a sophisticated programme with many agile components, powers and drives the digital transformation throughout the company. As such, it required an efficient, strategic and innovative approach to change. Rather than aiming for perfection with the website factory, the focus was on enabling brands' quick and correct web implementation.

Two factors influence the digital transformation: (a) design thinking, which depends on digital transformation, as they work together. The duo is helpful for most companies but thrives in more mature and agile corporations; (b) finding the right balance between business and user experience and asking questions such as 'Who are our users, and what problems are they facing?' and 'How are we promoting the design to boost consumption, engagement and improve performance?'

And when design thinking and Agile were applied together, it created a mutually reinforcing environment focused on user-centricity and rapid iteration as a means of reaching optimal outcomes. Design thinking brings a strong user focus while Agile is an excellent way to incrementally deliver solutions, ensuring user needs are kept front and centre throughout the entire design and development process.

Bank of America

In 2004, two Bank of America (BoA) vice presidents, Faith Tucker and Ray Chinn, put together a team of product managers, finance experts, software engineers and operation experts to brainstorm. The team held 20 sessions and generated 80 product concepts. They favoured one idea: the 'Keep the Change' programme. 'Keep the Change' is a service that automatically rounds up all purchases made with a debit card. These rounded-up cents are transferred to a savings account.

So how would this idea come up without watching, observing the customer, who is so far removed from the physical bank? Here's the back story.

Bank of America was especially interested in the customer segment of boomer-aged women with children. To conduct the required ethnographic research, a team of five BoA employees partnered up with four agency designers. In their user research, the group conducted interviews and observed families in Atlanta, Baltimore and San Francisco.

According to IDEO designer Sally Madsen, the team was 'talking to people who were great at saving, and people who struggled with it, taking inspiration from some of the existing, everyday habits people have around savings'. They observed a dozen families and followed mothers around when they went shopping or dining. Soon, they spotted an interesting pattern: in many families, mothers were in charge of managing finances. An extreme group in this pattern turned out to be single mothers, who are often on a tight budget and have to meticulously track their spending.

Many of these women kept chequebook registries, in which they listed their bills, expenses and ATM withdrawals. At the beginning of the 2000s, this was a common way to manage money, a time before widespread banking apps and online banking. When the design researchers looked at the chequebook of a woman in Atlanta, they realised that she rounded up numbers: instead of listing 22.73 dollars for a refuelling bill, she listed 23 dollars, for example. This simplified calculations, but it also added a little buffer each month. In the end, a few unexpected dollars were left over for her. A second, important realisation concerned the inability of mothers to save. Some of them simply did not have enough money to put anything aside, others could not control their impulse buying. The researchers realised that this behaviour revealed an unaddressed need in banking and offered the opportunity to create value for customers and the bank.

Once the 'Keep the Change' idea was mooted, a prototype of the service was tested. The team created a cartoon video displaying the rounding-up service and tested it through an online survey with 1,600 participants. After an extremely positive response, 'Keep the Change' was pitched to the consumer division and got approved. In an iteration of the idea, the product development team added three features, as a Bloomberg case study describes: first, a summary of the rounded-up transactions in the account; second, a feature preventing a rounding-up transfer from pushing the user's account into overdraft; and third, a promotion. As a treat, Bank of America matched the saving at 100% for the first three months up to a certain amount.

The 'Keep the Change' service turned out to be a huge success for Bank of America. After its launch in September 2005, the programme attracted 2 million customers in less than a year. Since then, more than 12 million customers have signed up for the programme and saved more than 2 billion dollars in total.

As much as 60% of all new customers enrol for 'Keep the Change', and 99% of customers who signed up for the programme stayed with it.

Closely observing user behaviour and interpreting their workarounds was a crucial step leading to this successful outcome: 'People couldn't tell us that they wanted a debit card that would "keep the change". It didn't occur to them,' IDEO CEO Tim Brown said in a Forbes interview. 'But we saw how many people were rounding up to the next dollar when they paid for things.' He describes that the success of this innovation lies 'in its appeal to an instinctive desire we have to put money aside in a painless and invisible way' in his 2008 *Harvard Business Review* article. According to Sally Madsen, the 'Keep the Change' programme 'meets Bank of America's goal of generating more business for their savings programmes, but it's also something that meets a core basic need that people have, which is finding ways to manage their financial security'.

Bank of America's former Senior Vice President and product developer Faith Tucker underlined the feeling of empowerment for Bank of America customers in a Design Better interview: 'There was an almost unexpected and very emotional effect from this new service. People who previously never had savings suddenly did. And it wasn't the amount that mattered; even a small amount of money in their savings account gave them a sense of power and control over their finances.'

THAT WAS THEN. AND THIS IS NOW

In the entire narrative in this chapter so far, the protagonist of our story has been the customer—the same protagonist is a starkly different beast today who is cocooned at home and only connected to the outside world via devices. These devices though are sending out hundreds of thousands of signals out on her behaviour, his mood, her aspirations, his retail needs, her hunger pangs, his job hunt, her favourite IPL cricket team, his favourite series on Netflix and much more.

Compare that to the isolation of the Spanish Flu or the Black Death discussed earlier, when this plethora of information was non-existent. Businesses today have the good fortune of having the opportunity of knowing the customer even remotely, just as the customers are much more fortunate today in having services at their doorstep that will keep them from going hungry and provide entertainment at their fingertips, all while continuing to have a job that they can handle via a WFH or which is more fashionably called WFA (work from anywhere) now.

But of course, in the absence of good digital engineering, all this data could be vapour for the uninitiated enterprise, a lost opportunity.

Customers today are always connected, are highly impatient with poor experience and are sorely spoiled for choice.

And the newest customer has changed even more drastically in a matter of a few months, a few days or we daresay, literally overnight. COVID has caused extended lockdowns, pervasive uncertainty and sustained attention on health, immunity, self-care and fitness. All of these factors are reshaping customer behaviour. The challenge for companies is to understand which customer trends and patterns will endure over the longer term. In this scenario, how can companies adapt to the future that is unfolding as we speak, and more pertinently, how soon?

Enhanced Engagement

Digital engagement has accelerated tremendously, and leading companies have innovated quickly to replace or augment traditional in-store experiences. Out of necessity or convenience, companies have created many new offerings. Indeed, 80% of companies believe that their core business model should be digitised to remain economically viable.

Increased Safety

Companies must build safety into the customer experience, especially in the near term. Rethinking contactless commerce to promote safety across products, services and processes will be critical to putting customers at ease and increasing their satisfaction.

A four-part framework can help executives select, prioritise, and implement the solutions that matter most to customers.

Analytics

In the next normal, companies will need to be more proactive and nimbler as well as anticipate customer expectations and needs. Now is the time for executives to invest in the data, technology and systems required to deliver exceptional experiences. Organisations that understand customers better—and do it faster—are likely to be the next customer-experience leaders.

The impact of COVID on customer behaviour has been massive and immediate. Spending across most industries is down, purchases have shifted from in-person to digital channels and public safety has become a top priority for companies and consumers alike. Executives who had carefully crafted omnichannel strategies to create unique, compelling customer experiences have had to throw out their playbooks and improvise to keep pace. Some companies have just had to perish as they were just not ready for this onslaught of uncertainty.

CUSTOMER JOURNEY MAPS

For companies that drew out customer journey maps, this is a good time to return to the playbook and remap customer journeys.

And for those who are unprepared for this discussion on customer journey maps, a customer journey map is a visual representation of the customer journey helping map the customer's experiences across every single touchpoint with the brand, lending a 360-degree view of how the customer engages with the brand.

Here is a brief glimpse of the steps involved in customer journey mapping:

- Set your targets. It's easier to navigate when you know the destination you're headed to.

- Create detailed buyer personas. Who is this person interacting with the brand?
- Identify motivations and pain points. What's driving the person? What's the problem or need?
- Map out the buyer's journey. When, how and how frequently does the buyer interact with the brand?
- Find your moments of truth—a term coined in 2005 by Lafley, Chairman, President and CEO, Procter and Gamble—referring to the specific touchpoints that mark the switch of the phase in which the customer is in on her/his journey with the brand.
- Revise. Make the necessary changes. Evolve. Adapt.

Journey maps could be a great resource, especially in times of change like these. How has the current environment impacted your customers' experience of your brand? The maps will help with the following:

- To find points of friction for your customers so that you can reduce the effort for them;
- To uncover duplication of efforts or ways siloed organisations create inefficiencies or irritations for your customers;
- To stress-test new processes, products, services or offerings for your customers;
- And to envision long-term changes to improve the experience for all your customers.

Journey maps are not about the final deliverable, nor are they in themselves the desired outcome. They are a way to understand your customer's real journey, not the one you assume is happening. That knowledge can inspire actions throughout your organisation to create better experiences that lead to real business outcomes.

As COVID sends the entire world in a spiral, multiple things will need to be addressed about your customer. A journey map could help find many of the solutions to the issues and can help set immediate goals. For example:

- If the priority now is to review expenses, a journey map can help identify points of high and low expenditure and identify areas of cost reduction.
- If the priority is to find ways to improve customer retention rates, journey maps can help identify points that hold high potential in terms of customer value.
- If the priority is to launch a new product or find a new audience segment, a journey map can help provide a more seamless experience to customers.

For your journey maps to be rich, consider gathering data in three categories:

- Customer feedback and emotional data,
- Customer behaviour and actions and
- Systems, procedures and touchpoints.

Once you have your map, it is ready for action and not to catch dust. The exercise of drawing out the journey maps can be really valuable, but the value can be unlocked when followed through. The maps can guide you in enhancing customer experience through insights that can be built into product or service design. And one must remember that a customer journey map is never something to consider 'done'. It's a living, breathing and evolving tool and must be referred to as such. It must be modified with every changing customer behaviour, and in today's environment, it may change at an especially rapid pace. It is important to keep track and adapt the business to large customer behaviour trends.

If you strive for a customer-centric culture, you have to understand the customer's journey—every step of the way. Customer journey mapping is a powerful way to find pain points and opportunities in your customer experience.

Picture an enterprise that has a design thinking culture has all their customer journey maps drawn out, has an Agile technology approach and the right kind of creative thinking adaptive leadership. And now picture the same enterprise in the eye of the COVID storm. They are already set to adapt to swift changes.

They know to continue to keep the customer at the centre of all plans despite the odds, they know how to visualise their customers' journey evolving with changing times, they know to quickly check in on what the customers' new needs are in the throes of all the unprecedented action and are enabled by technologies to make the necessary changes to enhance the customers' experience.

Among the most vexing challenges is determining which customer behaviours and trends are here to stay and which ones will eventually recede. Companies that invest in the wrong capabilities could find themselves on the outside as competitors that can offer exemplary customer experiences cement their advantage. The key at this point is to provide empathy to the customer and show agility to adapt to the new normal.

In the near term, it is clear that three top customer experience priorities will top everyone's agenda globally in the post-pandemic era: digital excellence, safe and contactless engagement and dynamic customer insights. Each organisation will pursue these priorities differently based on its industry and starting point as well as the competitive landscape. Many companies are already demonstrating their understanding of what matters to customers as well as innovative ways to meet their old and new expectations. These early movers offer a valuable point of reference for how to proceed.

5

Transformation through Data and Analytics

Data and analytics have been the two key drivers for the progress that industry and society at large have made in the last decade or so. Let's take a look at the connection between data and analytics and how analytics as a domain has evolved over the years and has become a game changer.

Business success has always been measured based on data. Data management by itself is not a new phenomenon as for a very long time, organisations collected, stored and disseminated data to various stakeholders based on statutory, legal, business, customer-specific or industry requirements. In the beginning, the efforts towards data management were all manual, and maintaining records of data and having the ability to convert some of it into information helped organisations in decision-making. Today, data that is available in multifarious formats and from multiple sources has to be collected and synthesised meticulously, as the survival or growth of businesses is dependent on how they relate to the data and information generated from within or sometimes outside it. The evolution of information technology and the progress in telecommunications technology have had a huge impact on the maturity of data management practices.

DATA PROCESSING

Fact-based decision-making overcame gut-based decision-making possibly due to technology enabling organisations in the processes related to storage, retrieval and presentation. Initially, this involved tedious data entry for large computer systems as well as data crunching to present reports and even assembling data from multiple locations to make it available at the central location where the computer was based. It was also time-consuming. With the advent of minicomputers in the 1970s, the cost of computing was brought down substantially, and data management systems at different locations became feasible, making it convenient to store, extract and analyse data. It was possible to store the data for posterity and use it for post-mortem analysis with the help of desktop computers at this stage. The databases could be available for decision-making support systems.

BUSINESS INTELLIGENCE

In the beginning, users were keen on data solutions that could lead to findings both accurate and reliable. Most use cases were exploratory rather than predictive in nature. Hence the products were designed keeping these objectives in mind and were easy to use, not requiring specialist analyst skills. The ability to crunch data and derive insights thereof is based on three main skills—technology, mathematics/statistics and the business acumen to define the problem and derive an appropriate business solution. While these three skills would continue to shape data science, the dynamics of changes in technology, statistical techniques and the frameworks for analysing business problems are making the field of data science more and more sophisticated.

The first phase in the evolution of analytics was to recognise the importance of business intelligence (BI), which as a discipline emerged in the 1950s. Relational databases (RDB) in the 1980s allowed users to retrieve data from a database on demand. The combination of cheaper and easier data collection, storage and retrieval technology opened up the possibilities of what could be done with data. Initially, all of this required a lot of time, even for tapping into a small amount of structured data available from internal sources.

Right until 2010, organisations had to be contented with the low speed and huge efforts involved in gathering and synthesising business intelligence. However, with the rapid development of cloud-based infrastructure capability and the lowering costs of telecommunications, it has now become feasible to create data warehouses where business transactions and production transactions can be brought together and stored in one system, thus creating enterprise consolidated data warehouses. BI and ETL (extract, transform, load) tools have made it possible to capture and store the data as required, thus enabling querying on specific requirements. Conversion of data into intelligence became feasible, which in turn could facilitate the decision-making process. The output was used within the business, and the analytics performed was primarily about the past, descriptive—what happened—and diagnostic—why it happened—with no available support for upcoming trends or predictions for the future.

BIG DATA

The next big thrust for analytics was the large-scale impact of the internet, wide access to mobile phones, cloud infrastructure and related technologies in addition to innovation around the social media paradigm. While the data generated within the organisation continued to be small, organisations were beginning to face the challenge of handling the large quantum of data being generated outside the organisation thanks to these developments. That is when, in 2010, the term 'Big Data' got coined to define the large amounts of data emanating from multiple sources as compared to 'small data' being generated from within the business entity.

Another interesting development took place in this phase related to the open-source community which extended support for building new processing frameworks such as Hadoop and new databases such as NoSQL to store and manipulate data. The Human Genome Project in fact gave an impetus to data being sourced from multiple public sources and created the momentum for large-scale data projects in business. In due course, various other frameworks emerged that would help in ingesting, transforming and processing big data around enterprise data warehouses to discover patterns, correlations and valuable insights to make informed and timely decisions. With large amounts of data being available, customer needs could be understood better by businesses in every sector, whether retail, banking, travel or healthcare, which resulted in the ability to create new products or services aimed at their customers. All of this led to data warehouses becoming more and more sophisticated. The concept of a data lake was developed, which could provide the organisation with the required foundation for predictive analytics.

PERSONALISATION

For a very long time, data remained in the preserve of the IT group. For every requirement of data or reports, help from IT teams had to be requested, and this normally involved a waiting period. Further, the reports were outdated and did not provide meaningful and timely insights. As user-friendly tools and self-service analytics have become available, business users have been able to access the datasets or part of them in the form of spreadsheets, thus making real-time data analytics feasible. While independence and flexibility on personalised access to databases and analytics were seen as a welcome departure from the centralised approach, working in silos led to mistrust and questions of data origins and accuracy. This led to the realisation that it was essential to create intelligent infrastructure addressing the needs of agility and customisation for users and the requirement for security and common governance for IT and digital teams. Therefore, lately, the thrust of many organisations has been to build a single repository centralising all datasets that can be accessed by all users, with IT retaining governance and access oversight. Machine learning algorithms are being embedded into what seems like a simple repository, making it a constantly evolving smart learning system capable of making recommendations. The recommendation engines are trained to suggest datasets, propose data models, share previous results and help in presenting smart models that meet current requirements.

Instead of working in silos, users are now aware with whom they need to collaborate with the help of smart recommendations from the data models. They can obtain superior insights upon blending their respective experiences and knowledge, leading to better decision-making. Further, the ratings of outcomes and datasets used from the central databases could be shared with others, thus making the data access, quality and analytics processes more efficient and relevant. Customer tech giants such as Amazon, Google and Facebook figured out how to use consumer data to deliver a superior and personalised experience to their users, thus empowering them with the information to make decisions on their purchase or making recommendations for alternatives or repeat purchase. Soon this approach of building analytics solutions around transaction data began to be adopted by traditional companies too, who learnt to leverage vast amounts of data they were generating from their distribution and suppliers' network to derive predictive and prescriptive analytics. This led to reduced costs and also brought innovation in their offerings.

PREDICTIVE AND PRESCRIPTIVE ANALYTICS

With data being internally available along with externally generated data, the two could be combined with cloud infrastructure, becoming robust and elastic and meeting the data storage needs of organisations. Crunching data for predictive and prescriptive analytics became feasible and complemented descriptive analytics. Prescriptive analytics uses techniques from statistics, data mining, data modelling, AI and machine learning to make predictions using both current and historical data to understand patterns, behaviours, trends and outcomes to predict future trends, as well as the likelihood of the occurrence of events and outcomes. Although predictive analytics has been around since the 1940s, it has developed into a well-defined domain with the arrival of big data and cloud infrastructure at affordable prices. It is now supported by advanced tools to be able to use the insights to prescribe or recommend alternatives for decision-making.

AUTOMATED ANALYTICS

With humongous data being available and the ability to derive meaningful insights, the next challenge to be addressed was concerning the effort and time necessary for building algorithms and models for each requirement. This led to the evolution of automation through intelligent systems. The integrated approach of machine learning, deep learning and AI are throwing up a huge number of possibilities to impact transactional outcomes. As a result, chatbots and neural machine translation are slowly becoming mainstream. With the help of ongoing training of the automated tools on the data mining techniques deployed from eliciting insights from multiple data sources, it is now possible to keep the recommendation engines dynamic and up-to-date.

Since the potential and impact of artificial intelligence (AI) on businesses has been recognised, the demand for qualified talent has surged. This demand is not easily met by end-users' industry and software development firms. This has resulted in an exciting new trend—the efforts aimed at giving more teeth and power to AI by building automated tools to support the AI engine instead of depending entirely upon humans to train and build such engines. Tech giants such as Microsoft, Amazon and Google and several start-ups are racing to develop the new tools that will reduce costs as well as dependence on AI experts and are expected to help companies take advantage of the enormous data at their disposal and embed significantly more AI into their systems without necessarily having to invest in building their own AI capabilities.

Currently, robots being used in manufacturing or logistics applications are trained for specific tasks and not for complex tasks such as sorting or using curiosity to solve a problem. However, the recent robot developed by the University of Berkeley shows the machine trained by viewing hundreds of purely digital objects to be able to distinguish the items not seen in the digital dataset. Machines are learning from simulated models and applying it at the workplace. The interesting approach adopted in all this research is that instead of trying to define the programme behaviour for the robots, the focus must be to set up an environment where the robots can find ways of learning to do things on their own. As of now, this is the quintessential distinguishing factor of AI tools as opposed to humans, since humans are capable of learning on their own.

While attempts are aimed at machines emulating humans in developing learning ability rather than learning to execute a specific task and be able to handle a complex array of tasks, humans will be required to closely monitor how machines learn and slowly move them away from 'what to learn' to 'how to learn'. The focus is thus more and more on software built around neural networks, which enables a machine to recognise patterns.

The coming together of neural networks and AI is being experienced in the art and music scene as well. Google's Project Magenta is aimed at teaching machines to create original music, sketches, videos and jokes to find new ways to communicate. Just as Facebook identifies faces in online photos or Android phones recognise voice commands, machines are now being taught to recognise music notes or objects and shades in the sketches to produce new formats of music or visual art.

At the same time, we need to keep a close watch on the frameworks and tools being used for analytics, as they may become obsolete or ineffective as competitors also use similar approaches. Therefore, finding new insights from the data is the key to stay ahead of the competition and deliver a superior customer experience. Zoom, the online meeting platform, has shot into prominence during the pandemic. Since it is easy to use and free, it has found patronage amongst everyone from governments to corporates to even individuals. Zoom added more users in the first two months of 2020 than in all of 2019. In March 2020, 200 million people around the world joined a Zoom meeting every day. Zoom has thus a huge head start with its customers, although several alternatives are now trying to compete with new features to retain their customers. Zoom is leveraging artificial intelligence and machine learning to eliminate adult content as well as identify accounts that may have been infringed. Zoom has been criticised for safety and privacy breaches, and it is planning to use AI to make its platform more robust and protect the identity of the users.

Users have expressed increased concerns regarding the usage of personal data, and companies too are becoming more protective of their data. The future development of AI will depend upon the broader distribution of and access to data and algorithms. This will mean possibly applying blockchains to access the required datasets by AI networks with no stakeholder, including the platform provider, controlling the data or algorithms and thus taking AI to the next plane of possibility.

COGNITIVE ANALYTICS

We have come a very long way since the time of data recording to using insights in real time to guide and change customer behaviour and using these trends innovate on products for greater commercial gains. This is not a one-time exercise of building IT applications as in the past. Organisations should be willing to commit to a continuous journey of making machines and tools smarter. As the celebrated writer and thinker Yuval Noah Harari says, over a period of time AI can be expected to develop a higher level of intelligence to solve more complex problems, but it cannot be expected to develop consciousness, i.e., the ability to feel things. Hence humans will continue to play an important role, although their roles will get redefined with every stride that AI takes. The success will largely depend upon the human mind to make the machines learn, become smarter and also design appropriate tools because emotional context and sensitivities cannot be experienced by automated tools. Hence the collaborative efforts of the power of the machines and the ingenuity of the human mind will play a dominant role in this journey.

Machine learning, deep learning and artificial intelligence have pervaded everyday life, moving beyond the domains of scientific research or programmers' screens. As they occupy centre stage in influencing every aspect of business and individual decision-making processes, the predominant question is the efficacy of such decisions and the resultant actions. Such concerns are expressed even though technology has been able to add tremendous value in doing a better job than humans in repetitive activities, such as in the case of retail checkout stations; activities that have high risks associated with errors, as in the case of banking transactions or could be life-threatening, as in the case of deep-sea diving in oil and gas exploration sites. These applications and several others—particularly when combined with advancements in voice recognition, sensors and natural language processing—are delivering solutions that are reducing costs, offering pertinent choices to decision-makers, making the processes more efficient and removing biases from actions.

Despite such obvious benefits, AI- and technology-driven solutions are often unable to factor in emotions, intuitions, experience curves and personal values to arrive at suitable recommendations. There is also the danger of algorithms influencing and shaping a whole new mindset and opinion forming, as has been highlighted by the recent cases of the role of social media and analytics in electoral behaviour. Organisations are also discovering the potential to build the right culture by shaping the attitude and behaviour of employees through the interpretation of behavioural stimuli. Since the bots and algorithms are developed based on available data and known patterns of occurrences or a series of actions initiated in the past, marginalised sections of society or under-represented voices would stand to lose due to their limited presence in the digital medium thus leading to lopsided recommendations or consequent actions. Ethical questions also arise related to tapping personal profiles through social networks within and outside the organisation and whether these could be fed into an engine for building an algorithm. Algorithms also falter at times due to common-sense failures or because they misunderstand the intent in a given situation. When a human interacts with other humans, they have a common knowledge of how the world works and how to transact in any given situation which is embedded in their DNA. However, machines do not have this advantage and can relate to only the clearly defined data and training they have undergone based on this data for predefined situations.

Therefore, before the process of building algorithms commences, it is important to address these issues in order to make the algorithms reliable, ethical and pertinent to situations. To facilitate this, a human-centred design of algorithms will be essential such that spontaneity and opportunity to relate to personal experiences or intuitions are encouraged to make the automated decision pathways more robust and practical. Users can also be informed of the potential limitations of the assumptions made while designing the algorithm and can hence complement the decision-making process by recalling from their memory of previous experiences. Organisations also need to be conscious of the biases that could arise both on account of humans as a result of personal and societal or corporate experiences as well as those that may arise out of machines on account of limitations of data and evolve new frameworks for decision-making that combine the best of both humans and machines. Repeated training and reinforcement will be required for both the AI tools as well as for those who will be using them to help them interpret the recommendations more accurately. It is therefore desirable that algorithm and AI tool creation are planned as a collaborative effort between digital experts and domain experts with the full cognizance of psychological, legal and social factors relevant to the ecosystem of the stakeholders. Algorithms with a human touch are the recipe for success!

Building Reusable Knowledge from Interactions

With the worldwide shift to remote work, our interactions with customers and colleagues have witnessed a concurrent evolution. Face-to-face communications and firm handshakes are giving way to interfaces such as Teams, Slack, Zoom or good old email.

Thus, internal and external communication are being transformed at an unprecedented pace.

Artificial intelligence holds new promise by recreating the in-person experience and reinventing the way we collaborate in the social distancing era. Unfortunately, most of the knowledge and rich context shared in these collaboration channels is lost in archives and forgotten.

The innovative approach of iEngage.ai facilitates building reusable knowledge from these conversations. The platform utilises AI to extract intelligence, insights and information and manage it within knowledge graphs (Figure 5.1). The platform provides APIs (application programming interfaces) to reuse this within your favourite applications.

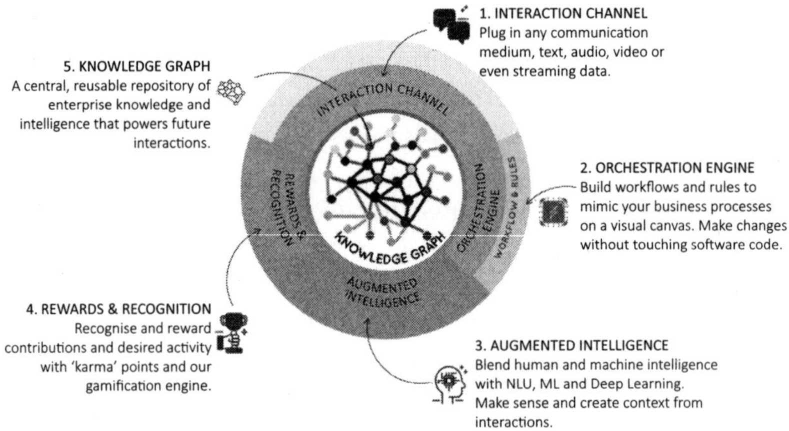

FIGURE 5.1 *iEngage Intelligence Framework*

iEngage.ai provides the insights that augment man and machine and increases productivity and delivers rich experiences.

Customer Service Experience Redefined

Any company with a customer service department is invariably growing their stock of unstructured data with every chat log, email exchange and recorded call. You have surely heard 'Your call may be recorded for quality assurance purposes.' The question is what to do with this data.

Short of replaying a contentious call for managerial review or using an exemplum for training purposes, most customer service (CS) calls fade into obscurity once the issue has been remedied. Since 89% of companies compete on customer service, the adoption of AI by CS teams is a key differentiator for a competitive advantage.

iEngage overcomes these challenges by triaging and monitoring channels that you connect such as email, chat messages and other communication exchanged each day and extracting relevant knowledge. The potential for real-time responses to what a customer says and inputs to how an agent should respond adds to productivity and experience.

The FreshEngage app for Freshdesk, powered by iEngage, learns from past tickets and resolutions. It automates numerous manual ticket processing activities to make support agents more productive. In addition to tagging, classification, prioritisation and agent assignment, FreshEngage lets agents discover and reuse issue resolutions within Freshdesk (Figure 5.2).

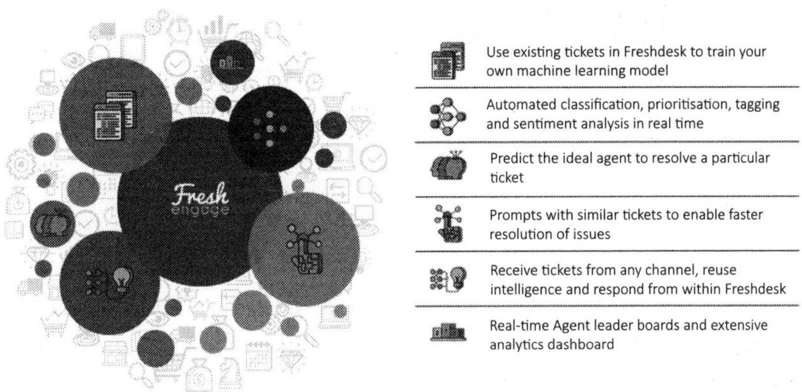

FIGURE 5.2 *Customer Response Mechanism*

Employee Insights, Analysed

Collaborative interactions in any business result in the sharing of knowledge. Tools such as Zoom, Slack and Microsoft Teams have invaded the remote collaboration space, recreating new remote working experiences for meetings, watercooler conversations and employee onboarding to cite a few examples.

These interactions lead to the creation of tribal knowledge—the know-how employees acquire on the job. Tribal knowledge can include shortcuts, workarounds, trade secrets or any other type of knowledge that isn't preeminent in written documentation. The more an employee learns about their role, the more tribal knowledge they gather.

Analysis of conversations by iEngage helps gather this tribal knowledge. This is the reason why Ariv.ai has been built, a personal knowledge bot that automates collection and discovery of knowledge from conversations (Figure 5.3). Just ask Ariv a question, like you would ask a colleague, and Ariv will sift through the knowledge graph to find you an answer.

FIGURE 5.3 *Framework for Personalised Response*

Ariv can also keep track of topics that interest you and deliver a digest at your convenience so you can achieve a deep focus on your work. Ariv incentivises knowledge sharing by recognising and rewarding such good karma. You can configure karma points to reinforce collaboration, and these points can be used to create leader boards and redeemed through redemption gateways.

Enterprise digital transformation initiatives dramatically benefit from these applications enabled by platforms such as iEngage.ai. The interplay between AI efficiency and human insight is a virtuous cycle. As the saying goes, 'Man is a slow, sloppy and brilliant thinker; computers are fast, accurate and stupid.'

APPLICATIONS OF ANALYTICS

Customer Analytics

Today's customer takes decisions on purchase or recommendations based on a wealth of information they have at their disposal. Unlike in the past, when customer analysis was seen as an important periodic activity by consumer brands with industrial brands not giving much attention to it, customers of every product or service today are very engaged and have an active interaction with businesses. Businesses have an opportunity and necessity to acknowledge the presence of customers in the digital world and influence them favourably towards their offerings. Customer analytics helps understand the profile and buying behaviour of customers based on insights drawn from each transaction, whether or not they have closed a purchase. Customer analytics is closely linked with the core functions of the business towards customers: acquisition, engagement, retention and revenue generation.

What was essentially once considered as the bastion of the new-age tech companies such as Amazon, Google and Apple, customer analytics that shaped the very survival and meteoric growth of these businesses, has become the prime focus of every business. Today, customer analytics has been recognised by every category of business as the essential growth engine, be it big or small, born digital or born as a brick and mortar venture, irrespective of the sectors that they belong to. It is fascinating to note that in just over the last five years or so, marketing managers and product managers are leaning heavily on customer data to gain deep insights to charter the course of their business. The customer analytics market size is projected to grow from 10.5 billion US dollar in 2020 to 24.2 billion US dollar by 2025, at a compound annual growth rate (CAGR) of 18.2% during the forecast period as per the report of Markets and Markets. It's the combination of two key factors that is driving such an astonishing growth—the maturing trends in technologies around applications of AI and the increasing desire of marketeers to understand customer buying behaviour.

Customer analytics frameworks are drawn up by mapping customer journeys and identifying different touchpoints such as websites, social media, specific contests, in-store visits and blogs and defining the nature of outcomes expected—descriptive, predictive, prescriptive or diagnostic. Insights drawn from such analytics could be used to increase footsteps in retail outlets, enhance stickiness to the products, upsell offerings to customers based on their interests and enhance referrals from satisfied customers. Customer analytics helps increase response rates and customer loyalty, decrease attrition by predicting customers who are most likely to leave, recommend the right proactive methods for retention and deliver the right message to each of the target segments. Further, the cost per conversion can be dramatically slashed and the overall advertising costs can be brought down considerably by focusing on specific segments of customers and by having a targeted messaging and strategy for each of these segments.

What many organisations are trying to do is not just build brands by focusing on their customers and using customer analytics to sell them more, but they are aiming to build communities and getting to understand the profiles of these communities. For instance, Harley Davidson is a recognised brand today with a set of followers who are emotionally connected. The company that was on the verge of calling it quits in mid-1980s has seen a resurgence in its business due to the loyalty factor of its customers. This has been assiduously cultivated through Harley Owners Group, where customers across the world connect and share their experiences. Hence, it's not just the brand value, it's the shared value of customers that needs to be understood and harnessed to grow the affinity for the brand, resulting in the success of the business. It takes time and perseverance to win the trust of the customers to be a part of the online brand communities as well as harness the strength of these communities to their benefit. Several Indian brands are attempting to build such communities as they recognise the importance of influencing the communities likely to have common characteristics. Brands are also beginning to recognise that in the long run, customer analytics of both groups and individuals will be important to developing winning strategies.

Marketing Analytics

Marketing was considered a cost centre as it was mostly not possible to track specific outcomes from the spend. This approach has changed considerably over the years as companies have started using a variety of digital marketing channels supported by different technologies, with monitoring mechanisms and metrics specific to each of these channels. As a result, analysis and decision-making have been conducted in silos. Marketing analytics provides an integrated view of all marketing efforts vs outcomes across all channels, thus making the planning and execution of the marketing programme efficient. Based on the analysis of the historical spend and outcomes, present status and predictions of future trends or the ability to influence future, marketing analytics help answer questions related to the marketing mix, channels hitherto not considered—on which new channels must be explored, how those channels compare with competitors, how effective the spend on the current marketing is vis-à-vis the likely outcomes from the new alternatives. Metrics need to be defined for each of the actions leading to outcomes, which are measured with the help of data. Marketing analytics place this data in the right context and indicate the impact on business results.

For building marketing analytics models, use of unstructured data along with structured data has become an absolute necessity in the context of the extended use of social media. Marketing analytics helps organisations fine-tune customer journeys with insights on product intelligence, competition, customer trends and behaviour as well as customer support. Some of the commonly used marketing analytics tools include web analytics tools (e.g., Google Analytics, Kissmetrics), visual behaviour and testing tools (e.g., Crazy Egg, Hotjar), SEO analytics tools (Facebook Insights, Hootsuite), content analytics tools (e.g., Google Alert, Scoop.it), email analytics tools (e.g., Mailchimp, Campaign Monitor).

Sales Analytics

Sales are the most important business parameter that all organisations are keen to track as it reflects the success of business efforts. In the fast-paced digital world where sales teams have to cope with several moving parts, sales activity can be broken down to micro nuggets and blended with external parameters. It is possible to provide dynamic insights in the form of sales analytics, which help enhance sales performance and prioritise sales activities. Empowering sales teams by directing them to the right opportunities, highlighting the need to acquire skills for increasing the effectiveness of sales calls and pointing out missed or hidden secondary opportunities for sales increase the success of the sales teams.

Metrics such as achievement of sales against the target, sales growth, product-wise sales, margins gained in each sale, customer-wise sales have been historically monitored and analysed as part of periodic sales reports. What distinguishes sales analytics is the ability to use such internal data along with external trends and be in a position to create models that can serve up the insights in a dynamic and transparent manner to various stakeholders, namely sales, finance, production, HR teams and the CEO as per their specific custom requirements. The predictions of future sales, AI-driven deep insights into customer behaviour and recommendations for enhanced sales or change of strategy help organisations make timely decisions.

Supply Chain Analytics

Business sustainability is often affected by the volatility of supplies and changes in demand forecasts. One of the key reasons for this is that planning is done around past data, and dynamic parameters are often not factored in. Supply chains of businesses generate huge variety and volumes of data. Analytics of this data provides huge scope to the business to cope with the dynamic nature of demand, optimise the deployment of resources, eliminate wastage and achieve savings in costs based on the patterns and insights derived from the historical data and the future trends data models can provide. The recent COVID lockdowns of economies in different parts of the globe put a spotlight on the supply chain of essential commodities. Upon lifting the lockdown, ensuring production, stocks, raw material supply, transportation and customer demand were closely aligned and could be achieved by those companies who had already invested in digital platforms. Supply chain analytics came to their rescue and helped them meet the demand in the best possible manner.

All types of analytics—descriptive, prescriptive, predictive and cognitive—could be applied to help solve problems, mitigate risks and predict future scenarios based on internal and external data, driving innovation and responding to customer needs in a timely manner. Critical functions such as inventory and operations planning, sourcing, manufacturing, storage and warehousing, logistics and sales are connected with one another through a well-planned supply chain analytics system and can transform the performance of the supply chain. Supply chain analytics cuts across functions and disciplines, and the insights highlight inter-related trends that help in internal and external risk assessment, scenario building for stock-out situations, identifying pockets where expenses could be contained and alternate models for safeguarding profitability.

Supply chain analytics is capable of providing real-time insights and help in speedy decision-making, thus providing a competitive edge to the business. In a study conducted by Melissa R. Bowers, Adam G. Petrie, Mary C. Holcomb and Gerald T. Neidert, less than 25% of the surveyed companies can respond immediately to insights from supply chain analytics. It is the speed of response that the authors call 'analytics insight cycle time', which is likely to become a key success factor. One of the key inhibiting factors for the inability of organisations to respond quickly is the presence of a number of diverse systems connecting various vantage points, where data is collected or transformed, and the lack of integration between multiple systems and touchpoints through which data flows in myriad types and formats. It is imperative to redraw the boundaries of the supply chain and consider building 24/7 connectedness with all internal and external stakeholders, including transportation and warehouse operators, with respect to demand for products and supply of raw materials through tightly coupled automated systems that provide real-time insights for decisions concerning the movement of raw material as well as manufactured goods to the locations of demand. Along with supply chain analytics, dynamic insights drawn from customer analytics need to be superimposed to arrive at viable plans for production planning and distribution.

In India, with many of the companies manufacturing consumer goods having geographically scattered factories, hundreds of distributors and thousands of retailers, planning and forecasting are even more complex. Gone are the days when forecasting used to be done on the basis of seasonal sales or sales done in the previous year. Real-time flexibility has become extremely important to cut down inventory carrying costs, demurrage or avoid overstocking and rerouting products from original destinations to new destinations. Thus, businesses have been able to see a direct correlation of investment in supply chain analytics with the reduction in working capital and the growth in business as the supply chain has become their lifeline in these complex times.

Finance Analytics

With the role of the CFOs extending beyond the responsibility of keeping accounts and executing traditional financial management to contributing towards strategic areas of business, traditional MIS systems are not equipped to address these requirements. Instead, they present revenue and expenses against the budget and have severe limitations. Data collected and presented have constraints, especially in large organisations, and being able to carry out an in-depth analysis and comparisons on micro-parameters could be time-consuming. Further, often when the data stored and managed by multiple teams is combined for the purpose of aggregation, inconsistencies emerge, leading to varied interpretations. There are also occasions when the finance department supports business decisions without validation or any independent analysis in areas such as negotiations related to customer billing and discount structures, resource planning, compensation reviews and competitor analysis. This happens on account of the finance function not having the required skills or tools to make suitable recommendations, the urgency of business teams to make decisions or the inability of business teams to articulate the financial analysis required to arrive at business decisions and so on. Hence the importance of financial analytics frameworks to be able to get as granular as required and use insights to predict future trends and provide strategic support to the business to take action with confidence.

To facilitate the system that is capable of providing financial analytics with the flexibility to meet the dynamic needs of the business, an integrated view of all financial systems would be required, which would enable centralised visibility and accountability of the data. Thereafter, it would be feasible to have an accurate and unified view of the data and analytics carried out with the help of automated tools. Self-serving analytics would not only aid in independent trends analysis of predictive sales analytics, customer-wise and product-wise profitability analytics, it would also enable better predictability of cash flow for each of the businesses with the help of working capital analysis. Finance analytics allows CFOs to combine internal financial data with external information drawn from social media and other industry platforms and support the business with strategic inputs in areas such as risks associated with doing business with certain customers, investment decisions, ongoing monitoring of key business value drivers, factors impacting shareholder value and impact of discounts on business returns.

People Analytics

In these times, when most businesses are going digital, HR managers are faced with the question of what the HR function should be doing and what the starting point for their own transformation journey should be. The question of the starting point is best answered by defining the problem the business is attempting to solve and how HR could play a role in the process. HR managers should tap insights from HR analytics that reveal the HR factors impacting business goals to help adopt the right approach to enhance business performance. They need to develop capability analytics, which dynamically measures the available level of expertise and skills, assesses the required levels of capability for each role and bridges the gap between the two with a dynamic talent development programme.

In the current context of employee experience being the key driver for employee retention, the critical prerequisite would be the ability to define the scope and metrics for the employee lifecycle with the organisation. This also means it is time we moved away from measuring employee satisfaction through surveys alone and instead combined surveys with data points and insights offered through people analytics for planning and devising the correct approach. And such insights will lead to appropriate analysis and proactive measures to avert likely dips in employee experience only when they are continuous. The employee experience journey has to commence even before the employee joins the organisation with innovative communication through the company website as well as social media channels.

Several factors impact the resourcing dimension, including cost, time, referrals, appropriate channels for tapping the right talent and analysis of profiles from social media. Talent resourcing managers need to be equipped with analytics on such factors to be able to support businesses proactively as required. Real-time productivity analytics of employees enables managers to give attention to idle time, redefine workflows or remove administrative tasks from high-paying roles, thus adding to the bottom line of the business.

Listening to the universe on social media and carrying out useful analytics on how the potential target segment as well as their influencers perceive the company and the roles offered must be the starting point with the view to enlarging the base of audience universe and their positive perception of the organisation. Eliciting insights from the experience of candidates during the interview and the selection process and building models to decipher the joining ratio and creating alerts for critical positions allow HR managers to further fine-tune their candidate engagement processes.

The ability to link business performance parameters with personal aspirations and the growth path of employees on the strength of predictive and prescriptive analytics should help create an environment of trust and transparency that is welcomed by employees. Hence, for a positive employee experience leading to enhanced retention, analytics should be the area of focus for HR managers. Digital platforms introduce transparency between all stakeholders about the assessment of capabilities vs opportunities available. Thus, they help set up customised career paths for employees without having to wait for the annual appraisal system to let them know where they stand. The annual appraisal system has traditionally been used by most organisations to determine salary hikes and a rewarding mechanism, using the bell curve as a guiding principle. However, with talent retention and engagement having become the key areas of focus, organisations are recognising the importance of continuous performance management with regular feedback and coaching of employees.

According to Stephen Balzac, an expert on leadership and organisational development, the best practices for creating new metrics for the modern workforce should include feedback on aspects employees can change rather than personality traits or characteristics they can't change. They must also focus on strengths rather than weaknesses. Therefore, HR managers have started moving away from the bell curve phenomenon for force-fitting employees in predetermined bands of the reward and retention system towards focusing on democratising the performance assessment system by providing a framework that leads employees to take ownership of their career, acquire the know-how necessary for the next role, receive continuous feedback and reach out to the right coaches to enhance their productivity and learn to adapt quickly.

In highly competitive businesses, where attracting and retaining the right talent is the key to innovation and continuous growth, HR functions must recognise the urgency of embracing an analytics-led approach. For the data-led approach to gain momentum, the first step is to integrate the existing systems in the organisation such as HR MIS, learning management systems and performance management systems on a digital platform and be able to pick the data sets that will enable the HR function to build a suitable model and train AI tools to support in decision-making related to employee experience milestones.

Lastly, performance is driven by leaders. Hence, their leadership style and interpersonal skills play an important part in the success of the business. Data about leadership performance can be gained periodically through the use of employee surveys and focus group studies, which can then be used to build models to form a correlation between business and individual performance, employee exits and referrals. The connection between HR and employees should not be restricted to just the emotional dimension. The connection will become strong and meaningful to the business when timely insights are made available to the business to aid in their performance.

NURTURING DATA-DRIVEN INNOVATION: OPPORTUNITIES AND CHALLENGES

Successful digital transformation initiatives undertaken by businesses are resulting in productivity gains, cost reduction, additional and new revenue opportunities and improved market shares. In addition to these benefits, the extensive data being generated from these initiatives, when tapped systematically and converted into useful analytics and knowledge, throws up a multitude of opportunities for innovation. The primary objective of innovation is to create value for the business. Innovation is a change that creates a new dimension of performance, says Peter Drucker. Organisations have recognised the importance of nurturing innovation in existing businesses; hence, as a part of the digital transformation initiative, organisations are also undertaking a restructuring of the business as required to support the innovation ecosystem.

Innovation in data-driven organisations is driving efficiency and growth in three possible ways—business process optimisation, enhanced customer intimacy and product or service innovation. Business process optimisation leads to opportunities in productivity gains and cost mitigation. Enhanced customer intimacy could result in brand loyalty and new upsell or cross-sell opportunities. Product and service innovation outcomes include reduced cost of servicing and new or enhanced income streams. Recognising the potential benefits of this, organisations are making significant investments in each of these areas in digital technologies and are acquiring knowledge and useful insights, then channelling them for fostering innovation in their businesses.

New knowledge is essential for producing distinctive products, processes or services that create customer delight. With the boundaries of knowledge being redefined on account of the access to deep insights into customer expectations and buying behaviour, the innovation potential has dramatically increased. Data-driven innovation has the potential to generate economic value through many channels, internal as well as external to the business. Data-driven innovation is relevant to citizens' services as well. For example, by tapping and analysing data to improve the well-being of citizens through accurate profiling of their medical needs and targeting the appropriate medical care, an improved healthcare system can be implemented. This can result in savings and more importantly help prioritise the services required based on available expertise in different healthcare centres, proximity to the community, criticality and affordability. Further, by sharing the data related to diseases, treatment and success rates with the citizens, not only is better awareness created and citizens can make informed decisions concerning their health, they are able to make timely decisions regarding hospitalisation and access to the right experts without delays.

Farming is another segment that has huge opportunities for productivity gains through innovation. In New Zealand, farmers are using a product called Farmax to manage complex issues related to farming activities such as ideal time for buying stocks, grazing and prevention of diseases. They have thus transitioned to more data-driven decision-making and actions instead of relying entirely on intuition and experience. In India too, farmers are using mobile-based applications to their benefit. With the increased adoption of such systems, farmers will be able to adopt better farming techniques and take timely decisions that will increase productivity. The Smart City project undertaken in various cities in India aims for greater convenience and access to better public services on the strength of data analytics in areas such as traffic management, electricity distribution and crime detection.

BUILDING A DATA-DRIVEN ORGANISATION

Despite the several potential advantages of data-driven innovation, many organisations continue to face challenges in taking full advantage of the possibilities. The primary challenge relates to the definition of data needs, lack of required processes to tap into the data pool and the linkage between various forms of data. For an organisation to become a data-driven enterprise, it is important to bring together data from different sources, both structured and unstructured and from multiple devices and social media. Building robust IT and data architecture is also necessary to derive meaningful insights. Data quality is most critical, with the quality of data determining the quality of decision-making. However, it is not necessary to wait to start until 100% accuracy on all data is achieved. There will always be some parts of the data which may be inaccurate, and it would be best to call out levels of uncertainty in such cases and try to enhance the quality of data over time.

Data silos are quite common in organisations. The starting point to create trust with the data systems is to have a framework with transparent and clean data that has defined access rights. Data collection and cleaning up should not be seen as a one-time activity. Therefore, systematic repeatable processes should be put in place with verification and security controls. It is always useful to first implement a simple system that touches all the key functions and addresses their core needs. This ensures organisation-wide acceptance and anticipation for more to come. Thereafter, more sophisticated systems can be built for specific areas. Data consistency should be the priority, while flexibility in studying the data from multiple angles should come next. There is no single approach that is the ideal way to address the analytical problem. Therefore, whichever approach is used, the rationale for the choice of including alternatives considered should be first shared with all stakeholders so that users understand the context for the approach. The ultimate benefit of data-driven frameworks is to lower costs, streamline processes and professionalise the relationships with key stakeholders, all of which results in improved business outcomes.

In addition to putting in place the right processes and technology, getting employees aligned with the mission of the business to be centred around data is extremely important to become a data-driven organisation. To get the buy-in from everyone, data needs to be treated as capital and its use across different functions should be prioritised. Very often, employees complain about the lack of basic data or difficulty in accessing basic data. Building a solution to address this should be the topmost priority to get people to believe in the data-centred organisation approach. Company-wide data and analytics proficiency should be encouraged, and employees should be upskilled as required. As far as possible, self-serving analytics should be provided to employees so that data becomes a part of their routine. They should be encouraged to explore and discover new facets of doing business on the strengths of the insights drawn from the data.

It is also important to find ways of integrating data science specialists with the functional teams. This can be done by providing data science specialists exposure to business by forming small teams comprising functional and data science specialists in conjunction with making executives code-literate and familiar with the language of data. Data orientation and the resultant business outcomes should be included in performance assessment and reward mechanisms. For data culture to take strong roots in organisations, leadership should set an example by anchoring their decisions around data. Key metrics of deliverables to be measured and monitored should be clearly delineated. Data should become the language of communication both inside and outside the boardroom for data to take strong roots in the business. The ultimate benefits of data-driven frameworks will be the lowering of costs, streamlining of processes and professionalising of the relationships with key stakeholders, all of which will result in improved business outcomes.

6

Impact on Business Processes and Domains

Six years ago, the CEOs of the industry association NASSCOM (National Association of Software and Services Companies) were in a brainstorming session on the future of business with the managing director of a global strategy consulting firm. He predicted that every customer of the software services and business process management industry would radically change their business models and purchasing behaviour in the next five years. Many incumbent vendor partners would simply fall by the wayside because they would not adapt to the evolving needs of their customers. In some cases, digital attackers would simply take away all the business of traditional incumbents. While many CEOs around that room didn't quite believe that our clients would change so fast, events of the last five years have made it abundantly clear that the world has indeed changed. There is every reason to believe that the change will continue and the pace may indeed accelerate in every industry domain in the years to come.

The purpose of this chapter is to explore these changes in the context of the rapid advances in digital technologies, with a focus on digital data engineering, data sciences and analytics and new stakeholder journeys that we have already discussed in some detail. Many trends cut across industry segments and yet some are very industry-specific, and it would be wise for any researcher, consultant or practitioner of digital transformation to understand these well. To build a logical sequence, we will explore the domains through the sequence of the customer's eyes—retail, banking, insurance, manufacturing, education and healthcare—and examine specific processes in these domains. The discussion will then move to common processes and how they get reengineered and transformed with digital.

RETAIL: WILL THE STORE EXIST?

The retail industry has been one of the early adopters of digital.

In the early months of March, panic buying that almost bordered on hoarding led to a jump of over 20% in grocery purchases. The need for social distancing and keeping shoppers out of the store led to a sudden acceleration of all digital efforts for retailers. The key areas where investment focus has increased have been the tracking of potential buyer journeys to new methods of online customer engagement, including the building and nurturing of online buyer communities and digital brand influencers.

Digital reengineering in retail has also meant deep studies of buyer psychology, rearchitecting the process by which customers consider a brand and choose between competitors and making the online experience as friction-free as possible. All retailers are enhancing their web presence to ensure that top-selling and high-margin merchandise is most easily visible to customers and is optimised for ease of access from mobile devices. Retailers must always keep in mind the need for omnichannel simultaneous updates, as a customer is very likely to shop around on their mobile phone and complete price discovery and purchasing from an office or home computer.

One area of augmented experience that many frontline brands are investing in is the use of virtual appointments, where a store expert can be called in for a consultation on the best product to buy from the store. Virtual try-ons have also been adopted by most apparel jewellery and cosmetics brands using computer vision and augmented reality in 3-D to allow shoppers to preview items before they buy in an environment simulated to be as close to a private visit to the store. This is, in fact, one area where customers could have a much better experience from the comfort of their home and might arguably never feel the need to go back to a physical store again even when it is completely safe to do so.

The operations within the store are of course where digital can and will play the most important transformational role in the future. It is no longer the browsing or stay experience that will matter but the speed at which customers will be able to get in and out of the store for transactions that just do not lend themselves to self-service. Extensive use of robotics, sanitised products, display shelves and all surfaces and quick and proactive communications and efficient handling of payment processes. The other opportunity that has already been explored during COVID times and might continue even beyond COVID will be cross-brand partnerships. In the peak of COVID, an enterprising sweet shop in Kalyani Nagar, Pune, made its products available through all the open stores in the suburb and offered to modify their websites to add the last line, 'Do you want some sweets today?' As a consequence, their sales went up manifold during the period. They also installed a counter at these stores when physical shopping became possible after the initial lockdown. Such partnerships may initially have started as marriages of convenience, but if the brand values are similar and the digital storefronts can be integrated with ease, cross-selling serves the purpose of all partners.

Retail is one segment where the new normal post-COVID will have to be entirely reimagined. The physical store should and will exist, but it will be assisted by deep customer analytics that can predict which customer would do what at which store and how each customer's experience, from store entry to shopping to payment to merchandise collection, can be optimised in a manner that is most delightful to them. As mentioned, the product consideration, try-outs, price discovery and consultation can all happen through well-designed user interfaces and user experience design, but ultimately it is the full cyber-physical experience that will determine the level of satisfaction and delight the customer recalls. Extensive use of partners for delivery, robotics and store automation, AI and machine learning for prediction and prescription and the coexistence of humans and robots in the store will all have to be considered. Surely a dream for digital reengineering practitioners, since every one of the five forces will be simultaneously at play here!

BANKING: THE FUTURE OF CUSTOMER ACCESS AND EVEN MONEY

Banks as we know them have morphed many times over the last four decades and more, with core banking systems brought in by various vendors and the onslaught of digital introducing a plethora of new opportunities that allow users to manage their money with the bank, then without the bank and eventually without money. Instead of jumping to the radical, let us look at the way our large banks have progressed and the digital agenda they are now chasing on behalf of their customers.

There is a common cliché in the services industry that 'run the bank' and 'change the bank' are two agendas to be pursued concurrently. Given the importance of winning and then maintaining the trust of every customer of the bank, retail or corporate, the first goal has always been to build a secure IT infrastructure and trusted framework on which all new technologies can be implemented. Operating mission-critical transaction systems effectively and efficiently in an uninterrupted and secure environment has always been the priority, and banking is one function where for a long time the goal of IT and digital was primarily to be aligned to business objectives and serve the customer with the fastest transaction processing capability and the best user experience.

First among the goals and objectives for IT and digital in the banking sector is a flexible and scalable architecture built on cloud capabilities, advanced analytics and using new-generation products, cognitive customer contact centres and a sustained spirit of innovation as core to the data and information strategy of the institution. In the financial sector, fraud prevention and business continuity cannot be compromised at any cost, and the focus on disaster recovery centres and many layers of security is imperative. On the digital strategy front, conceptualising digital interventions and aligning them to the imperatives for a trillion-dollar digital India has been the focus for both public and private sector banks in India. New platforms have been introduced to ease access and delight retail customers on the one hand while providing banking convenience through digital products to large corporates as well as small and medium enterprises on the other.

Specifically, in India, the need for 'Phygital' is still strong. Physical activities such as cheque and cash collection have co-existed with e-collection services through NEFT, RTGS and QR code scanning. 'Anywhere banking' services, extensive use of UPI and the rapid rise of payment banks with excellent digital capabilities have pushed banks in India to offer a unique basket of services and also do aggressive digital marketing to promote the digital facilities they offer. Today, any bank that wants to retain a market share must focus simultaneously on its core banking applications, ensure that all channels through which customers contact the bank and get service are optimal through digital, build high-quality data warehouses and analytics as an integral part of its executive support systems and constantly upgrade and refresh its technology stack, setting up network opening centres and heightened security systems to satisfy the pulls from customers and the pushes of regulators.

To a lesser or sometimes greater extent, the other arms of financial services, such as NBFS, payment banks and the myriad fintech companies that provide point solutions as part of the banking and financial services ecosystem are all being transformed through the rapid onslaught of new digital ideas. In recent times, the biggest disruptions have indeed come from the fintech, probably more so in this industry than many of the other segments. Pricewaterhouse Coopers (PWC) has estimated that incumbents in this industry could well lose a quarter of their business to standalone fintech companies just in the next five years.

It also makes eminent sense for incumbents to make hungry fintech firms part of their innovation ecosystem. These firms have seen global investments of many billions of dollars into their product development and marketing proportionate to the market share they are chasing, which is the spending by the banking system on information technology, touching over 300 billion dollars. One key disruptor that is catching attention is blockchain technology, which may finally see its real application in this industry and move from historical retail focus to industry transformation. Blockchain public ledgers will be welcomed by regulators and become a significant focus area for industry and company technology integrators in future. The other trend which was started by Uber and Airbnb is the sharing economy trend. Companies will emerge that will match providers and users of capital, not in the disruptive manner that bitcoin tried to do, but in a more collaborative fashion, where banks and financial services companies become part of the provider group.

One realisation that is accelerating the adoption of technology investments is that core services are becoming utilities. These need not be proprietary and could actually be standard services used on a pay-per-use basis from public clouds. Credit rating, managing consumer payments, providing statements and so many other functions need no longer be trade secrets. In fact, consumers will demand standardisation of the way their work is done and reports are provided to them for physical or electronic access. Added to the myriad non-core functions such as basic accounting, human resources and customer relationship management functions that are already moving to platforms and software-as-a-service, the competitive differentiator will be service. Entities such as Bajaj Finserv amongst NBFCs and Fino Payments Bank in the payments industry have demonstrated their ability to satisfy and even predict every need of the customer. Just as Apple Computer does with its new introductions to discerning consumers, the leaders of the future in financial services will be those who use best-in-class digital capabilities in every segment of the value chain and serve the customer consistently faster, cheaper and better. With chief data officers today having access to predictive and prescriptive analytics capabilities for every customer type, all winning organisations will have access to customer intelligence, and customers too will not be shy of demanding what they want.

The good news is that every participant in the banking and financial services industry is acutely conscious of this.

New digital-edge technologies are finding their way into this sector as well. Robotics combined with AI will go far beyond just replacing a bank teller and will use natural language processing, social and emotional intelligence, sentiment analytics and pattern recognition to predict customer responses and prescribe financial solutions suited to the needs of each individual. Services robots, combined with robotic process automation, will show incremental value in the short term but truly accelerate impact in the medium term.

Innovative financial services powered by an ecosystem of fintechs are truly focused on customer engagement and are learning rapidly from the experience and expertise of e-commerce pioneers such as Amazon. They are guiding engagement with the digital services they offer, tracking usage and drop-off points, enabling mobile access to the maximum extent possible and coming down hard on customer attrition, realising the lifetime value that loyal customers can give the institution. Building digital marketing capabilities is no longer the preserve of 'digital-only' banks and institutions, it is imperative for every legacy organisation that wants to remain in business. Embracing Agile in software development and team organisation, and facilitating cross-functional discussions on product design and customer service management and office design like Citibank's Long Island facility where customers are encouraged to interact directly with service development teams are all examples of how quickly both thinking and actions are evolving in the digital world.

Extreme focus on digitally enabled customer journeys and facilitating personalisation to the largest extent possible needs significant investments in technology, a fact that is not lost on any forward-looking institution of modern times. Global entities such as JPMorgan Chase, Goldman Sachs and Citibank and Indian leaders such as State Bank of India, HDFC, Fino Payments Bank and Bajaj Finserv have realised and put in practice the sandbox approach to let a large number of nimble entrepreneurs co-create solutions for their customers and the organisation. They are also recruiting data scientists and digital experts in large numbers, embracing cloud for infrastructure and software in a big way, seeking an order of magnitude cost efficiencies and making the entire IT function much more exciting for innovators and pioneers to work in. In all this, cybersecurity remains one of the top risks. The extensive outsourcing to third-party vendors, use of cross-border information exchanges and fast-changing technologies, including mobility and the internet of things will make it essential for technology administrators and chief information security officers to be constantly on their guard even as strategists continue to explore the unknown.

INSURANCE

The opportunities of digital in insurance start with claims processing, underwriting, policy administration etc. at the core, and then takes some of the best of digital in retail to build a transformed relationship between the insurer and the insured. How much insurance has evolved and how many new products have become possible! What a journey from the early days, when individuals bought a life insurance policy and a couple home and car insurance and then forgot about it! In India, a transition has occurred from the ubiquitous Life Insurance Corporation and General Insurance Corporation of the old days to myriad providers, including aggregators such as Policy Bazaar.

Many core and edge digital technologies are empowering this transformation. None is so ubiquitous as IoT. One of our early discussions about the potential integration of IoT capabilities was interestingly with a very innovative insurance firm in South Africa which, as a late entrant into a crowded market, decided that their mission was to remove the stigma of something going wrong, which dissuaded young people from buying insurance. They took the very interesting step of setting up a chain of wellness centres to give their clients a feel-good factor with the idea that building a health-based relationship with citizens in the main cities would make them the insurer of choice when the time and resources came together and the search for the right insurance began.

The idea of digital transformation struck this firm during a brainstorming session on how the wellness chain across a major city could make unexpected offerings to the customer. One of the first ideas was to tie up with the key mobile phone operators and deploy IoT beacons across the city, particularly in the vicinity of the wellness centres. The minute the prospect or customer drove into the parking lot, the beacon would signal the command centre, and a welcome message would be on the person's phone to visit the centre. The receptionist at the wellness centre would be immediately alerted, and a welcome message would flash on her screen with a detailed routine to suggest to the client based on his previous medical history. Imagine the satisfaction and the high likelihood of enrolment when faced with a surprise like that!

The same elements of surprise and delight are being made available to the potential insured everywhere. Every aspect of every citizen's life is potentially available and the digital exhaust of people who are regular users of social media. With due consideration to privacy laws, insurers have a potential insurance plan for every individual based on habits and propensity for risks. Discounts to drivers who use in-vehicle tracking devices and incentives for using a Fitbit or an equivalent are elementary examples of this, but with more wearable digital devices gaining traction, the integration of sensing devices with the automatic repricing of premiums will soon be an accepted transaction between the company and the insured. Customers will also get an opportunity to save. Once privacy concerns are resolved and mutuality of interests is established, digital sensing, analysis and prescriptive analytics can ensure that truly sticky relationships are built and sustained.

The logical focus area when transaction volumes accelerate and personalisation moves up the need hierarchy for clients is big data and advanced analytics. From assessing the safety of civil construction and electrical wiring in commercial and residential properties to detailed medical records of individuals, accessing and analysing data from multiple sources becomes a real asset to precision risk calculations and premium assessment, all with the level of transparency now demanded by all digital natives and millennials who are entering the insurance ambit for the first time. The increasing deployment of chatbots makes the collaborative process easier and indeed part of the workflow. One may soon see innovative self-service mechanisms when premiums can be negotiated based on commitments and data on actual life-style adjustments and compromises. Chatbots and innovations such as social listening, machine learning and cognitive customer relationship management not only make the interactions more open and pleasant for customers, they substantially reduce transaction times and human costs for the company. Chatbots are also being deployed to help customers navigate and understand complex policies. Finally, as more and more claim settlements become easy enough to be transacted by AI without any human intervention whatsoever, claims processing time and costs are being shaved substantially.

As in the case of fintechs and financial services, in insurance too, many entrepreneurial digital attackers are changing the expectations from the industry. Emerging companies that help customers search for information, enrol quickly and get the best and quickest deal are Metromile and Root for auto insurance. Metromile uses a telematics device installed in the car and, in many American states, can save money every month for the driver and the insurer in addition to supporting car health checks, optimisation of routes and car theft warnings. Root is an auto app that tracks driving habits such as hard turning and braking to dynamically adjust insurance rates and save as much as half the insurance costs for safe drivers, again a sure deterrent to wayward driving habits of customers, following weeks of test driving before a quote is given to a client. Only the best and most steady drivers qualify for the benefits. Insurify uses an expert virtual insurance agency called 'Evia' to track driving behaviour and provide quick quotes with multiple auto-insurance partners and software-enabled optimisation of the auto insurance options available and recommended for each client.

Similarly, home insurance is being optimised by 'AI Jim', an app used by digital insurer Lemonade that provides a variety of policies with even jewellery and personal high-value item add-ons and offers a guarantee that 20% of the paid premiums will be used for handling claims while the unused premiums will go to a non-profit of the customer's choice, a big hit in the philanthropy-conscious USA. Oscar Health Insurance operates in partnership with Mount Sinai Health System to provide guaranteed 24×7 doctor call back services and prescription management with nearby pharmacies. It also offers add-ons such as expectant mother training and yoga classes for discerning clients. Ladder Insurance, in partnership with Fidelity Security Life, disintermediates the insurance agent and offers direct access to life insurance to customers without any annual policy fees with policy transactions completed in less than five minutes. Dynamic scale-ups and scale-downs of coverage based on anticipated events such as weddings and long-distance travel are possible, and it is now expected that such usage-based insurance and premiums will soon be over 20% of all insurance coverage in advanced countries with very discerning customers.

The process of buying insurance online has also been made truly user-friendly in recent times, with a full range of insurance products available online and no intermediary or long conversation needed to view, get queries answered and make effective choices. Insurance-on-demand will soon be the order of the day, designed to be fast and friction-free and completely customised to the needs of every customer.

MANUFACTURING: THE DIGITAL FACTORY

Delivering the keynote at industry association NASSCOM's annual summit, the CEO of one of the world's largest manufacturing organisations spoke eloquently about a new factory for producing factory robots they had established in China. The entire factory was run by robots working on a bed of automation, and the only human was the person in the control centre monitoring the movement of the robots and materials on the shop floor and tracking variations from the digital twinning methodologies that had been used to design the operations before the plant was commissioned.

Our own experience as digital transformation advisors to a large facility in Shenzhen was similar. Three years ago, this microprocessor manufacturing facility had 3,000 hard-working Chinese girls employed who would work dawn to dusk with just half an hour for a quick lunch, a nap at their worktables and frequent sips of Chinese tea to keep them going. A few months before COVID hit, this factory now employed just 400 women, each trained to have four robots as co-workers and managing the new work process as diligently, with much higher productivity than before. The digital factories empowered by smart manufacturing and Industry 4.0 may be like one of these two examples, but the new narrative will certainly be substantially superior to anything the world has ever experienced.

Indian manufacturing companies, particularly the SMEs (small and medium enterprises), have been slow starters in the adoption of digital but recent data from News Analysis and PWC show that Indian companies are at a digitisation level of 27% in comparison to a global level of 35% and before COVID struck were expected to reach a level of 65% in the next five years. With big data, robotics and simulation seen as the biggest levels for transformation, the expectation has been that 10% additional revenues and 10% reduction in operating costs could be the targets to achieve in this period. In fact, the shipments of autonomous robots to India were expected to be double the 2017 level in 2020. Even SMEs have started moving, some influenced by their larger OEM customers such as Suzuki, Tata Motors and Kirloskar and most prioritising frugal investments in automation and analytics and showing a preference for smaller digital solutions that connect legacy machinery on the shop floor to control systems easily operated by blue- and white-collar employees.

The trends that have shaped smart manufacturing and powered Industry 4.0 can be broadly categorised into six. The first is an extension of the materials planning and enterprise resource planning that have been implemented outside the shop floor, which are expected to start from a structured scenario analysis and demand forecasting, inventory optimisation using statistical modelling techniques, lost-sales scenario analysis and inventory stock level planning at all stages in the supply, production and demand cycle. The second trend is smart predictive maintenance, based on a constant feed of performance data from machines and production lines on the shop floor, with machine learning applied to provide contextual insights on scheduling machine or plant downtime for predictive maintenance. Organisations such as Kirloskar Oil Engines have extended this even to their finished products, which leave the factory with IoT sensors installed. Through their life cycle on customer sites, performance data is automatically transmitted and monitored from a central control centre in Khadki, Pune with self-healing tips and shutdown warnings to maintenance personnel on-site being sent out as and when required.

The next three trends impact the shop floor directly—the application of digital twins, human–robot collaborative operations and intelligent factory operations. GE Aviation has always been held up as one of the perfect examples of digital twins to model performance, predict failures and allow rapid testing of potential improvement on the production line. Over 5,000 performance parameters are captured by the 100 and more sensors installed in every engine, and mechanical and thermodynamic performance analysis is obtained from the engines while they are in operation. The digital continues to learn how to track the operations, evaluate different scenarios and improve uptime and operating efficiency. In conjunction with the move to 'everything as a service', folks in GE began to predict that one day, GE would not be selling aircraft engines but the actual uptime of the engine, charging more if the engine had higher uptime and less if it came in any period below the sold benchmark. GE also decided to introduce 3-D printing for site production of desired spare parts and components, further reducing wait time and downtime.

Digital Twin applications in Siemens and other advanced manufacturing companies such as ABB allow full production lines to be designed and operated virtually for many cycles before the first equipment is physically laid on the production line. PWC and BCG (Boston Consulting Group) have predicted that the digital design, simulation and integration market would be worth 45 billion dollars by the year 2021. And once the factory is laid out with the installation of plant and equipment, the new generation of robots would come marching in to take over precision operations on the shop floor with voice and speech recognition. The only role for humans on the shop floor would then be to manage the programming and coordination of robotic operations. Possibly the most evocative visualisation of the robotised shop floor we have even seen was in a workshop in Japan, where a slide photograph was shown of a factory in full production in the night shift at a major Japanese automobile manufacturer. The photograph was just a black frame with a white dot on it. The darkness was of course the factory, and the dot of light emanated from the torch of a security watchman looking around for any disturbance to the smooth human-free operations of the factory! This is also where IoT truly benefits intelligent factory operations, constantly improving performance against key metrics such as production yield rates and overall equipment effectiveness while enabling real-time production process monitoring.

What then will the digital factory of the future look like? One successful niche company from India, Onward Technologies, with operations in Europe, the UK and the US, has articulated its value proposition in this area extremely well, from engineering to shop floor automation to enterprise resource planning and analytics (see box on page 141 on Onward Technologies). In essence, a truly digital factory would have fully automated its market research and customer listening processes and built product lifecycle management and product engineering solutions to minimise time to market. Generative design principles and artificial intelligence would be used to schedule the production of custom-built products. When production starts on the automated shop floor after the digital twin simulations, it will be with machines that can optimise all production parameters based on material and process inputs. Operators on the cyber-physical production line will be supported by virtual agents supplying them information from IT systems as needed, and fully automated material handling systems would deliver parts as needed from an intelligent warehouse where stocking patterns are dynamically adjusted based on predicted demand patterns and adjusted production schedules. The role of the robots would be to respond to human intervention where needed and automatically adjust to moving part locations and machine settings.

Artificial intelligence will run like a stream through all the operations of the shop floor, from quality issue prediction to quality defects analysis using computer vision. It will also handle the prediction of maintenance needs and feeding back actual operating parameters into the machine learning processes to further improve intelligence for the future. AI will move well outside the shop floor to offer specific product recommendations to customers through the past transaction and preference data. AI can play a lead role particularly in call centres and service areas, with speech recognition, caller tone analysis and sentiment analysis used to suggest personalised responses to each customer and request. In the logistics area, AI can optimise route planning and substantially improve the efficiency of operations across the supply and demand chains.

A case in point is Jabil predictive factories, which have operations in Malaysia and Mexico. These use the Microsoft Cortana Intelligence Suite to provide real-time predictive analytics by connecting equipment and sensors with business intelligence for people, enabling comprehensive optimisation of factory operations. Jabil factories claim 10% savings in energy and scrap, and 17% savings in rework and decrease in manufacturing cycle time with an overall 80% accuracy in predicting early equipment or process failure.

While smart manufacturing and Industry 4.0 are truly exciting globally and adoption in the Western world and large parts of China and Asia has yielded superior business results, we should expect some continuity of sluggishness in India, particularly in the SME segment. The reasons are many. Labour wages continue to be low, particularly because of the large proportion of contract labour in use because of difficult labour laws. A large installed base on legacy equipment on production floors exists, with data islands being created everywhere. The skills in shop force blue- and white-collar employees still leave much to be desired. Hence frugal initiatives will continue, except when some companies take a leap of faith with leapfrogging capabilities such as SCADA and manufacturing execution systems, and it is more likely that a cluster approach with multiple companies investing in a shared services solution will be the interim solution. With quantum computing and 5G substantially reducing the cost of data processing and data transmission, there can be optimism that digital factories across India are just a few years away.

Featured Solutions Provider: Onward Technologies

Onward Technologies Ltd. is a publicly listed company in Mumbai, India, and has built a reputation for world-class computer-aided design and engineering solutions over two decades with clients in India and worldwide who are among the top global manufacturing majors. In the last two years, the company has expanded its solutions set to embrace the digital factory and fully connected plant operations.

Onward's core premise is that factories of the future will build intelligence and automation into all layers of their operations, from field level inputs provided by sensors and signals to sensing and control of plant operations through programmable logic controllers and IoT to monitoring and supervising on the shop floor using SCADA and other available software, comprehensive manufacturing execution systems to better business planning with intelligent ERP systems, AI, machine learning and predictive and prescriptive analytics.

The company's work encompasses four pillars of services. The first is automation, where it provides design automation, finite element analysis and traditional CAD solutions, simulation of shop floor performance and digital twin implementation, standalone and collaborative robots, process automation and robotics, manufacturing and robotic process automation and after-sales issue management. The second pillar is IoT and integration, involving connected devices and wearables on the shop floor, process automation and robotic simulation and after-sales predictive maintenance. The third pillar is cloud and edge computing with real-time data processing and cloud architecture to enable hybrid and private clouds for manufacturing master data management. The fourth and constantly evolving pillar is the broad area of analytics, comprising augmented and virtual reality solutions, time series analysis, inventory optimisation outside and in the factory, demand forecasting, cost analysis, after-sales warranty planning and customer loyalty analytics.

Onward delivers this wealth of capabilities through a very calibrated approach to clients. Discovery workshops are conducted over six to eight weeks at the customer's factory and office premises to understand the existing products, processes and systems, analyse gaps and opportunities, develop a technology deployment strategy and choose areas where there would be a maximum return on investment. With the major shift happening from an outsourced market to locations and ultimately to home markets or alternative locations, the company expects digital factory planning and implementation to be the core of its growth plans for the future.

EDUCATION

In the beginning, there was a piece of chalk and a blackboard. And then there was light! One wishes this were true in the field of digital transformation in education, but the reality is that there are miles to go before we can rest in peace that the future of our children, youth and even adult learners is truly safe. Most of us readers of this book would have come through fairly traditional education processes, adopted in schools by teachers and in colleges by lecturers and finally in graduate schools and universities for masters and doctoral programmes, where we learnt the art of critical thinking and analysis. We may have been fascinated by some glitzy new ideas and experimented with e-learning, massive open online courses (MOOCs) and assumed that transformation is truly underway. But what is the reality of this journey?

Our own first experience with e-learning was in the late 1990s when, as CEO of APTECH, Ganesh had the opportunity to engage McKinsey & Co to explore partnerships for technology-led learning across our 1,000-plus global network of training centres. In various discussions with universities and at that time fledgling e-learning providers such as Skillsoft, the charter was clear: what kind of technologies were available then and were on the horizon to come close to or even exceed the learning effectiveness of attending a class taught by a Tom Peters or even an Abdul Kalam? Twenty years later, the course completion rates for e-learning were still less than or just about 10%, reflecting the rather sorry state of technology's success in enabling education and ensuring good learning outcomes.

To understand the problems and also the emerging solutions, a dive into history is needed. One of the first evolutions was the Smart Class in schools with the deployment of DVD players, projectors and videos while colleges moved from 'chalk and talk' to epidiascopes, overhead projectors and eventually the ubiquitous PowerPoint. Books started getting converted to PDF formats and page-turner computer-based training software emerged. These were more a refresher of classroom materials than specifically designed for a new medium. By the year 2010, there was some sense of happiness that students were adapting to e-learning for pre-requisite, remedial and reinforcement learning, but the primacy of the class and the great teacher remained unquestioned for delivering the core lecture.

During the same period from 1995 to 2010, the increasing popularity and proliferation of television made it possible to use this medium as a large-scale delivery platform. In India, the first humble experiments of the national channel Doordarshan with its Countrywide Classroom programme met with a lukewarm experience. A bold experiment with the private channel Zee Telefilms conducted by author Uma in partnership with APTECH saw the launch of edutainment in the form of computer courses for adults and kids, all of which saw over 100,000 engaged learners and the creation of both Zee Education and a national network of support centres called Zed Points. In the meantime, the Indian Institutes of Technology decided to launch their own video series called NPTEL, which was a repeat of the rather weak national television experiment because it did not account for the reality that even the best professor of a subject could not be watched for two hours without allowing the students to interact in some manner. The maturing of satellite communications also provided an option to tele-education in the form of satellite-delivered education, which enjoyed brief popularity before waning away.

The need for interactivity resulted in a disaggregation of learning content, and instructional designers started creating courses with a mix of video, online tutorials and short interactions to ensure better understanding. Blended learning formats were adopted both in schools and colleges. The era of Google as the universal source of truth made it feasible for core content to be absorbed independently by students and the classroom to be more of a place for interaction. And in an almost innocuous manner, asynchronous learning, where the student was left to their own devices to manage the timing and pace of the learning process was replaced by much more interesting formats of synchronous learning. Blackboard, an American educational technology company became a standard medium for university integration, and with 'hand raising' now a possibility, classes became more engaging even when many learners were not in the same physical classroom as the teacher.

It is in the last five years and a bit more that online education has matured to a large extent. The most important example of this is HBX, the online offering of Harvard Business School (HBS). This has incorporated some of the best ideas of a galaxy of some of the world's best educators and industry professionals. Delivered from a studio in Boston, it gives a visual to the professor at the console of all 80 people in the class. Akin to the process followed in an HBS classroom, the professor is guided to see students who raise their hand and also engage with those whose attention span may be wandering. Stemming from this, many new experimental platforms for digital learning are emerging, including one revolutionary Indian product called Skills Alpha from our stable of digital innovations at 5F World. More about that in the chapter on skills.

The ideal future way of harnessing digital technology for better learning would be to ensure that four features of outstanding universities such as Cambridge in the UK and Harvard in the USA are integrated into the content and pedagogy of learning. The first of course is offering a full suite of career choices to students at the university level and not force a choice too early. This can be facilitated by AI bots that indicate clear pathways to students as well as corporate learners on employment options along with career growth pathways as the case may be. They must also provide an estimate based on an individual assessment of the effort the individual must put in to acquire the skills needed for that pathway.

The second feature would be to enable the skills on the chosen path to be acquired through an adaptive and personalised learning approach using the nest of asynchronous and synchronous pedagogies. A personalised approach would mean choosing the medium of delivery—whether text, video, quizzes, etc.—that are best suited to the learner. An adaptive approach would alter the learning level and pace of the course based on progress as evaluated by intermediate testing.

The third feature would be to encourage peer group learning, which is the biggest benefit of being on campus with other learners. AI can allow learners to interact in a curated manner, with students at similar stages of learning and also with others who have been on the pathway earlier and mastered a particular subject.

And finally, the fourth feature would be where technology can truly score over even the ideal university experience would be by offering a wide choice of mentors and coaches, both from within the campus and from the corporate environment and even a large group of willing senior people from the whole world.

We have seen the wonders of this approach work, even in the social sector where we run a large initiative called the Skills Lighthouses in the city of Pune in Western India. Attempting to transform the lives of 200,000 slum dwellers from 600-plus city slums, the lighthouses take in youth who wish to pursue sustainable livelihoods and help them through this full process. A multi-week 'agency' or aspiration-building programme supported by digital technology is the first step, followed by counselling on various opportunities where AR and VR are deployed to create near-lifelike experiences. Skilling is provided on-site and online in over 40 different skills, following which job placement or entrepreneurship opportunities are provided. The AI bot on the mobile phone is a constant companion for the person through the initial difficult years and keeps them engaged with their lighthouse peers and mentors. Our initial experiments have shown that placement records are over 50%, three times the national average for such initiatives, and the subsequent dropouts are less than 10% against the national number of 50%.

Into this promised land, let the learners of the future waken. If we harness commonly available technology uncommonly well, it can happen in the near future!

HEALTHCARE

Healthcare systems all over the world have become increasingly complex over the years and stand to benefit most by the thoughtful assimilation of digital technologies into all aspects of the patient enrolment and health delivery value chain. Digital healthcare holds the potential of living in society a more healthy and joyous experience, with precision in diagnosis and treatment personalisation. It can also make the provider–patient relationship friction-free.

At a peripheral level, member enrolment and linkage with payer services such as health insurance and government-run welfare programmes have been integrated with hospital information systems over the past decade and more, but the real value is expected to come by helping patients with wellness services, health tracking, tele-diagnostics, medical procedure necessity reviews. Hospitals and provider systems can be helped with care coordination and nurse triaging, optimising equipment utilisation, 3-D printing of materials at remote locations such as war zones and rural camps and patient case management across time and space barriers. Health education for patients as well as all members of the community served by the providers is a more recent and essential part of the service that can benefit from digital intervention.

In an outstanding report on hospitals of the future, Deloitte has called out five use cases for the future of healthcare delivery inside hospitals for very ill patients and home and outpatient ambulatory services. This is based on a simulation created with crowdsourced ideas by futurists, technology leaders, physicians and health administrators. The five categories identified in the Deloitte study are as follows:

1. Redefined care delivery
   Emerging features include centralised digital centres to enable decision-making as with an air traffic control function for airports, continuous clinical monitoring, targeted treatments including 3-D printing for surgeries and the use of smaller, portable devices for constant monitoring of acute-care hospitals.
2. Digital patient experience
   Digital and AI technologies can facilitate on-demand interaction and seamless processes to improve the patient experience. While not explicitly stated, one expects that a whole range of predictive and prescriptive analytics solutions to perceived and reported symptoms will be part of this area of work.
3. Enhanced talent development
   Robotic process automation (RPA) and AI can allow caregivers to spend more time providing care and less time documenting it. Most of the support and documentation process can be automated intelligently. This is a far cry from the early work in medical transcription, where doctors spoke into recording devices all over the USA and the transcription was done in back-office centres in India. Intelligent automation can

truly enable checks and balances to be incorporated into the documentation process.

4. Operational efficiencies through technology
   Digital supply chains, automation, robotics and next-generation interoperability can drive operations management and back-office efficiencies. This is not different from the data continuum from the shop floor through materials and production planning and customer servicing that manufacturing companies are already mastering. To continue the analogy, digital twinning might well become a possibility, using which complex operations can be simulated and their possible impacts analysed before the patient is wheeled into the operation theatre.
5. Healing and well-being design
   The well-being of patients and staff members—with an emphasis on the importance of environment and experience in healing—will likely be important in future hospital designs. Every aspect of wellness, diet management, symptoms tracking and post-operative care will fall under the ambit of this factor.

Digital health in its widest sense can encompass every digital journey that can benefit the patient and provider systems and explores the intersection of digital technology with health. From mobile health tracking apps to robotic surgery, AI and machine and deep learning, digital health can help a community improve and track their health, need fewer visits to a physician or hospital, ease symptoms before they become overly aggressive, shorten the lifespan of a disease and even trim the medical bills which have been crippling, especially in the Western world. While the recent dithering with the unknown COVID virus may not inspire too much confidence, there is no doubt that the data gathered will help ward off future pandemics. Healthcare practitioners the world over should have learnt from their experiences in 2020 and be better prepared for unusual and large-scale future illnesses.

The encouraging trend is the active participation of tech giants in digital health research. Bill Gates received his share of bad press and a lot of credit for jumping in wholeheartedly into the vaccine development process soon after COVID hit the US. Predictably, a leader like Google has jumped into the wearable health market, launched health platforms and put serious effort into artificial intelligence for healthcare. Verily, the health sciences unit of Google's parent Alphabet has undertaken a longitudinal study of patient health and is designing wearables to track physical biomarkers of mental trauma. Their other health entity Calico is committed to combating ageing processes and defeating death. Readers of the book *Homo Deus* by Yuval Noah Harari will recall that Professor Harari has predicted that future generations will live well beyond 100 years, albeit with multiple metallic parts, and will call for substantial new investments in geriatric care, new skills and occupations every 15 years and new ways of prolonging human relationships, definitely a topic for future research and many future books!

The other FAANG companies are not far behind in their focus on digital health. Apple Computer is creating an ecosystem that extends from the provider to the consumer with medical parameter and even fall detection features built into the Apple Watch and new research and health records management facilities made available to hospitals. Amazon has bought a medication delivery firm and is building a health benefits platform that will see it compete fiercely with Microsoft in the healthcare domain.

Lifestyle measures of the future are also coming into the purview of the healthcare digital pioneers. Sleep quantity and quality measurement are now fairly common, and reproductive health and diet management are becoming new areas of interest. Interest has also been sparked in exomedicine, or the study of the impact of a micro-gravity environment on medical treatments which could then be applied on earth. The potential impact this could have on research, development and commercialisation of new medical solutions will be the subject of work in laboratories in space.

The real challenge that providers working at the intersection of digital and healthcare will face will be to add to the capabilities while reducing the costs of availing newer diagnostic, treatment and wellness services. While high blood pressure, cholesterol and type II diabetes are already being controlled by blood pressure cuffs, connected glucose monitors and digitally enforced habits and lifestyle improvement, the future lies in the management of addiction, depression and other diseases. Digital tracking will certainly be one way of detecting cases early and reducing the overall costs of disease tracking and management. The digital health market is currently valued at over 250 billion dollars. Transparency Market Research forecasts that this figure will double by 2025, with 'patient-centric healthcare' and mobile health itself contributing close to 200 billion dollars and wearables, a relatively new phenomenon touching 30 billion dollars in a couple of years.

Digital healthcare offers many other potential benefits as well, primarily among them the creation of large data repositories which can provide actionable insights to treatment providers, takers and government systems to help improve the effectiveness and slash the cost of healthcare worldwide. Privacy concerns will continue to be a niggling area of worry as also the lack of awareness or use of these innovations by a large segment of the population, premature and possibly faulty diagnosis for people who get overly obsessed with symptoms. On the flip side will be avoidable incidents with people who exercise excessively or follow regimens suggested for athletes by their wearables and avoid visiting the doctor even when it is advisable to do so. Implants for everything and everywhere is also a concern. The Harari prediction of every human being walking around like a humanoid with large amounts of metal in various parts of the body cannot be over-emphasised.

Medical regulations may also prove to be a dampener to the excitement around digital health, though the digital health action plan launched by the US FDA in 2017 has been joined by the likes of Apple, Verily and Samsung. Similarly, the European Medical Devices Regulation plan due to come into force clarifies and broadens the definition of medical devices and apps and strengthens traceability. The American Hospital Association has produced a reassuring report that over three-quarters of US hospitals now have partially or fully computerised telehealth systems in place. The ongoing pull from the medical ecosystem and the push through rapid developments in key technologies such as robotics, AI, AR/VR and 5G communications hold out a very real promise of digital health transformation and massive growth opportunities for the future.

The future of digital healthcare depends on the wisdom of health regulators in each country, the investments that hospitals, physicians and clinical chains are willing to make in process reengineering, analytics, technology and people and the willingness of the citizens of the community to adapt to the changes and adjust to technology rather than the friendly face of the family doctor. The benefits for individuals, providers and policymakers are likely to be staggered—the upfront investments will get more than the expected financial returns in terms of operational efficiencies, patient satisfaction and staff comfort. Developing a culture of service orientation and encouraging demands for more information will ensure that the healthcare systems in many countries, which have been suffering from legacy technologies and poor attention to patient satisfaction, are transformed to create the healthcare systems of the future.

The Healthcare Digital Platforms of Citius

CitiusTech: Overview

CitiusTech is a specialist provider of healthcare technology services and solutions, serving more than 100 healthcare organisations worldwide. CitiusTech's strong and deep understanding of healthcare technology has enabled it to track the industry evolution closely and build capabilities and platforms ahead of the industry. It focuses on multiple areas of digital technology, such as business intelligence, mobility and IoT, big data, cloud computing, predictive analytics and data science. It serves four different markets across the healthcare ecosystem—healthcare providers, healthcare payers, medical technology companies and life sciences organisations.

CitiusTech has four key proficiencies, each focusing on a unique part of digital innovation:

- Enterprise applications: Architecture, design, development, testing and deployment of healthcare applications. Focus on next-gen technologies, architectures and deployment models such as cloud, mobile, IoT, DevOps, telehealth, automation, etc.
- Data management: End-to-end support for the data management needs of healthcare organisations for data sharing, real-time patient care, data analytics, enterprise data warehousing and big data management.
- Performance management: Leveraging healthcare data and analytics for clinical quality performance, financial performance and regulatory compliance.
- Data science and consulting: Focus on AI/ML, consulting and UX expertise and tools to analyse and solve complex problems in healthcare.

CitiusTech Digital Health Platforms

CitiusTech offers specialised platforms and solutions to help healthcare organisations address core digital innovation needs. This involves:

- Aggregating and leveraging diverse healthcare datasets (including big data)
- Driving value-based performance through business intelligence/analytics
- Leveraging AI/ML and data science to enhance health outcomes
- Enabling effective interoperability between healthcare organisations, physicians, consumers, etc.

CitiusTech's platforms include the following:

H-Scale (Healthcare Data Management)

Due to the diverse and distributed nature of health information, aggregating, normalising and leveraging structured/

semi-structured/unstructured healthcare data is a key challenge for the global healthcare industry. H-Scale is a next-generation platform for healthcare data acquisition, processing, governance, quality, security and advanced analytics. It has a unique set of features designed for healthcare data, such as pre-built data quality rules, healthcare data pipeline, big data processing and real-time streaming analytics.

BI-Clinical (Healthcare BI/Analytics)
BI-Clinical is among the world's leading healthcare BI and analytics platforms. It is used by some of the world's leading healthcare organisations to address challenges around clinical, financial, operational and regulatory reporting. The platform has some specialised features that address quality and performance management needs of large health systems, such as rules management, 700 pre-built healthcare measures and real-time audit. BI-Clinical has been deployed across more than 5,000 locations, impacting over 40 million lives.

FAST+ (Healthcare Interoperability)
CitiusTech's FAST+ is a specialised solution designed to help organisations deploy the FHIR (Fast Healthcare Interoperability Resources) standard. (FHIR is a new standard released by HL7 for exchanging healthcare information electronically.) FAST+ gives healthcare organisations the ability to accelerate their FHIR strategy by helping them set up FHIR APIs, implement identity and access management, manage data ingestion and store data.

Embedded Intelligence (AI/ML Solutions for Healthcare)
CitiusTech has a healthcare-focused data science team that provides AI/ML modelling and implementation solutions to healthcare organisations. It uses a unique embedded intelligence framework that designs data science models to drive incremental enhancements to clinical, financial and operational processes within healthcare organisations.

FINANCIAL INCLUSION

In India, the three great digital innovations in the last decade have been what is famously known as the 'JAM trinity', with 'J' standing for Jan Dhan (wealth of the people), 'A' for Aadhaar, the unique identity system for every citizen which now covers almost 80% of the 1.3 billion population and 'M' for mobility, the revolution with handheld phones that is slowly reaching every person in every corner of the country. This has made every citizen directly reachable for communication as well as for benefits transfer when required with minimum friction. One of the biggest benefits of this digital capability in the country has been financial inclusion.

Financial inclusion is an aspiration, not just in India but in every part of the world. Billions of lower-income individuals, as well as billions of medium, small and micro enterprises, lack access to banking insurance payment transfer and other basic financial services. Among the developing parts of the world, Africa was probably the first to attempt financial inclusion with the assistance of telecom operators such as Vodacom, but financial and operational costs continued to be high, limiting usage till the broad sweep of digital made it more feasible to access the entire population. The expectation is that 5G going mainstream will transform the access and make inclusion a reality everywhere. The other concern of data security will continue to linger like a cloud over the expansion potential of inclusion, but over time, the benefits will far outweigh any fears or concerns in this regard. This also presents a large future opportunity for public–private partnerships in the financial inclusion and microfinance space, where customers near and at the bottom of the period can be better served better through strong digital leverage to reduce costs, increased security and total trust.

Developing an ecosystem, ideally enabled by a collaborative digital platform, is the best way to get all participants to contribute towards true financial inclusion. The digital ecosystem will have to educate small traders and show owners, home businesses and every individual, at home or in the office, and make them financially and digitally literate. It will also need to give access to credit for small businesses.

Our own experience in the social sector with entities such as Social Venture Partners India and Pune City Connect has been that digital literacy, which we started implementing in 2015 after the announcement of Prime Minister Modi's National Digital Literacy Mission, is the first step to creating expectation and then generating demand for these services. In the city of Pune, where digital literacy has moved to digital empowerment and nearly half the eligible population in the 600-plus slum communities in the Pune Municipal Corporation have been covered. The confidence and entrepreneurial instincts that have been aroused in these beneficiaries have led to the conviction that the next stage is large-scale entrepreneurship and digital autonomy. Women at home and even youth will seek vocations to apply their digital literacy, which will create a good livelihood. This will also create the necessary demand pull for financial inclusion. Soon clusters of small businesses will evolve, very similar to the early Indian experience of village *haats* or local marketplaces. Digital platforms will emerge that connects the small businesses, capital providers and potential collaborators and customers. This will also create a peer-lending opportunity between participants in the ecosystem. Over a period of time, in every community and across the country, the digital platform has to make a trusted financial ecosystem and be able to provide insurance, working capital financing and simple 'Know Your Customer' (KYC) mechanisms that enable businesses to collaborate and grow in an environment of mutual help and trust.

The government of course as a large role to play in this, both in terms of setting up simple regulatory mechanisms for these clusters and enabling a digital infrastructure such as the BharatNet, which serves through a national optic fibre network. The government must also maintain the financial histories of the hitherto unbanked. Financial institutions too, particularly payment banks and small savings banks, must develop and launch personalised financial products for small customers and leverage social listening, sentiment and behaviour analysis and collaboration to further refine their understanding of small consumer needs and facilitate better service. And as in the case of Africa, technology companies, particularly providers of voice and data networks, cloud services and business correspondents, will need to be key partners to this ecosystem. Finally, service providers for national and foreign remittances, skills development agencies and other participants in every small town, *gram panchayat* or village will need to be available with the expectation, not of making a fast buck today, but of being a participant in the growth and value creation story of tomorrow.

In India, it is not just the small firms but also leading software companies such as TCS that have played a stellar role in building and supporting financial inclusion networks. TCS leaders have been quoted as saying that the next wave of solutions will leverage digital technologies and data science to analyse the dynamic needs of customers and have services on offer when the need arises. Use of machine learning models to predict customer response to new financial products and quick launches of products that meet risk management criteria without compromising the stated or implied need of the customer is seen as a tangible opportunity for the future. As more and players with a long-term orientation begin to participate in financial inclusion, innovation with products and business models will expand the market and make financial inclusion a profitable and scalable opportunity for all.

DIGITAL TRANSFORMATION OF PROCESSES

The discussion on business processes has been active for over 30 years since the seminal work of Michael Hammer and James Champy on business process reengineering (BPR) brought the process view of organisations into sharp focus. In two earlier books on BPR co-authored by Ganesh and Indian BPR specialist M.S. Jayaraman, we have explained that a functional or departmental view of an organisation tends to be siloed and also results in orthogonal workflows because decision-making and the need for approvals from department heads often flow orthogonally to the desired streamlined flow of the process.

The process view of any organisation normally has three core processes—product or service design, order fulfilment and logistics. Of course, these will have different nomenclatures for different industry segments. But in a very broad sense, any successful organisation is known for the speed and relevance of its new product and service launches, the end-to-end management of customer journeys and all administrative and support systems working with the maximum possible efficiency. These ensure that the customer gets the product or service with the minimum fuss and maximum happiness.

What then is the role of digital? Every technology should be lining up to ensure that it is not an end in itself but a true enabler of customer-focused business processes. To go down the list of the technologies already explained, our core SMAC stack enables overall efficiency and cost optimisation of all processes by moving software, infrastructure and platforms to the cloud. It allows easy access through mobile devices to all permissible data, engages with and listens to the voice of the customer and the supply-and-demand chain partners through social channels. It also builds the data marts and warehouses while providing the fishing rods necessary to get actionable analytics from the data lake. The edge technologies, IoT, AR/VR, blockchain, 3-D printing, etc., are all additional enablers for both the customer and logistics process efficiency and effectiveness. The third wave of digital, including quantum computing and 5G, are constantly looking for ways to enhance the speed of product introduction, customer access and smooth partnering with other players in the ecosystem.

For the CXO reading this book, the recommended approach would be to take stock of the efficiency of every process and sub-process and apply both incremental improvement ideas and reengineering breakthroughs to put digital at every possible touchpoint. Within the domain or industry in which the company operates, it would be good to understand who is 'best in class' and attempt to benchmark process efficiencies against these players. The constant benchmarking and process quality enhancement will lead the company through the reengineering process and finally deliver the Holy Grail of comprehensive transformation!

7

Talent and Culture: Force Multipliers

DIGITAL TRANSFORMATION: IT'S ALL ABOUT WINNING THE HEARTS AND MINDS

It is possible to make a strong case for digital transformation on the strength of quantifiable metrics such as reduction of costs from better control of inventory or improvements in the supply chain, enhanced customer experience leading to enhanced sales or retention of customers, expansion of market with the introduction of new products and services and so on. These potential outcomes can be expected to be achieved when the organisation radically rethinks its use of the right technology, processes and talent under a capable leadership. However, digital transformation is much more than adopting new technologies or nurturing the innovation ecosystem. The fundamental factor that can spell success with the digital transformation journey is the business leader's ability to create the right culture and environment to embrace and facilitate the change. Unlike in the past, when organisation strategy once developed would have three to five years to be implemented, organisations committing to digital transformation should be prepared to make changes and adapt daily.

Therefore, the importance of aligning the values of employees with those of the organisation has to be the top priority of the organisation as it embarks upon the digital transformation journey. It's as important to assess the culture risks of the organisation as it is to assess the business risks to ensure that changes in processes or the planned technology adoption are successfully implemented.

Employee reluctance or cynicism in some quarters if ignored or not sensed by the management can have a major negative impact as organisations move forward with their transformation plans without the total-buy in from all concerned and may be forced to pause or take a few steps back to address such issues, thus losing time and the momentum with the digital plans. The organisation runs the risk of losing its market relevance or even revenue. Hence cultural readiness has to be accorded a high priority for moving forward with digital plans.

In this context, businesses need to take care that digital strategy is not developed independently. The first level rollout plan should be in sync with the culture that exists and take advantage of those elements of the current culture that supports the digital strategy. It may not be possible to bring about changes overnight in the way organisations work. Therefore, while the ideal status should be conceptualised, it is prudent to take advantage of the existing strengths in the current organisational culture, identifying departments or functions that are willing to be the change champions and the first movers and set examples for the rest of the organisation. Every organisation and its culture is unique, and so will its digital transformation programme be. Hence it is also extremely important to blend informal interventions along with the changes in the approaches for metric-driven performance management, ensuring continuous communication and personal touch of the leadership is sustained with the employees. The goals for digital transformation can be achieved only by winning the hearts and minds of people who are part of the journey and by inspiring them to raise their level of aspiration.

TRANSFORMATION IMPERATIVES: THE HR FUNCTION FOR THE DIGITAL ERA

The fundamental premises around customers, customer needs, the business model, the competition landscape and offerings are all changing the context of digital transformation. Hence the HR function too needs to become agile and supportive of the dynamic needs of the business. Building a culture of flexibility and bringing a shift in the focus towards delivering solutions have become important for a company to be considered a reliable partner to the business. Familiar hierarchical structures must be replaced with a networked organisation design that allows work to be defined around teams based on specific business needs. The duration of the team and its composition must be reconfigured as required. Teams need to be coached about new work principles and performance assessment—the need to move away from following instructions and being able to lead in different areas even within a project and to be able to collaborate while being respectful of each other's areas of strength, thus adapting to new working relationships that are no longer 'command and control' but 'collaborate and win'.

If the HR function develops analytical capabilities and useful insights juxtaposed with business parameters, they could actively contribute to the strategic trajectories of the business. The insights drawn from analytics could go a long way in deciding effective spending on employee engagement as well as in building links with learning and development to maximise performance management. The HR function also has an important role to play in fostering innovation in the organisation. Building communities of practice and strengthening the knowledge repositories within the organisation to nurture best practices, new ideas and innovation and connect them with the expertise available in academic and other institutions in the ecosystem will be essential for sustaining its competitive advantage in the marketplace. Ultimately, for digital transformation to take off and gain acceptance within an organisation, HR has a big role to play in managing the change and nurturing the new culture essential for millennials and others to thrive and succeed.

WINNER TAKES ALL: THE WAR FOR DIGITAL TALENT

With talent being the key differentiator for businesses embracing digital transformation, the tasks related to acquiring, grooming and retaining quality talent for growth and sustenance of the business would have to be managed with extreme care. This is because resources would expect personalisation and customised employee journeys during their association with the organisation. HR heads must therefore be willing to revisit all dimensions of the traditional HR model and using a design thinking approach, visualise the new age employee journey. Unlike in the past, when skilled resources were required only to support the IT function, organisations need digitally empowered resources across all functions in the context of digital transformation. This makes the matter significantly more challenging. Further, since digital capability is the combination of multiple technologies where each evolves simultaneously, some independently and many interdependently, the talent readiness and profile requirements have become even more complex. The talent pool that is well adapted to such an evolution while at the same time being well prepared for future trajectories of technologies is difficult to find.

It is to be noted that in the past, IT upgradation was primarily driven by the IT function. Since the skills required pertained to mostly the IT function or limited to training on the usage of systems built by the IT department, the IT function took the lead in the skilling or reorientation of employees. Today, the requirement is a combination of capabilities in areas such as customer behaviour or psychology, design and analytics, along with the technical skills as most of the new application development work is centred around the external world. Further, it is equally important for technical professionals to have an understanding of business domains and for business teams to have the basic technical skills to function successfully in a world where every aspect is digitally driven.

HR managers will have to deal with this significant change and get ready to reorient the employees and also put in place new methods for recruitment of such resources. As newer technologies and innovation would have to be rapidly absorbed by the organisation, a young talent force with cutting-edge capabilities would always be in demand. Therefore, the longevity of employees and rethinking employment contracts would become important areas to be addressed. Customers will favour organisations that are 'fashionistas', i.e., those who are first to market with savvy technology-based solutions.

Employee experience is central to this function. HR managers are applying design principles to reimagine the employee lifecycle journey with the opportunity to remain always connected with the employees. The learning and development (L&D) function is expected to be aligned with the aspirations of the employees while the digital learning solution, supported by AI tools, augment their learning effectiveness manifold by constantly shadowing and keeping the employees up-to-date with the necessary knowledge and skills. Personalisation of learning paths becomes possible thanks to digital learning platforms. Along with these, coaches who help employees get equipped with competencies required for current and future roles are welcomed by employees, as these initiatives are viewed as positive indicators highlighting the value of individuals. In the digital era, quality talent will be drawn towards organisations seen as winners—those organisations that place individuals at the core of their functioning and create an environment of trust and opportunity for ongoing learning and career advancement.

Talent analytics has become crucial in the context of large-scale hiring and retention needs of businesses. Detailed profiling of candidates based on information about their background and experience in the public domain, coupled with social media analytics, provides useful insights to recruiters about leadership and other qualities and the potential stickiness of a candidate. Alerts about likely exits as well as recommendations to managers for proactive actions to ensure employee satisfaction provided by the HR analytics engine are being embraced actively by managers. Talent retention involves an ongoing review of compensation, and it now comprises a comprehensive mix of activities aimed at employee engagement. Therefore, leadership capability that brings together an understanding of technology, business processes and people management required to drive digital transformation has to be carefully cultivated.

THE IMPORTANCE OF LEARNING FOR THE SUCCESS OF DIGITAL TRANSFORMATION

Organisations big and small have recognised the impact of digital and are gearing up for transformational changes in their business models. They are redefining processes, technologies and people capabilities aligned with the emerging needs of their customers. When it comes to people and the need for change, the focus must be on equipping them with the skills required to function effectively in the digital world. While this is indeed an essential prerequisite for the success of the transformation programme, with the realisation that 'business as usual' would have to change in every aspect to be counted as an effective partner in the transition process and beyond. The learning and development function must rethink its approach to learning design and outcomes.

Design Imperatives for Corporate Learning in the Digital Era
Gone are the days when the learning and development function used to be viewed as a tool primarily for motivating employees. Despite the frequent discussions on the return on investment (ROI) of learning initiatives, it was generally accepted that effectiveness and outcomes are difficult to measure. Hence surveys and feedback from learners and their supervisors were the main metrics to establish the relevance and the usefulness of the programme. While these will continue to play an important role in the digital era as well and there are several excellent tools to capture and analyse the usefulness of the programme, the fundamental shift taking place in the context of digital transformation is the feasibility of establishing close links with business goals, the ever-changing dynamics of the business landscape and the possibility of measuring outcomes and impact in real time—all of which can now be factored into the learning design process. With in-depth analytics available on multiple fronts, designing the learning programme is no longer an art but is blended with science. The principles of agility built into the design construct and make it capable of adapting to the dynamic elements of the business. Thus, learning design today is enmeshed with the business goals

of the organisation, and the L&D function is expected to play a proactive and central role in aiding business success. This is a huge departure from the past, when L&D function mostly played a reactive and passive role. Let's examine the key elements that would require attention to make the learning design for the digital era a success.

What Millennials Want: Individual Learning Needs and Style

Even when an organisation provides a set of L&D pathways, employees, especially millennials, prefer their own learning pathways and prefer to learn at their own pace and use the style that best suits them. This may be different from the plan that organisations work upon. Therefore, the moot question is how organisations recognise individual needs and styles of learning and align their talent development plan with them and how they can keep them motivated with training initiatives while building a sense of connectedness between the employees.

First, organisations need to have a mechanism to redefine the competencies required for existing and emerging roles at regular intervals, given the dynamic nature of the business and the resultant employee performance expectations. Employees should have an opportunity to continually assess their readiness for the future and have the ability to access the learning pathways and the required learning content. The transparency and flexibility that organisations can provide in this context using digital platforms will build motivation and confidence in employees towards their own future.

Next, L&D has to come forward to redraw the boundaries of learning by not restricting learning to the classroom or the already-created e-learning content repositories and find ways of expanding the horizons of learning from multiple new channels. These channels may include content freely available on the internet, tapping the knowledge of colleagues and coaching by experts and others. With digital tools and technologies available, learning can take place outside the organisation at the convenience of employees in areas of their interest and choice. Employees are consequently not entirely dependent on the organisation for self-development.

Some organisations may already be facilitating these avenues, but the challenge with most is that these learning channels work in silos. Therefore, neither does the L&D function have the visibility on how the learning and development of individuals are shaping up nor does the organisation have the ability to access and expand on the knowledge assets—tacit and explicit—on an ongoing basis. This calls for a robust digital learning platform that is plugged into all the existing HR systems—HRMIS, performance management system, competency dictionaries and the learning management systems. It must also create a comprehensive approach to enable all stakeholders, including business, HR, employees and the content partners to come together and create a vibrant ecosystem for talent development (Figure 7.1).

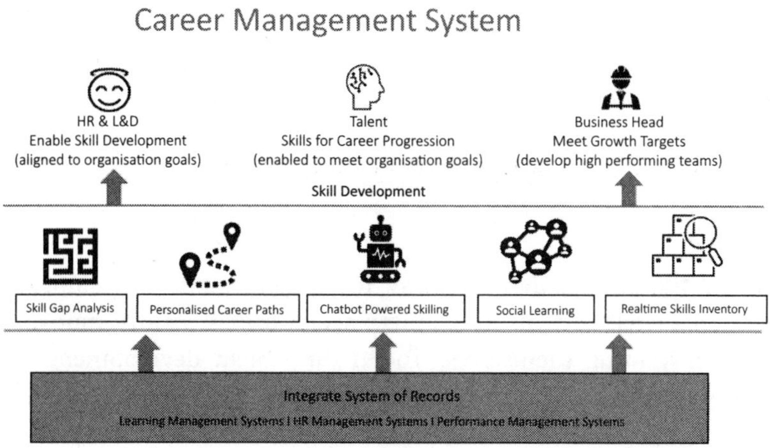

FIGURE 7.1 *Framework for Integrated Career Management System*

Content-centric Approach to Give Way to Learner-centric Approach

The other significant advantage for the organisation from these interactions between employees is the ability to understand the gaps in current offerings or how customers are being serviced and speedily address them. The digital platform can thus also act as the fountainhead for breakthrough ideas and innovation. By assigning weightages to such healthy interactions and recognising and rewarding employees for their answers to queries and the personal initiatives demonstrating their competencies, HR managers will see a significant return on investment on the digital learning platform by nurturing a positive culture in the organisation.

Why a Skills-focused Training Approach Is Necessary for the Digital Transformation Journey (Figure 7.2)

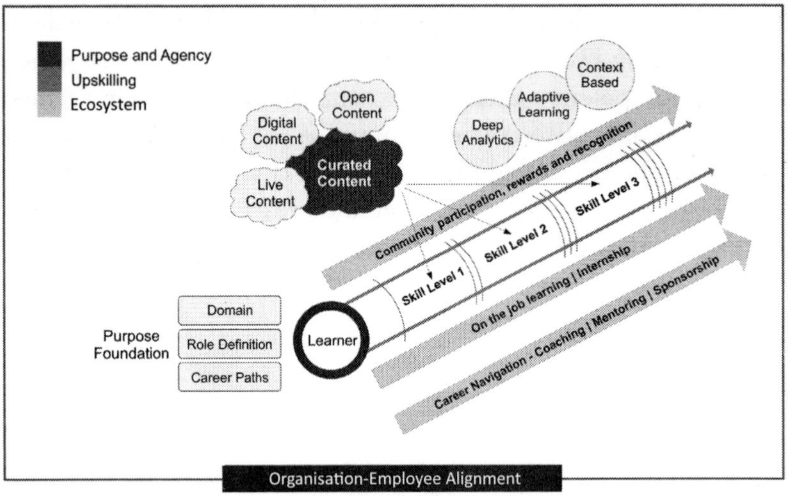

FIGURE 7.2 *Framework for Upskilling*

In the digital era, the only way for organisations and employees to remain relevant in the marketplace is by constantly innovating and reinventing themselves. To do this, talent development must recognise that by acquiring new skills, capabilities can be enriched or enhanced. It should be feasible to identify specific skill sets required for specific roles and, along with the previously acquired capabilities and experience, equip oneself to handle new assignments. Hence organisations need to start mapping the skills inventory, help employees draw up aspirational career tracks based on the skill gaps against role requirements and provide upskilling opportunities to attain the desired goals. Businesses can thus leverage the experience of their talent pool and simultaneously create pathways to acquire the required capabilities in the shortest possible time. New talent acquisition will also have to be made based on skill requirements, and new hire orientation and induction can be focused on the skill gaps mapped, thus shifting the ownership of upskilling to the individuals as their success is intrinsically linked with continual skill development.

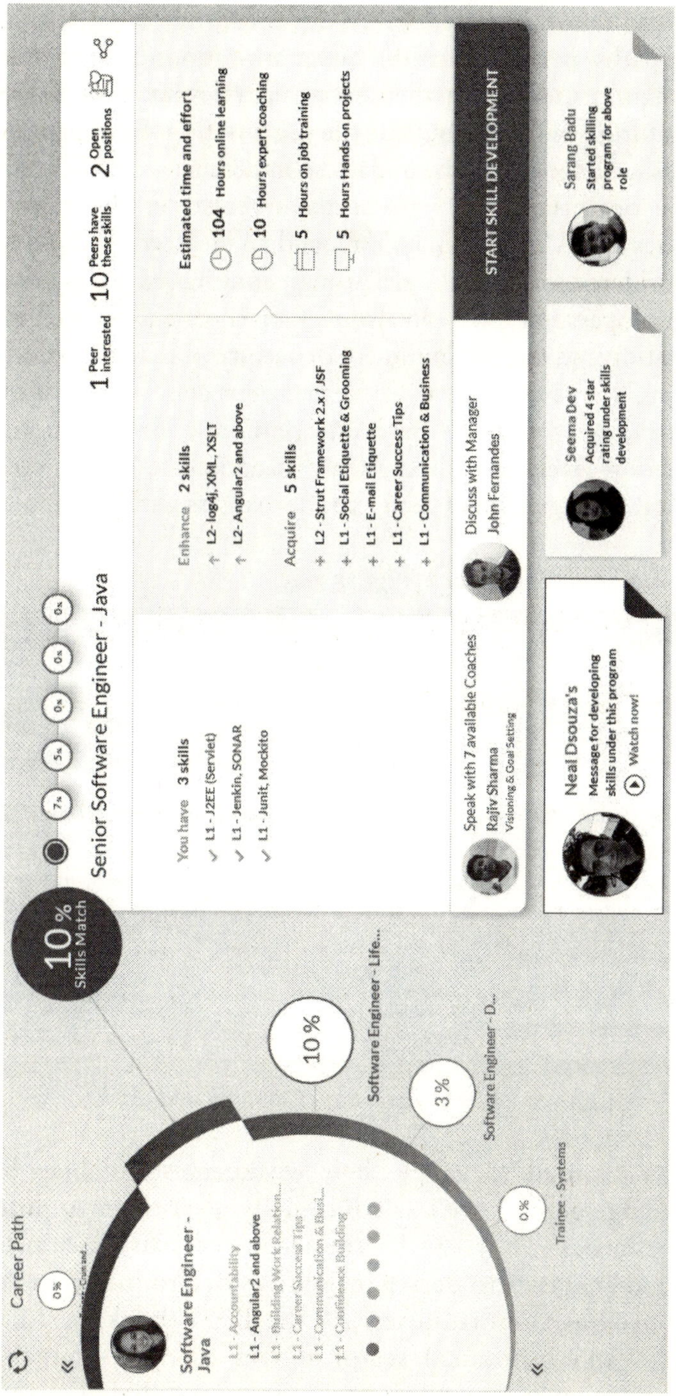

FIGURE 7.3 *Career Navigator (Courtesy: Skills Alpha)*

An organisation powered by AI tools can first suggest the ideal career pathway or support the career aspirations of the employees (see Figure 7.3). It can then serve up relevant and customised content from within or outside the organisation. Further, based on the business needs and the updated competencies or skills required by the organisation as well as the interests of the employees, analytics and AI tools can recommend an ideal set of employees to be considered for upskilling. Through continuous interaction with the employees, AI tools can also pick up silent cues related to their motivation and predict imminent departure or dissatisfaction, thus bringing forth timely alerts to the managers about the need to have conversations with them. Such interventions addressing both their motivation levels as well as their customised learning needs can help HR managers build better connectedness with the employees.

Mapping Skills Inventory (Figure 7.4)

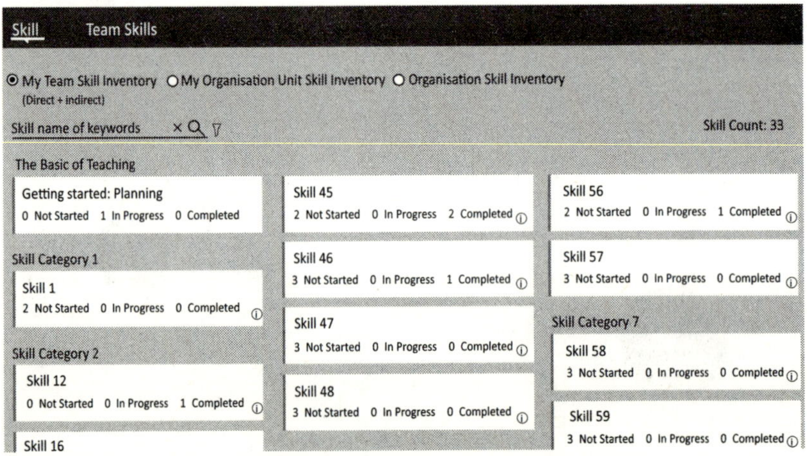

FIGURE 7.4 *Skills Inventory (Courtesy: Skills Alpha)*

AI can be used to gauge their weaknesses and help bridge knowledge gaps as well as continually alert them to potential opportunities. They can be trained to use customer profiles, data and analytics to derive insights to determine cross-selling and upselling opportunities. As the BFSI (banking, financial services and insurance) sector moves towards omnichannel strategy encouraging employees, agents and digital channel to work in tandem, all the stakeholders will need to be oriented to work in this new environment. For this, the training will have to be centred around individuals and their need to become better at catering to the needs of their end customers.

One significant factor affecting most performers in organisations is the urgent need to embed analytics-driven approaches into their functioning as the roles have become more and more complex over the last few years. Digital learning platforms provide analytics support to business managers and L&D managers to effectively manage their training budgets. The customisation experience aligned with the business requirements can also be fine-tuned as a result. Deep analytics can help teams develop personalised plans and monitor their progress. Investments in technology can be justified only if the correlation can be established between learning and business outcomes such as sales growth, employee engagement, customer satisfaction index, attrition rates and employee engagement score. Just as the customer engagement parameter has become more and more scientific and data-driven, the measurement of learning effectiveness is expected to become more accurate and reliable. Digital learning platforms with their built-in analytics and the capability of bringing together multitudes of relevant content promptly may be the game changer for businesses working on the transformation agenda.

The successful translation of learning design into learning outcomes has been largely dependent on the content and the trainers. In the digital era, the 'content is king' approach is no longer valid, as the content has to be contextualised and adapted to situations, learner profiles, learning styles, speed and format of learning. Above all, the focus is shifting to the learner experience, which is defined by the environment and the peer-to-peer and group interaction, which have substantially improved the quality of learning. Learning effectiveness is therefore no longer determined by the content and the profile of trainers alone. Curation of content based on learning design is more important than being dependent upon a single source or known sources of content. This is because content is available in plenty in multiple formats and can be multi-sourced from various content publishers, experts within and outside the organisation as well as through social media. It can then be stitched together to create learning mosaics based on patterns of learning assimilated with the help of learner analytics without losing sight of business objectives or their expected learning outcomes. Moving away from an approach that involves a mason building everything ground up, to assembling prefabricated modules, the construction industry could expedite the speed of delivery and also increase customisation. A similar approach is now expected with learning architecture that facilitates quick assembling and updating of content at higher speeds and lower costs and supports smart deployment of digital tools such as gaming, simulation, augmented reality and machine learning, significantly enhancing learning productivity.

However, even in the digital world, there is definitely space for brick-and-mortar and face-to-face learning. The debate about the digital environment should not be about whether there would be a role for trainers. It must be about how well-thought is the learning design that comprehensively brings together the best of both worlds. It is the ability to combine best of digital tools, curated content, insights from analytics and online and offline interactions with trainer- or expert-led training that will eventually determine the success of learning programmes in the corporate environment.

Digital learning platforms recognise that individuals can access multiple sources of content. Hence, they are designed to facilitate this requirement. Apart from organisation-designed content, digital learning platforms such as Skills Alpha provide access to numerous external channels of learning and also nurture networked learning and user-generated content. Coursera, YouTube, Udemy among others are frequented by all. By integrating these channels into the platform, it becomes feasible to appeal to varying learning patterns and styles of the employees and thus add a significant depth and dynamic edge to the content. Further, byte-sized and video-based content is increasingly preferred as learners have a short span of time. This trend has to be addressed by the digital platform. Coaching and feedback from on-the-job training are other useful dimensions of learning that should be added to the learning platform, thus providing a seamless experience for the employees. As a result, training managers need to spend more of their time in content curation rather than original content creation (Figure 7.5).

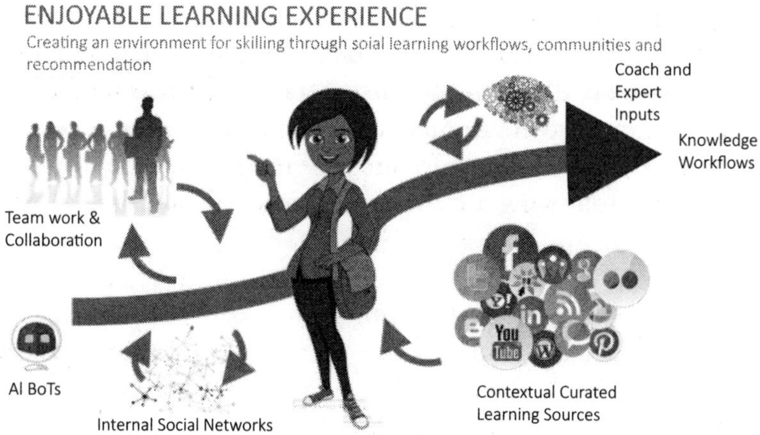

FIGURE 7.5 *Learning Experience Framework (Courtesy: Skills Alpha)*

Banking, financial services and insurance sectors are in the throes of tumultuous changes leading to a significant focus on the ongoing training of employees. Not only is there competition from within the sector to scale up and acquire the maximum market share in the shortest possible time, but new digital service providers are springing up with alternate options for customers.

Further to this, ongoing statutory and regulatory changes are impacting the business, necessitating new processes and compliance. The BFSI sector has been at the forefront of using the power of digital technology not only for creating a superior customer experience but also for recognising the advantage of using digital technologies for retooling and reskilling their employees. Given the large number of employees required to be trained, high levels of attrition, particularly in sales roles, and the challenges of geographic dispersion, technology-led learning has been adopted by several organisations as the catalyst for talent transformation.

In the insurance industry, for instance, it is observed that there is very little contact with the broker in the period between the sale and the claim. This leads to the problem of how insurance agents are perceived by customers. In the banking sector too, employees are used to customers walking into their branch to seek their services even today. Many of them are not comfortable when they are mandated to seek out their customers proactively for their needs. The traditional approach of being seen as a trusted advisor has to be reiterated to win the customers' confidence and, in the current competitive environment, also enable the customers to choose the right products, provide new insights and guidance in the after-care following a claim or a deposit or purchase of any other offering.

Linking Social Media with Learning

The role of social media in the context of communication, collaboration and network-building has been well understood. But understanding its potential impact on learning and incorporating it as part of the learning strategy is at a nascent stage. The opportunities that social networks present for learning and the advantages of integrating social networks with online learning are important to recognise while designing the learning plans for individuals and professionals in future.

With a plethora of information available on the internet, searching for the right information or ensuring you are not left behind through timely upgradation of knowledge have become cumbersome tasks. That is where professional learning networks could address these concerns and act as a dynamic feed for continuous learning and upgradation if conceived well. How are these professional learning networks different from the online learning systems set up by companies? Online learning portals are mostly based on 'push' strategy whereas professional learning networks are designed around a 'pull' approach and are successful when integrated with social media networks. The starting point is to decide the extent of content curation on the portal. This is because of the humungous amount of content available on the internet and the consequent need for skilfully discerning what content is relevant and how to present it to the learner. Thus, the role of the curator is to artfully filter the information that would suit learners, tastefully present the content using smart labelling and descriptions, understand the profiles of the learners and their styles of learning and use language and idioms including humour suitable for the learner group.

Once the building blocks of the learning network are defined, the dynamic components of the learning system must be carefully planned. Managing the network for the ongoing feed of content is a crucial success factor for learner adoption and usage of such networks. The types of content that need to be made available in the learning network calls for specialised skills in browsing the web regularly to understand what is 'in' and what is 'out', listening to peers and industry specialists to identify the best solution for aggregating the content. The other task that has to be done diligently concerns who to 'follow' and who should ideally 'follow' the members of the network. There would have to be timely responses to posts and that would create interest amongst the learners and facilitate active interaction. To make socialising of the learning process effective, knowing where the expertise and resources reside and linking up to them on an ongoing basis is essential. This includes an understanding of how to post, making posts effective, whom to target for response and generating a buzz on key topics to ensure the participants stay connected and interested. In short, the etiquette and the dynamics of interactions that take place on typical social media networks would have to be adapted for social learning networks.

Being able to expand the horizons of learning by systematically facilitating engagements with social networks is indeed a great boon for learners, but it comes with some important challenges as well. Performance tracking through assessments is an essential part of the learning process, and the tools available for it are currently at an embryonic stage. Based on the context of learning and the expected outcomes, designers of learning programmes will have to think through this dimension and invest in developing relevant assessment methods. Social media networks and the associated technologies are still evolving and may consequently not provide a stable structure as required for facilitating the learning environment. Those networks and features that can significantly add value to the learning process will have to be carefully picked out and those which may be glamorous but may not provide a steady framework left out.

It is easy to be drawn into the maze of social media, and attention can get diverted from the focus areas of learning. Therefore, it is necessary to exercise caution while identifying the social media linkages as well as ensuring the boundaries of interactions if required through manual interventions by a nominated coordinator. Training departments and the career development assessment centres in organisations need to be familiar with the possibilities of social networks playing a role in the professional development of managers. Organisations beginning to conceptualise and design customised professional learning networks should also plan to tap into the multitudes of data available for carrying out the required analytics and making the learning process responsive. These are exciting times for training managers, who now have the opportunity to make learning more targeted, customised and real-time. It can also be device agnostic and supported by the right experts within and outside the organisation through social networks ably guided by smart analytics.

Augmenting Corporate Learning with AI

The biggest value AI could bring to learning is a better understanding of learners, their learning styles and their evolving learning needs. AI may fully or partially replace trainers in some cases, and by following the learning patterns of the trainees, will empower training managers to come up with customised and varied offerings. Often, learners do not wish to expose their weaknesses and may therefore be reluctant to learn. An AI-powered environment facilitates learning through trial-and-error methods and encourages learners to experiment without fear.

AI systems can provide expertise and answer queries intelligently. Through this process, it can become more intelligent with every transaction, thus slowly becoming a synergistic companion for the learner as well as the trainer, whose role will slowly become that of a facilitator. AI can even take on grading and evaluating the students and providing occasional feedback. At times, the learning content and pedagogy may not be just right, because of which learners may struggle with their grades and the learning outcomes may not be satisfactory. AI systems enable large organisations to study these patterns to arrive at the exact course corrections required to bridge such gaps and to make learning purposeful. They bring together the vast amounts of data about individual learning, social contexts, learning contexts and personal interests, allowing insights to be derived from interactions and used to make learning adaptive as well as contextual.

When knowledge is served up as required and contextualised, it becomes much more valuable than when it is static and has the same flavour at all times to everyone. Contextual support at the time of addressing a customer query or resolving a problem makes the executive more productive and allows them to efficiently tap into the knowledge. The organisation knowledge repository also constantly grows in this process and becomes more intelligent over a period of time. The examples of Siri, Cortana, DeepMind acquired by Google and driverless cars are well known, all of which highlight the potential of machine learning unleashed by AI systems applied in different ways. IBM's Watson is a classic example of the deep commitment to ongoing learning, which has seen brilliant results in a variety of fields such as oncology, travel, law and finance. The device can perform text mining and complex analytics on huge volumes of unstructured data and serve up the knowledge that we are seeking. OpenAI, the artificial intelligence company invested in by Tesla and SpaceX boss Elon Musk, is building out a new kind of free training 'gym' for computer programmers. Known as OpenAI Gym, it's an open-source tool to get developers around the world to train computer systems better to learn and develop more complex reasoning systems.

The measure of success in such an exercise is not just the short-term outcome but the impact it is capable of creating on an ongoing basis and the longer-term intelligence the tool acquires that helps in coaching and providing expertise in a just-in-time mode. The significant change from the past is that organisations need to gear up not only for upskilling their employees and associates but also plan for continuous training of the automated tools to keep pace with the dynamic needs of the organisation. The critical success factor will be to train the automated tools and employees to collaborate. It is important to note that AI tools will be only as smart as they are trained to be, but we can train our talent to think and act even in situations never before experienced, in ways that only they can do.

THE NEW AVATAR OF KNOWLEDGE MANAGEMENT IN THE DIGITAL ERA

Knowledge management (KM) started occupying centre stage in organisations in the 1990s, with companies beginning to value their knowledge assets in addition to traditionally valued physical assets. Knowledge assets were repositories mostly comprising explicit knowledge objects and some tacit knowledge inventories that employees and other stakeholders could access with relative ease. This happened as knowledge management became responsible for the coding, documenting, categorising and sharing of knowledge objects to help users save time and efforts in locating such assets. KM practitioners faced the challenge of motivating employees to contribute to the repository on the one hand and, on the other, encouraging them to take advantage of the painstakingly built repositories. With organisations engulfed by digital technologies and transforming as a result, KM practitioners are facing a new set of questions, including the relevance of knowledge management in the context of availability of information and knowledge from multiple sources.

For KM to occupy the centre stage of business, KM practitioners have to redefine what knowledge is meant to be for the business and make the knowledge acquisition and refreshing process dynamic. The conventional approach of viewing the KM journey as one of capturing data and converting it to knowledge and knowledge to wisdom is giving way to the emerging model centred around data. In this view, data combined with cognitive tools leads to insights, a combination of insights leads to new knowledge and the ability to tap and apply the knowledge wisely creates winners in the marketplace. KM has developed tentacles in its adjacencies and has thus become more responsive.

Over the last few years, the focus has shifted to tapping into external knowledge in addition to the internally generated knowledge because of the vast amounts of data available from multiple sources. This allows KM practitioners to redefine the scope and impact of KM practice in their organisations. KM today is not just about being able to support the just-in-time needs of the decision-making process or about making managers savvier at anticipating and proactively changing course on the strength of insights derived from time to time, but when coupled with digital transformation, it also has the potential to alter the business model and reposition businesses. The spotlight on KM is to go beyond the organisational boundaries and leverage its ecosystem in building a seamless value chain and linkages to the core knowledge system.

A good example of this is the possibilities that exist with primary healthcare centres. These health centres have access to a lot of data related to their patients gathered over a period of time, but most of the data has so far not been digitally catalogued and accessed for more understanding about the population. While there is definitely a need to digitise such data as the first step, the entire value chain connecting medical equipment providers, patients, hospitals, pharmacists and insurance agencies will have an enormous potential to generate huge volumes of data at every stage of connectedness. This data, when layered with cognitive tools, could be used to service the customers better by predicting illnesses in families and preventing the occurrence of diseases. This would help in delivering affordable and timely patient-centric solutions and enhance the overall wellbeing of the citizens. Another advantage is to enable all those engaged with the services to develop skills in those areas where there is a demand. Thus, learning becomes purposeful and aligned with the core expectations and needs of the community.

The approach to KM discipline is shifting from systematic storage and dissemination of knowledge to the users to dynamic creation, sharing and customised retrieval and access formats. As a result, the relevance of KM has not reduced but has significantly evolved. If managed well, knowledge harnessed and used by the business could become a key differentiator in the competitive marketplace. The process of adopting digital technologies, with its focus on heightened customer intimacy and enhanced customer experience, has led to knowledge insights drawn from every transaction with the help of intelligent analytics becoming the crucial drivers for businesses. Huge volumes of data are now being turned into relevant information that could be used for better decision-making.

The KM discipline had its foundation in a digital library of sorts and hence had a strong focus on creating robust processes for collating available assets from known sources and sharing them effectively. With access to multiple knowledge sources, especially outside the boundaries of the organisation, it is now feasible for KM to demonstrate its value and ROI through analytics and insights. As a result, what constitutes knowledge for the organisation needs to be redefined and prioritised, as it requires huge efforts and investment to manage these assets. In the past, KM managers had to coax employees to share their knowledge with others. Today, not only has the culture of sharing become a natural phenomenon, but due to collaborative frameworks available and seamless networking amongst various stakeholders, it is difficult to draw boundaries for knowledge source and ownership. This raises complexities regarding intellectual property rights of such knowledge assets and security considerations around sharing of knowledge across and within physical boundaries of organisations.

With organisations also beginning to inculcate an innovation culture, KM assumes another important dimension of fostering entrepreneurial zeal. In many organisations, instead of or in addition to setting up the repository of knowledge assets and taking a 'push' approach, employees are encouraged to ask questions through the intranet portals and respond to them based on individual expertise. Further, the patterns of seeking and providing information are studied to identify emerging clusters of new competencies and knowledge created across multiple teams in the organisation. As a result, such knowledge networks throw up new opportunities for organisations to design new products or services for their customers. It has also been observed that customers who wish to find quick or smart solutions to immediate problems are beginning to utilise the large networks comprising smart young employees of their vendors and thus drive innovation through their participation.

Depending upon the industry type and the maturity of businesses, different generations of KM are likely to coexist within an organisation. Knowledge assets curated to meet the business needs to be tapped by users as per their requirements, query-based responses leading to archival of such knowledge assets, mapping customer-centric knowledge through social media and other company-specific platforms and co-creation of knowledge by collaborating with specialists are some of the models followed by organisations. Some of them use more than one model to meet their objectives. We must remember that the tacit knowledge of the organisation also increases in tandem with large volumes of data being converted into explicit knowledge.

KM for Digital: Imperatives

Very often in the case of digital transformation, the aim is to consider one of the critical functions such as marketing or operations or an entire process that is reengineered with the help of digital interventions. We have come across successful case studies of enhanced customer experience or enhanced productivity resulting from integration with digital ecosystems. The success in each of these cases results primarily from the ability to generate and analyse the data and use these insights to transform the way the business functions. Thus, it is on account of the power of data that knowledge management has assumed renewed significance in the digital transformation context.

The potential advantages of data are driving the investment decision towards IoT, robotics, AI and embedded systems, which are throwing up a variety of data leading to exhaustive analytics. The knowledge base that the organisation can create through the insights from predictive and prescriptive analytics is exciting and is adding quantifiable value to the business unlike in the past, when it was a challenge to correlate its contribution to business outcomes and attribute a value to it. A constant and regular update of the knowledge base in the wake of digital technologies has become the bedrock of business processes on account of contextualising the data on a continual basis. Structured and unstructured data is not only accessible by interested stakeholders for addressing operational issues but can be used to build scenarios and simulate possibilities, making organisations better prepared to deal with the changes in the marketplace. With the help of AI and advanced analytics, the signals and cues businesses are in a position to get make the decision-making process more precise. From being mostly restricted to tapping and addressing the stakeholders inside the organisation, KM now has become richer and contemporary because of the extensive reach and direct connect with customers through the business network.

KM in Business: The AI Factor

Now KM is witnessing a new phase where we are experiencing the exciting possibility of new knowledge nuggets being added to the repository not just by its employees and other stakeholders but also through deep learning and machine learning. The deployment of bots and the ability to extract valuable insights with the help of AI tools have broadened the horizons of knowledge capture, storage and retrieval capabilities. The machine–human interface and the ability to mine new knowledge at a rapid pace augment the knowledge repository in real time as the new facets are discovered. These are adding significant value to the knowledge assets of organisations. As enterprises embrace digital technologies and redefine the value they could offer to their customers, leaders need to be mindful of the significance of the enormous volumes of data that would be used and get generated through the multiple touchpoints created by digital systems. Successful business models will be centred around data, harnessed through cognitive tools leading to insights and a combination of insights with new engagement mechanisms leading to new knowledge.

With the availability of digital tools, a three-tier system of recording data, deriving insights and developing engagements with the stakeholders has started to gain momentum. Several new and existing businesses have demonstrated enhanced customer experience or productivity resulting from integration with the digital ecosystems. The success in each of these cases is their ability to reorient the organisations around the ability to access and analyse the data and use these insights to transform the way businesses function.

The potential advantages arising out of data is driving the investment decision towards IoT, robotics, AI and embedded systems, which are throwing up a variety of data leading to exhaustive analytics. The knowledge base that the organisation creates through insights drawn from predictive and prescriptive analytics is exciting. It is adding quantifiable value to the business, unlike in the past, when it was a challenge to correlate the direct contribution of data to business outcomes and attribute a value to it. Structured and unstructured data available are not only accessible to interested stakeholders for addressing operational issues, but it can be used to build scenarios and simulate possibilities, thus making organisations better prepared to deal with the changes in the marketplace and introducing precision in decision-making. The deep insights obtained through access and analysis of data are leading to exciting new possibilities to engage with each of the stakeholders—whether employees, customers or partners. The new knowledge derived helps produce distinctive products, processes or services to create delight for the stakeholders. The scope and impact of engagement are consequently enhanced. The issues around ownership of data, intellectual property rights and privacy also need to be addressed, as these could be pivotal in the success of future businesses. Owing to the heightened importance of data for building the framework of future organisations, it is important to harness the data using appropriate technologies. This involves multiple steps starting with defining data, capturing data, accessing data in multiple combinations with ease, analysing data as required and storing data systematically.

The data management process has become complex. Therefore, organisations need to have a strategy around data management and identify technology platforms that suit the business requirement. Data therefore must be extracted not only from everyday transactions but must be focused on the emerging phenomenon of AI. Industries and individuals connected to the digital system are seeing the impact of AI in one form or the other. Until now, businesses have been dependent on individuals for harnessing their knowledge and building knowledge repositories for supporting the business in future. AI and machine learning are not only now capable of tapping the minds of employees but also determining behaviour patterns. They are also capable of predicting scenarios and actions. While cognitive systems can be trained to respond to complex problems and even situations with ambiguity, they should be viewed as necessary support for augmenting the knowhow rather than replacing the function or losing the human touch. AI brings in a new dimension of knowledge to businesses whose boundaries and scope of impact can be defined by humans alone. Defining and managing these trajectories as well as redefining the boundaries of human knowledge and productivity as a result become challenging. AI capabilities required to develop talent and organisational knowledge feed on one another, and their effective combination is crucial to empowering the talent available with the organisation.

Learning and KM: Linkages

In this context, learning and knowledge management are getting closer than ever before, as both functions have started relying upon each other for freshness and contemporary relevance. Repositories built over some time are providing a head start for building a smart knowledge ecosystem powered by cutting-edge digital tools. These are leading to ease of access and consumption of knowledge nuggets. With millennials accounting for over 50% of the workforce in most organisations, the style and the duration of learning are also changing rapidly due to learning through tech devices and the acquired habit of accessing the internet for short nuggets on any topic of their choice. As a result, organisations are reworking their knowledge repositories to have chunks of short-duration content supported by microlearning videos of three to four minutes by experts, thus ensuring the rich content built over the years is put to effective use. At the same time, embellishments can be added to the content by tagging their usage patterns, with additional ratings and user insights. The automatic updating of content in the knowledge repositories in the organisations, along with peer ratings and links to other related content available elsewhere, keeps the knowledge assets fresh and relevant. By being able to contextualise the content to support adaptive learning needs, it is also making the learning experience more productive. While vast repositories of knowledge assets are available and have been stored and catalogued well, employees may still not be aware of how they could make them more effective. The new trend is to align the knowledge assets with the roles employees have to perform and assign the mandatory knowledge objects to them. Employees are then assessed periodically on the levels of competencies they have managed to achieve and on the effective use of knowledge resources assigned to them, which may also include mentors and experts in various domains. Effective KM approaches adopted by organisations create confidence in the teams that they have easy and quick access to support while dealing with complex customer requirements.

As a result of these developments, the outcomes from the investment in the KM function are much more quantifiable and measurable than in the past. In the past, KM practitioners often struggled to justify how knowledge repositories could be seen as contributing to the wisdom required for decision-making. Now the pathways of KM to wisdom and the effective utilisation of knowledge assets at various levels in the organisation are becoming clear to both the practitioners as well as the business heads. An exciting dimension of the new-age KM function is that it has now the added responsibility of identifying the relevant knowledge nuggets from bots and coaching them on an ongoing basis to become superior performers and learners competing or complimenting the human learners and performers.

Therefore, the KM function has to reorient its attitude towards defining knowledge objects as it recognises that the challenges in tapping and building knowledge repositories would be very different. In the digital era, KM and L&D practitioners have to adapt to the characteristics of these new channels of expertise and balance the training and coaching methods for both human and machine learning environments where they would feed each other and get smarter with every such transaction. While businesses may be creating intelligent systems to aid in their respective functions, it is important to create linkages of data, knowledge and business need and redesign systems such that they can deal with dynamic situations and address the emerging demands of the organisation. The traditional production thinking would have to make way for design thinking. The requirement is for more and more interdisciplinary skills along with analytical competencies that are becoming critical for every job. The leadership challenges will include the organisation's ability to nurture the right talent and foster a suitable culture for the digital era to encourage employees to upskill and adapt to the changing times.

The Emerging Role of CKOs

Businesses are increasingly keen on developing better connectedness with external stakeholders inspired by the power of social media. Three key factors are leading to the need for a radical change in how chief knowledge officers (CKOs) function. First, it is no longer just the sales function that is interacting with the customers and is solely responsible for bringing in a new understanding of the marketplace. In the context of businesses going social, barriers of communications have ceased, with all the functions having numerous touchpoints with the external world. Therefore, knowledge creation is no longer restricted to specific functions—it is co-created by multiple stakeholders. Second, the multiplicity of data forms and channels have dramatically increased in the last few years, which is expected to increase manifold in the coming years. This is posing a stupendous challenge to businesses to sift and prioritise the data from which relevant knowledge is derived. They also recognise that knowledge objects are no longer required to be boxed in unidimensional constructs—the multidimensional potential of knowledge objects could be powerful levers for decision-making. The intelligent combination of content, technology and contextualisation can lead to knowledge discovery about the use of their products and profiles of end customers, which could prove strategic to businesses. Third, in the new world order, motivating people to share knowledge per se is not as much of a challenge as the question of how much to share and the rights to ownership of co-created knowledge.

These tumultuous changes impacting businesses call for a new look at the role and expectations of CKOs. CKOs have to become externally focused and align knowledge management systems to support all functions to be market-centric. In the past, if they derived strength from their experience with quality, systems or processes, now the success of the CKOs will significantly depend upon their ability to put their arms around multifarious data and bring an analytics capability to their function. A sound understanding of the interplay of social media and the psychology of players as well as machine-to-machine and machine-to-person interactions is expected of them to design systems that can draw upon the huge amounts of tacit knowledge being generated and convert them into explicit knowledge that could be put to smart use by the business heads in the areas of design, service delivery and new product creation. CKOs will also be expected to develop market research perspectives and help functional heads on how to use tools such as crowdsourcing to tap into the explicit knowledge of potential and current customers, the skilful interpretations of which could lead to conversion as tacit knowledge that could be used in serving customers better. In short, CKOs now have the unique opportunity to play the pivotal role of helping CEOs to steer the course of the business. The success of the CKOs in the digital era will depend largely upon their ability to redefine their roles with the customer as their primary focus and clearly calling out the business value they can generate.

While the specialist teams are being tasked with managing explicit knowledge, KM practitioners need to continue to focus on methods and tools to elicit and manage tacit knowledge because it is the wisdom derived from the combination of explicit and tacit knowledge that will drive the strategy of the business. In this context, KM practitioners must examine their current systems supporting KM and make their platforms intelligent by adding cognitive power. While a business may create intelligent systems to aid in their respective functions, linkages of data, knowledge and business need and the systems redesigned such that they can deal with dynamic situations and address the emerging demands of the organisation. The other challenge businesses have often experienced is how to convert tacit knowledge to explicit knowledge. Patterns are discernible from the transactions that take place via emails, portals, social networking sites and other such avenues. Companies have the tools and the ability to tap into and maximise access to hitherto unavailable tacit knowledge in easy-to-interpret formats.

THE CASE FOR LEADERSHIP

Most businesses, be they small or big, have acknowledged the urgent need for organisations to adapt to the digital trends as they recognise that the alternative of not doing so would be to perish. As a result, many of these organisations are developing strategies to take advantage of the potential of digital technologies to take their businesses to a new opportunity zone. Some of the businesses are focused on building and enriching customer relationships with the help of new insights received through digital technologies as witnessed in the retail segment; those in the manufacturing and product development businesses are reengineering their processes to rethink supply chains, inventory management and after-sale service on the strength of redefining their networks. Other businesses are rethinking their business models, as has been witnessed in the financial services sector, an example of which is the current debate about the future of brick-and-mortar retail banking outlets and which of the current standard offerings will become extinct in the next few years. Each one of these strategies calls for taking certain risks and embarking on a bold, new and hitherto unventured path. Hence, it would be pertinent to consider the challenges that are likely to be faced and the leadership imperatives to be successful in the digital era.

While embarking on the journey of digital transformation, choosing from the various options of digital pathways available is the first step. The first decision point for the leadership is to arrive at the key thrust area that will create distinctiveness in the marketplace and strengthen market positioning. Related to this question is the sizing up of the investment required for the change and justifying the investment to get a buy-in for the digital transformation proposition. Reallocating the available resources and budgets to showcase proof of concept and its benefits is a good way to test the initial hypothesis. That could help in finetuning the eventual roadmap. Further to the pilots, zeroing in on the areas of maximum impact results in either savings or higher business volumes as a result of the proposed investment. This is essential to create ownership with all stakeholders of the transformation journey.

Vision can be translated into action by nurturing a strong digital culture in the organisation. Imbibing digital culture involves being harmonious with the use of digital technology in the daily routine. Coping and adapting to the change in processes or the redefined jobs, readiness to think digital and helping employees and other stakeholders envision the change can pave the way for embracing the digital culture. The fundamental change that the digital era is bringing about is the need to work more and more collaboratively as opposed to working in functional silos. This calls for new organisational design thinking and also encourages people to reach out to pockets of expertise inside and outside the organisation for superior output. This is a drastic departure for the existing workflow systems, the system of recognising individual contributions and performance management systems that organisations have been accustomed to for several decades. This is important to manage the transitions with sensitivity and through consensus building. In the past, when new technologies were introduced in the businesses, the framework of regulations and business conduct that organisations had to comply with did not by and large undergo significant changes. In the digital context, leadership has to deal with a plethora of data from multiple sources and must have the ability to drawn insights from these for decision-making. This also raises questions about ownership, confidentiality and intellectual property rights on the creation of new ideas/products. Hence one of the key challenges of leadership in the digital era is to rethink types of resourcing talent and terms of engagement with customers and vendors, thus ensuring fairness and integrity in transactions.

While the opportunities offered by going digital are immense and businesses may be ready to make the necessary investments to reap their benefits, one of the key constraints is how to deal with the legacy systems and the restrictions they place in accessing free-flowing data critical to making real-time impactful decisions. Since digital technology advancements are impacting the customers faster than businesses can cope with them, businesses have to deal with the myriad changes in customer expectations happening rapidly and have to drive the required changes to swiftly replace or modify legacy systems as well as pick the relevant priority applications for a replacement. At the same time, the newly designed systems for doing business in the digital space would bring about further changes in the customer behaviour in the new connected world, and organisations should be prepared internally to deal with the ongoing changes in customer behaviour. Therefore, leadership success lies in not just the ability to paint the future but to prepare the organisations to develop resilience and speed in learning and adapting to the new expectations of the customers as well as to take advantage of the unexpected opportunities that may arise from unknown quarters due to the tectonic shifts and the several moving parts of the connected world. The journey of digital transformation is indeed exciting, but the critical success factor lies in the quality of leadership and its ability to win over all its stakeholders to commit to the journey.

The calibre of leadership required for the digital transformation journey is unique and comprises layers of capabilities. This has been explained by Pearl Zhu in her book *Digital Master*, in which she defines digital leadership as consisting of five characteristics:

1. Thought leader, the capability to be tough in facing the market and competition change
2. Creative leader, a digital leader who has a creativity and innovation mindset to formulate the idea into reality
3. Global visionary leader, a digital leader who can provide direction and to orchestrate the digital business transformation
4. Inquisitive leader, with the complex and dynamic ecosystem due to volatility, uncertainty, complexity and ambiguity (VUCA) factors, a digital leader who has a learning capability

5. Profound leader, a person with digital leadership capability to lead in complex times and having in-depth knowledge and understanding, to use their knowledge in interpreting, speculating and synthesising the information for decision-making.

What is also important is to recognise that leadership style and form that succeeds in born-digital organisations is very different from the leadership required for the digital transformation journey. As research by Korn Ferry shows, born-digital leaders are comfortable with a digital environment as they have grown in it and there is no 'selling' required. The essence of change required from time to time in processes or technologies is fairly well understood by all stakeholders. As compared to this, leadership in organisations undergoing digital transformation is vastly different as the transformation journey impacts several dimensions of the business and therefore requires the combination of a gamut of experiences, skills and knowhow to put together teams and motivate them. In fact, leadership capability required in this context is also vastly different from the leadership capability required to bring about other previous organisation-wide changes successfully in the past. This is primarily because the current time can at best be described as 'fuzzy' and calls for not only envisioning the future for oneself amidst the fuzziness but for also enabling other various stakeholders who would be part of the journey to reimagine the future in the same way as the leaders. Further, leaders will have to risk redefining the future from time to time based on how technologies evolve and redefine the industry and society. Yet leaders will have to keep a sharp eye on the bottom line, define success metrics for short periods and be able to assess achievements against these every so often to build confidence with the teams and also redefine strategy and success metrics. Such complex manoeuvres call for exceptional capabilities that will require clarity of purpose and articulation of the ideas in the core of leadership.

Leadership Quotient for the Digital Era

- Implementing design thinking and envisioning new paradigms every so often
- Storytelling and influencing
- Having learning agility
- Having change agility
- Navigating through the newness of technologies
- Managing aspirations of people
- Getting the best out of the people–machines mix
- Collaborating within and outside
- Nurturing innovation
- Being comfortable with data models and decision-making through insights from these models
- Having emotional intelligence
- Risk-taking

Leadership Act in Balancing AI and EI

Competitive forces impacted by AI are acting as triggers for large well-established businesses to rethink their business models to survive in some cases and in others to create new growth trajectories and build on their brand legacies. Therefore, rather than fighting the progression of technology and AI, the success of leadership lies in deploying AI in smart ways that will benefit the business. Unlike in the past when information technology played a supportive role and was left to experts, the need of the hour is to develop versatile leadership acumen capable of not just handling AI but dealing with the transition from AI to extended intelligence (EI).

Extended intelligence is the use of artificial intelligence to enhance human intelligence. Human intelligence and AI are good at balancing out each other's weaknesses and complementing each other's strengths. Hence it is important to change the mental model about what is important in one's role and begin focusing on what humans can do better than any smart machine.

By recognising that machines and AI have a greater ability to crunch enormous amounts of data in a short period, improve outcomes and lower costs and that competing on these fronts with it is pointless, leaders can use their emotional intelligence, superior comprehension capability and decision-making capability that machines are not equipped to address. It is important to recognise the boundaries of human and machine intelligence and their interdependence for success. Therefore, leaders should develop the competency to work with AI systems and assimilate a large quantum of data and synthesise it into meaningful insights.

Leaders also need to learn to appreciate the dynamics of machine-to-machine relationships along with human-to-machine relationship and groom teams to manage teams comprising both machines and humans. What this would also lead to is the ability to constantly adapt to a shifting balance of power and influence of both humans and machines. Collaboration with teams and valuing the contribution of partners and interest groups would become even more critical in the coming years in fostering innovation. All of this would mean investing huge amounts of time and energy for thinking divergently about ways of doing things and in occasionally trying out new ideas, failing and trying again until the ideal state is realised.

In this context, the emotional intelligence which has been considered a critical cornerstone for successful leadership assumes even more significance. How to better manage, influence and relate to people and motivate them for better performance by adapting to technology trends is what leaders have to offer. This is where they can excel as compared to AI and machines. The contribution of an outstanding leader who is a great listener and motivator of people, even when technology changes take place, will continue to be valued. Machines do not have feelings. The empathy that business leaders demonstrate can go a long way in establishing trust and building positive relationships. Business leaders must also ensure that they go beyond the immediate benefits of AI to monitoring the ethical impacts of AI technology on their workplace, customers and reputation. They need to expand their limits of tolerance of risks and ambiguity while showing resilience in the face of constant change as well as develop the confidence to take the lead in driving change. In summary, leaders in the age of AI have to play the game differently by thinking, acting and reacting differently, thus requiring transformation in the cognitive, behavioural and emotional domains.

THE EMERGENCE OF DIGITAL CULTURE

History tells us about how civilisations have been shaped over millennia by various events and discoveries. From the Stone Age to the Industrial Age, there have been significant changes to the culture of the society, with new learnings and intermingling of people brought about by science, the wars won and lost and the socio-psychological impacts of globalisation. Human migrations, travels, trade and conquests have acted as catalysts of cultural change from time immemorial. There have been distinct changes to the identity, the relationships, the customs and the ethos of civilisation from time to time, and careful studies by anthropologists and historians have helped us appreciate the evolution of culture in different societies. Unlike in the past, when the impact of changes took time to materialise and, in the process, formed several subcultures, the Digital Age is heralding a new culture with fascinating and sweeping changes to our everyday life. These changes are being experienced simultaneously to a greater or less extent throughout the world. Understanding the trends and the patterns of these changes is important for appreciating the societal evolution as culture is a core factor that impacts the customer mindset, which in turn impacts the organisational mindset that defines the organisation culture.

Cultural changes are brought about by two key developments—discovery and innovations from within society and by borrowing and adapting to ideas from the outside. In the digital world, values, beliefs and practices are being shaped on both these fronts, leading to social change. Digital tools such as the internet and social media are examples of inventions that have radically impacted society at large and are driving the culture change. In the past, human agents played a key role in bringing about the change. In the digital age, while human interventions continue to contribute immensely to the dynamics of change, technologies and tools themselves act as the medium of change, resulting in the stupendous pace and the rate of adoption of change. Digital technologies have also led to the spread of new ideas and practices, making a dent on some cultures and also possibly unconsciously enabling the evolution of a common cultural code.

Closer collaboration between groups of people and inspiration and borrowing of ideas have started impacting the lifestyles of society and the DNA of businesses. We have witnessed a powerful transformation in the political landscape in recent times in countries such as Egypt, where social media interactions played an impactful role in the political upheaval. We have also been experiencing the emergence of user-friendly mobile apps that have brought about changes in consumer preferences through concepts such as Uber and Amazon simultaneously in both economically advanced and developing countries around the world. Digital memory and privacy are just two of the key issues being debated on their merits and demerits and aiding the progress and the emergence of a new culture.

If in the 1980s and the 1990s we attributed global cultural changes to the medium of cinema and television, in recent decades, digital technology has expanded the scope, depth and numbers of people impacted, thus creating the new social order. Referring to the emerging phenomenon of digital culture, the Israeli Professor Ilya Levin mentions three different cultural spheres in the digital era: spiritual, social media as a new way of forming social consciousness; social, personal identity as a new way of forming personality; technological, data-intensive science as a new methodical paradigm of science. What is distinctive about cultural change in the digital era is the speed of adoption of change, the simultaneous adoption of changes and the likely impact on subcultures.

A McKinsey survey of global executives has highlighted three digital culture deficiencies: functional and department silos, fear of taking risks and action on a single view of the customer. Therefore, a cultural risk management initiative should address factors such as accountability, collaboration, transparency, willingness to learn, risk-taking ability and broadening the scope and definition of customer and performance measures. Cultural risk assessment can be carried out through surveys, town hall interactions and ongoing social media sensing of employees, customers and other stakeholders. Based on this assessment, it may be necessary to revisit organisation values that will encourage changes in performance assessment metrics as well as organisational behaviour. The basic insecurity of people, which stems from mindset patterns or a lack of the right skills for the digital world, should be addressed with appropriate talent development programmes.

Since digital transformation is an ongoing journey and digital reengineering is a necessary prerequisite at frequent intervals, culture in the organisation must facilitate its ongoing learning and adaptation capability. Therefore, the paramount focus of the businesses must be on nurturing learning and creating a transparent and democratic environment to provide opportunities for people associated to keep learning and growing in their professional acumen. Innovation is the key differentiator to remaining successful and can be fostered only with the help of learning organisations.

Fostering the Learning Organisation

In his book *The Fifth Discipline*, Peter Senge discussed 'learning organisations' and their unique practices. According to Senge, a learning organisation discovers how to tap people's commitment and capacity to learn at all levels, where people continually expand their capacity to create the results, they truly desire, where new and expansive patterns of thinking are nurtured, where collective aspiration is set free and where people are continually learning how to learn together. Senge propounded five learning principles—shared vision, mental models, personal mastery, team learning and systems thinking and prescribed tools and frameworks for each of these principles.

In the digital era, organisations have recognised the importance of ongoing learning and adapting to the swiftly changing environment. The principles of learning that Peter Senge highlighted consequently assume even greater significance. One of the key challenges to becoming a learning organisation is ongoing communication with people, consistent action at all levels and transparency to remove concerns or disillusionments along the way. Learning today does not only take place only in the realms of the organisation or within the boundaries of organisation teams, but there is a constant flow of information from multiple stakeholders and through multiple channels. Digital tools and frameworks provide significant support in addressing each of these challenges effectively and aid them in their objective of becoming a learning organisation and sustaining their efforts thereafter. The communication and knowledge retrieval and access tools are beneficial in building transparency and fostering alignment of aspirations with the vision of the organisation. Identifying the potential roadblocks and challenges and proactively supporting the learning needs of individuals are being made more and more simple and customised to individual needs thanks to the concentric circles comprising artificial intelligence–machine learning–deep learning. AI is what we experience externally; it is manifested through the capabilities of machine learning.

AI possesses characteristics of humans and can perform tasks as well as or, in some cases, better than humans can. These technologies exhibit some facets of human intelligence, and this has been made possible by machine learning. Rather than coding a specific set of instructions for performing specific tasks, machine learning uses algorithms to parse data, learn from it and determine or predict actions or events. This is made possible by 'training the machine' using large amounts of data and algorithms that give it the ability to learn how to perform the task. Machine learning is further enhanced by deep learning, which is made possible by artificial neural networks that have discrete layers, connections and directions of data propagation. Organisations are connected through myriad digital networks. The success of *The Fifth Discipline* and the rewards of being a learning organisation were thanks to the capability of converting large data volumes from various transactions between people within and outside the organisation as well as between people and machines into useful knowledge and learning assets. Broadening the horizons of learning and recognising the layers of learning that ultimately emerge as knowledge are the first steps towards this possibility. Further to this, applying appropriate AI and deep learning tools to data volumes allows us to handle hitherto-unknown nuances in the transactions and bridging the gaps in human thought process and behaviour, thus paving the way to making the organisation a winner.

Social Listening Shaping Organisation Culture

Social listening is considered the new mantra for understanding customers and their buying behaviour patterns. Social media has become a livewire platform for conversations and sharing of ideas and experiences. Hence social listening is the new art of listening to the customers to know who they are and profile them accurately. Never before have researchers and product managers have had access to such an expansive set of data about their customers. This leads to innumerable possibilities of shaping their strategies. While social listening is often connected with customer service, product management and marketing, it is immensely beneficial for the HR function to be able to understand their employees' aspirations and expectations better as well as to map the brand equity with erstwhile and potential employees and decide on the appropriate communication strategy. All of this helps shape the organisation's culture.

What began as a pleasant note of music has become a cacophony of sounds lately with businesses being besieged with large amounts of data and thus challenged to derive the right insights. Hence organisations are recognising the need to build a sound social listening strategy that would enable them to identify the right strands of conversations to follow, analyse and act upon. It is not only people-to-people communications supported by technology that creates a case for social listening. Machines embedded with digital technology are also capable of sending valuable information and insights from the field and customer locations straight into the core of the organisation, functions and teams that can act upon such information in a timely fashion. Such machine-delivered information, when further curated and presented to communities for a response, can throw up amazing insights on preventing problems or predicting future scenarios. Social communication has also led to fake information in many cases that we need to be vigilant about. To make social listening truly impactful, it is important to construct the end-to-end strategy addressing aspects, such as who will listen, what we will do with what is being picked up, who will act upon them, how we will monitor the actions being put in place and measure the effectiveness of such actions. Glassdoor, in-house employee forums, WhatsApp groups, Twitter and Instagram are examples of channels available for social listening and social influencing that are considered a necessary part of how culture is interpreted and communicated.

Redefining Culture for Work from Home

In the wake of COVID, with offices having shifted to the homes of employees, the norms of working and productivity definitions have radically been changed overnight. This poses a new challenge for both the employees and businesses, as working from home is an unfamiliar phenomenon for most people and they are only now getting used to it. Employers were comfortable with bosses keeping a close watch on the employees and peers glancing at one another. Armed with timesheets, employers believed they were getting the most out of the employees at the workplace. Working from home has led to a big question for HR and business managers about how they are going to measure the productivity of 'unseen' employees and how to motivate them to deliver on their designated responsibilities. While downsizing or use of robots on the one hand are being touted as possibilities for certain jobs, most managers are concerned about how to continue to meet their commitments towards their customers and support employees as this trend is likely to continue for a while for some sectors and employees residing in certain locations. For others, the possibility of the blend of workers preferring to work from home and others from office has opened up exciting new avenues to access hitherto untapped talent and strive for better outcomes.

It takes several years for an organisation to align its culture because of frequent formal and informal interactions. It is a real challenge to preserve this idea of organisation culture. It is even more of a challenge to get recruits to understand and imbibe this culture in an environment where most people are not working from offices. Hence sooner than later, organisations will try to get back to working from the office as the conditions for doing so are safe. Until that happens, the new work culture triggered by COVID will need to be supported by a collaborative work environment, thus continuing to maintain the human touch and connectedness with the organisation despite physical distances and tightened security measures.

Readying for the New Mix of Workers in the Organisation

Since the beginning of the year 2000, India has been experiencing internationalisation of businesses, particularly in the services sector. On account of this employees working in India have been familiarised with the global ways of functioning, processes and interactions with people. This has resulted in a culture with a global flavour. In many cases, employees have been sensitised to similar cultures across all locations. This was just the start of redefining cultures in many organisations on account of boundaries of work being revisited. The digital era and automation have brought in their wake the urgency to redesign work definitions and rethink current roles. AI, sensors and cloud technologies have been invading workspaces and have begun to disrupt established processes and workflows. With fresh talent coming into organisations with digital skills and the ability to learn and adapt, we should expect a sea change in the work environment. Almost half the workforce is made up of millennials familiar with digital technologies. This also means readying the organisation and the current talent pool to work differently and acquire new skills and capabilities.

The key question for most is whether their current jobs will vanish and what new jobs will be created. Depending upon the type of automation being planned and the tools that are emerging, a displacement effect or productivity effect can be expected. As Georgios Petropoulos states in his book *Work in the Digital Age: Challenges of the Fourth Industrial Revolution—The Impact of Artificial Intelligence on Employment*, there will be a reduction in jobs that have started incorporating more technology in the core tasks, such as clerks, assemblers and secretaries. There will also be an increase in the demand for traditional higher-skilled jobs, especially in engineering, such as design or research and development, and business tasks such as marketing or service requiring skills in digital technologies such as data analysis, network management and cybersecurity. As is already being experienced, several new roles that did not exist until recently will emerge around content, user engagement and analytics along with innumerable technical roles in new technologies. What is of importance is to recognise that the total automation of most jobs will not be feasible. The biggest hurdle for the full automation of a role is that most jobs are varied and require adapting to situations that cannot easily be simulated or predicted for robots to handle. Therefore, while some standardised roles in retail stores or shop floors that operate within predefined boundaries may be replaced by robots, new digital roles will be created and current roles are likely to be centred around technology.

It is therefore important for employees not only to be able to learn how to adapt to digital technology and the changing flavour of current roles, but they will also need to learn how to work along with the robots as co-workers instead of humans, as has been the case until now. Every employee will need to be digitally savvy and have a good understanding of digital technologies such as IoT, cloud, AI and analytics and how to embed them in their work areas. Social and emotional intelligence will gain importance in everyday functioning. While robots will make those roles extinct that involve carrying out routine and repetitive tasks, humans will be required to do all original thinking work and continue to play 'high-touch' roles that will help build engagement with customers and other employees.

HR managers will need to find new ways of attracting and retaining talent with the required skill sets. The traditional approach of finding employees with a 'loyalty' factor will no longer be applicable, as a large number of millennials will want to function in a mobile work environment and prefer to work for a specific period with an organisation on the strength of their specific skills. Changes will thus occur in the relationships between employers and employees and in creating a meaningful employee experience. Providing challenging work opportunities and flexibility in the work will require the utmost attention of HR managers. It is also quite possible that career growth or the career ladder will no longer be of interest to the new-generation workforce. Instead, companies will need to build a strategy around creating a career experience to attract talented personnel. This will determine the primary reason for associating with the company. In the gig economy, skills will carry a premium, and steady jobs will no longer be the attraction. New work and social contracts will emerge, and businesses will need to cope with a diverse set of workers—full time, part-time, freelancers, virtual workers, assignment-based workers and robots. As a result, the new work culture and new mindset towards work and organisation need to be managed very differently from the culture built over a while, thus giving way to greater transparency and democratic decision-making and priorities for quality of life and personal values as the basis for which organisation workers want to be associated with.

Individuals today have easy access to what they want to learn and how they want to learn and are not necessarily guided by or restricted by what their organisations can offer. As the individuals take charge of their learning paths and career goals, the L&D function will not be expected to direct and provide learning opportunities, but it will need to act as facilitators for learning by curating learning experiences based on the dynamic needs of stakeholders.

The COVID pandemic has sounded a wake-up call to businesses that have already been in the throes of digital transformation to consider further changes empowered by a combination of commonly available tools and some custom solutions. This has led to an urgency to understand and redefine the needs of customers as well as learn to do more with less, resulting in new opportunities for optimisation of costs and enhancing productivity in their operations. Businesses are now trying to rethink their paradigm and show resilience in their strategy. This is also the time when employees have to be coached to recognise that success as defined in the past is no longer relevant and that they need to adapt to the new normal defining new metrics for success. Along with continuous communication and engagement facilitated by digital technology, the effort should also be to enable employees to act with more confidence, speed and resourcefulness in the current scenario as well as in the post-pandemic era. Employees will be empowered to think and act together by digital tools with a greater emphasis on collaboration, thus allowing them to create a new culture in the organisation.

8

The Post-COVID Organisation

COVID will wax, wane and resurface in pockets, and its effects will linger in the psyche, the processes and the culture of organisations for years and change the world of business forever. Digital technologies, processes, data management, culture and stakeholder journeys will drive the way transactions are done in the new world, and businesses will transform in ways we can only conceptualise today and design for tomorrow. Some aspects of this design will certainly be new ways of thinking about serving customers, digital platforms for multi-stakeholder business transactions and ambidextrous innovation within and outside the organisation to serve stakeholders better and maximise the organisation's financial benefits and impact.

We have been on a journey exploring various facets of the digitally reengineered organisation, analysing the technologies, the processes, the domains and the skills and culture needed to deliver the new organisation forms that will play out in 2021 and beyond. Let us now attempt some synthesis and put together a model for the future organisation that will develop through the next phase of growth we all expect to see.

RETRACING THE DIGITAL JOURNEY FROM YESTERDAY TO TOMORROW

We know through the discussions in the last few chapters that the digital journey for organisations is not very new. It began in

2014 or 2015, when companies started experimenting with cloud and mobility and the mobile phone became a ubiquitous part of human attire. We then moved to understanding the power of data. The term big data was coined and people realised that data was hitting us from everywhere, inside the factories, from the ERP systems, from various supply and demand partners. We realised that we had to have tools to analyse this flood of data and present it better to create actionable insights for people. We then moved to understanding that digital could actually change the business model, in which case there was an opportunity not just to improve efficiency, but to create new customer engagements, fruitful employee engagements exploiting the myriad digital touchpoints that new technologies and reimagined processes were making feasible for us. And finally, in 2020, the year that COVID taught us not to take anything for granted, we had many moments of epiphany and began to realise what it means when we have true digital collaboration.

The excitement with technology has given way to the quiet realisation over the last few years that true cyber–physical combinations can transform organisations everywhere. From robotics, augmented and virtual reality, IoT and computer vision on the shop floor of the digital factory to AI assisting, autonomously augmenting and occasionally replacing human intelligence. Automation of knowledge work is the current excitement because automation of factories was already happening through manufacturing execution systems and robots on the shop floor. But the minute all knowledge processes became candidates for automation or at least augmentation, new paradigms of performing services have emerged. Then, of course, big data and advanced analytics have taken the corporate world by storm because people have very quickly realised the real value of data will not just be a good post-mortem analysis of what happened last month or last week, but moving forward and predicting what could happen next month and prescribing what steps could be taken to obtain desirable outcomes and avoid undesirable consequences tomorrow of today's actions. We are already seeing this with Amazon, which is prompting the customer to look at what people with similar tastes have bought. What are they doing? They are prescribing a book that people like you bought and enjoyed. And if it helps them move some stock out of their warehouses, that would be just a collateral benefit.

The entire world has changed in the last six or seven years as businesses first understood the value of the SMAC stack and deployed social media, mobility, analytics and cloud into their strategy and implementation processes. Social listening has gone mainstream today, with software being deployed to listen actively on Twitter and LinkedIn to figure out what is being spoken about a brand, make those adjustments to offerings, use social influencer marketing and get a positive turnaround in brand perceptions. That is the true power of the social matrix. And finally, it's anything as a service thanks to the internet with large amounts of capital expenditure moved to large server farms owned by Amazon, Google, Microsoft etc. It started with software as a service, where applications were moved to the cloud. It meant infrastructure could also be moved—why would you have heavy-duty data centres inside your company when everything was being outsourced? Finally, with the advent of multiple business platforms, being a tenant in a multi-user platform or building and offering a multi-user platform to a company's ecosystem became the 'new normal'. So, whether it is in education, healthcare, manufacturing or any form of service, shared resources with secure data drives the deployment of digital in business today.

How do business models get driven by technology pushes and pandemic pulls? The most obvious area of change is productivity. We all believe that work from home during COVID pushed up productivity because people could focus on the tasks at hand and there was no stress or time loss on account of travel from home to office or city to city. Productivity improvements have also been enabled by automation, artificial intelligence, robotic and cyber–physical collaborations.

The other big area is user experience. Technology has given us better touchpoints at every stage of the digital journey of customers, supply and demand chain partners and employees, and rapid evolutions in user interfaces and user experience continue to improve the comfort, satisfaction and delight of both digital natives and digital immigrants. COVID has also had a role to play in this, with physical proximity frowned upon and a maximum reliance on digital handshakes and screen-to-screen interactions. The downside of all this is the reduced social interaction endangering collaboration of all forms and a real risk of social isolation and problems at home, as too much time at home intrudes on the private space of non-working members of the family.

Finally, what we are seeing in terms of leveraging digital is completely new business models. All of us know that the most successful digital companies that emerged from the dot com boom in the late 1990s, survived the bursting of the bubble and became dominant forces are Amazon, Facebook, Google, Netflix, Airbnb, Uber and a rejuvenated Apple Computer. Except for Apple, none of the other success stories owns any assets. It's their ability to optimise the use and sharing of other people's assets that make them invaluable in the marketplace. This is also giving every business the option to choose between exploiting digital to be a cost leader or become an experience maximiser or a true platform model.

What is the cost model? If you look at how a Google or an Alibaba or an Amazon or even a Facebook and an Airbnb started, it was all about aggregating buyers. The model provides full transparency to a price where you can do price discovery on the internet. It provides a free service initially with the option of upgrading a certain category of user to a premium service for a fee like Amazon and LinkedIn or staying with a lifetime free commitment for users like Facebook or Google and making money from advertisers. Reverse auctions can be held, where a customer can name the price at which they seek a service or an activity, and they can also shop around and get it wherever they want. A case in point was priceline.com, one of the first entities to do reverse auctions and greatly helped fill last-minute capacity in hotel rooms or airline seats, which would go waste if unused. In the same vein, usage-based pricing is the commercial model of choice. The consumer has for too long been buying a large piece of software and using barely 10 or 15% of its features and functionality. This is as true for office productivity software as it is for an insurance policy. But today, we find it more useful to shun life insurance and avail usage-based insurance, which maximises the coverage in a period where high risks are being incurred.

Moving from this exciting world to what we call the experience model, companies such as Netflix, Disney and even BMW and Tesla have optimised the experience model. This model, unlike the cost model, is all about personalisation so you feel that the brand has been made just for you. What you are served up by a Siri or Cortana is personalised to your likes and adapted to what you would like to see from the brand. Customer empowerment these days is all about instant gratification—what you want is what you get almost instantaneously, including the best flight, the movie you may most want to see and everything served up at your time, place and pace. Reducing friction is a critical element of this model because there is no need for long waiting times in dialling a call centre and certainly none of the queues encountered when going to a physical bank branch or movie theatre. Today people will not go back to terrible customer service experiences of the past.

The platform model is arguably the most exciting innovation brought about by digital through the creation of multi-tenancy marketplaces, where every player in an ecosystem can participate. For instance, a company could host a platform for every supplier, every dealer and every distributor, providing complete visibility of the supply and demand chain and facilitating transactions with due authorisation. This obviates asking for information because aggregators place it at the consumers' fingertips and all services are ready to be consumed. This also enables crowdsourcing, because various people can participate in these platforms. The whole community can be included in the design thinking and building of a multi-user platform, and all participants can share both its cost and utility. This is where platform providers become more of data orchestrators as they do not necessarily create the product or service but orchestrate the availability of services when customers wish to avail of them. And finally, a digital community or a digital marketplace is a full ecosystem coming together. This enables fundamental visceral changes in the way participants view, consume and pay for anything in the future.

The transition from cost to experience to a platform is being seen in every industry. We have referenced usage-based insurance. In 2019, it already accounted for 15% of the global insurance market. In e-commerce, the prediction is that 40% of e-commerce is enabled by cognitive personal shoppers, which is a collection of bots and the social network. In retail, thanks to COVID, people are placing orders on the internet and then driving to the parking lot of the store to merely pop open the car boot and have the ordered items placed there. Soon, a day will come when people won't be needed for even that. Robots will come out of the store and put the consignment in the car, or better still, send it by delivery drones to your doorstep. The use of robots will also be in customer-facing roles in retail, including the roles of store greeters, assistants, service mechanics, etc., almost eliminating the need for any form of human contact.

In manufacturing, the shop floor is being completely transformed. Many factories today don't have a single person on the shop floor. Everything is planned around digital twins, robotics, computer-aided manufacturing and manufacturing execution systems. But what is also interesting is that many field services are becoming self-serviced—equipment goes out with IoT-embedded devices and can self-heal or ask for maintenance when required. We don't need people monitoring machines all the time—it's all done by intelligent control towers constantly receiving a data feed from remote sensors and the internet of everything. In financial services, blockchain has moved out of the initial shadow of bitcoin and smart contracting and distributed ledgers. Socially distanced transactions are going to be the way people are going to avail of finance. And finally, healthcare is probably the most exciting opportunity for digital, because telemedicine, which was a doubtful case even six months ago, is now going mainstream thanks to COVID. Investments in field-ready 3-D printers, which can print every form of assistive equipment if not medicines, right out in the field. These will give us probably the entire capability of hospitals, doctors and medical services without ever having to physically meet them.

There is of course a very real possibility that if we are not careful, a combination of robotics and automation could take over our lives. What we also find is that it will be a choice for all of us. So, we need to be very conscious and thoughtful about the role we allot to digital technology. Do we want it to be assistive, do we want it to augment our capability, do we want it to completely transform us or do we want it to automate everything being done by human beings? This is where digital reengineering methodology can help every organisation to be truly thoughtful about the way they perceive the future and plan their distinctive position in the new world. When we practice digital reengineering, we need to recognise the importance of the six forces that can assist us in the transformation or hinder our success in achieving the desired results. These are forces to be simultaneously understood and managed.

The first force is technologies, which we have mentioned goes beyond the traditional digital SMAC stack of social, mobility analytics and cloud. We need to consider edge technologies—computer vision, AR/VR and even mixed reality, audio and video interfaces, IoT, 5G, quantum, cyber-physical—and choose based on need and not because each one is fascinating in itself. The second force to consider is process adaptation, how your business process and your manufacturing process can be made more market-facing with optimised digital touchpoints. The third force is more of visualisation through design thinking of all new stakeholder journeys, for customers, supply and demand chain partners, employees and shareholders. The fourth force naturally focuses on what is critical in the modern world, the ability to manage data well as it flows into our consideration from within and outside the organisation and how we can generate actionable insights through predictive and prescriptive analytics. The fifth is the creation of an innovation ecosystem, with internal motivated employees and external entrepreneurs who can craft new solutions for the firm. And most important, apart from technologies, processes, journeys, data and analytics, is culture. Very often, even large organisations manage the first four forces pretty well but underinvest in the fifth and sixth. In the early days of business process reengineering, we used to talk about the problems of fifth-generation aspirations and fourth-generation technologies colliding with third-generation systems, second-generation processes and first-generation people. Today, COVID and digital have pulled and pushed us respectively to a very asymmetrical situation where aspirations and technology are both fifth-generation, systems and processes need large doses of reengineering and people throughout the organisation have to be moved from a legacy mindset to a truly 24×7 digital existence.

At the end of this chapter we will present the model for moving towards digital maturity using these six forces, but let us first dive deeper into the opportunities and new thinking that have emerged on truly building new capabilities for the new world.

THE FUTURE-READY ORGANISATION: A MODEL FOR REENGINEERING

Let us understand the whys of the why-what-how thinking on future-ready organisations. As the world limps out of the wreckage caused by COVID and targets recovery and then resilience powered by digital tools, what are the deep areas to understand that all readers of this book who will be future practitioners of digital reengineering?

COVID: Key Influences on Customers and Businesses

The major influence will be the propensity for social distancing and absence of face-to-face communications for a substantial period. Online communication channels will continue to receive major attention, comparisons and significant funding. Zoom moved to a market value greater than the multi-decade leader IBM. Eric Yuan, their CEO, has said that technologies are being explored by which Zoom users can communicate collaboratively, even 'feel' a high five or hug given by the person on the other side and possibly even 'smell the coffee' in a conversation! Remote working, remote learning and remote family chats and singing will be the norm. Shopping online with virtual try-outs and alternative product and price discovery will be the norm.

Companies will increasingly search for, interview, recruit and deploy people online, and it is quite conceivable that some employees may never actually have a physical chat with their bosses or colleagues for months or even years. With the increasing use of digital labour, the exploration of robotisation and automation will also encourage businesses to become first workplace independent and eventually worker independent at least for many government and services jobs. There will be a proliferation of self-service and a 'Do It Yourself' culture, and the gig economy will be a mainstream method of paying for time and outcomes rather than just showing up at a workplace.

Increased social consciousness by customers, businesses and brands will surely be one desirable outcome of the COVID catharsis. Going 'Vocal for Local' will not only encourage national self-reliance but also support local businesses whose capabilities will be strengthened by being part of clusters that share best practices, technologies, digital platforms and customer knowledge. The consumption of digital content will accelerate and digital influencers will be much in demand by brands as they seek to expand their digital awareness.

The Impact of COVID on Digital Adoption Timelines

Digital transformation has firmly become more than an afterthought in many boardroom and management team meeting agendas. Competitors seek to attack incumbents in every sector, and the original relaxed timelines of three to five years for total digital transformation have been brought down to 6–12 months. This call to action is evident from many examples.

In banks and financial institutions, the transition to remote sales and service teams and providing flexibility for omnichannel interactions has been done in most cases with flexible payment arrangements offered for mortgages and loans. In a country such as India, where private banks took the lead in digital, large monoliths such as the State Bank of India have pivoted to a digital-first operation with alacrity. The overall digital transactions in the financial sector exceeded 100 million a day by end of August, with a transaction value of over 65 billion dollars (5 trillion rupees). Manufacturers have developed plans for fully automated 'lights out' factories, and supply chains are being enhanced with digital and AI. Retail has adopted online ordering and safe deliveries, and the visit to the ubiquitous mall or retail outlet will soon be more for the food courts and casual inspection of merchandise rather than for serious purchases. Healthcare in countries like India, where a visit to the family doctor was the only way to seek advice for decades, medical practitioners aided by new legislation have begun practising telemedicine and customers ordering online have enabled pharmacies on the net to double their sales. Robotics, 3-D printing, AI and machine learning will find rapid adoption in all hospital and health systems. Medical care will never be quite the same again.

The biggest disruption of course will be in the delivery of skills and education. The Lighthouse Communities Foundation in India has demonstrated the power of using augmented and virtual reality immersive experiences to build agency and aspiration in underprivileged youth. Digital literacy is being delivered online to full families in slum houses because nobody has to travel to a centre. In education, we have mentioned in the earlier section that the open universities of the future will not stop at experimenting with e-learning or even blended learning but will redesign the entire content and pedagogy to ensure that career counselling and management, choice of courses and style of personalised learning, peer group learning, coaching and mentoring and even job assistance and alumni interactions are completely managed by AI-powered digital platforms.

Can all this be done in less than a year? If the right set of factors are addressed, yes. Read on!

THE EXCITING WORLD OF DIGITAL PLATFORMS

Digital platforms began to catch the attention of both large firms and significant service providers six to seven years ago, and the adoption, like all good things digital, has been slow to start with and has taken off like a rocket in the last two years or so. In the work author Ganesh did with McKinsey & Co as their Senior Advisor in 2016, the state of art in this area was explored. A lot has remained relevant while a lot more has changed or evolved in the last three years. Let's start at the beginning and explore this exciting world.

What Is a Digital Platform?

In digital transformation, as we have already seen, business data, processes, applications and infrastructure are all candidates for substantial change. In many industry segments, the need for refreshed and reengineered versions of each of the areas is fairly similar, though some competitive advantages are introduced to delighted stakeholders in companies within an industry. In a similar vein, the needs of horizontal areas or business functions such as accounting, order processing and supply chain management tend to be similar, definitely within an industry segment and even across industries. In a world where CAPEX has moved to OPEX, the cloud has become omniscient and shareable software a reality, it is becoming increasingly efficient to have an integrated offering for each vertical domain or horizontal functional area that addresses all information and processing needs, integrates infrastructure, business processes and applications and becomes a digital platform that can be used by multiple companies. Customisation can be done at the periphery to suit each group of users.

Good digital platforms tend to stay fairly lean so that customisation and feature additions are possible through application programming interfaces (APIs) and microservices. Since these terms have not been properly defined for the readers of this book, let's do so in simple terms. When certain services such as processing a purchase order or invoice are fairly standard in a country or location, time to market for a platform is significantly reduced if these areas made available as microservices to be called upon and used as part of the functionality provided by the platform. Apart from these microservices, some tools enable different software programmes or an in-house platform and external platform to communicate. For instance, an interface that enables an AI bot or full functionality capabilities such as the Skills Alpha learning platform to be accessed or called when needed by a large human resource management application is what the API economy is all about. In this case, the enterprise platform can just expose its API to this platform, and the service can be called and used without being integrated into the platform. The difference between microservices and APIs is that the former target mainly internal users who are limited and definable whereas an API-exposed third-party application can serve large numbers of internal and external users. Abundant availability of these provide an entrepreneurial opportunity for microservices and API-accessible business application developers and also facilitate elegant design and easy deployment for the platform community.

Global examples of platforms that have gone mainstream apart from the well-known Facebook, Amazon and Netflix examples are Predix from GE for the manufacturing segment, Watson Health from IBM and Trizetto, which was bought by Cognizant and integrated into its healthcare platform. Among the large service provider community, Accenture chose a platform strategy to grab dominant opportunity share in digital services and built a galaxy of vertical and horizontal platforms. The investments made in substantially higher R&D, frequent acquisitions and high double-digit percentage spends on sales and marketing as a percentage of overall revenues have paid off for Accenture. They have obtained multiple 200 million-dollar-plus digital transformation deals and their average revenue per employee is an order of magnitude higher than Indian competitors such as TCS, Infosys and Wipro.

The other important aspect of successful platforms is that they have emerged as a true plug-and-play model that allows producers and customers to connect and create and exchange value. Platforms truly integrate all the new terminologies, sharing economy, IoT, social networks, idea crowdsourcing and the gig economy that characterise the way today's businesses function and are preparing for the new narrative.

What Platform Providers Should Know

Platforms can be built on top of existing industry ones, built afresh or acquired from a provider. In all cases, there is an ongoing investment in keeping the platform updated and relevant. Netflix retains its dominant share because of its efforts to personalise, use artificial intelligence and be highly responsive to every customer's habits and needs. On a wider canvas, Amazon gets customers addicted to the ease of their service and product offerings, and Facebook and Google launch new features and offers at a staggering pace. Platforms hold the potential to be spun out as a separate business, harking back to the 1970s when American Airlines built the Sabre platform to create ease of online reservations and spun it out to become a more profitable business than the airline itself. Today's platform companies dominate the tech space and indeed the market capitalisation in the US. There is no doubt that a good platform strategy is good for business and value creation. The logic for that is obvious. The network effects of platforms are direct, indirect and even cross-side with more direct users creating more value for each other, more application developers for the platform adding to the user value and more merchants participating in increasing value for all platform participants.

Platform creators must also clearly identify the purpose that the platform will serve. For instance, Facebook, LinkedIn and Twitter are the most obvious ones that enable social interactions among individuals. Quora and Stack Overflow and even to some extent Google are slightly different platforms because they serve as fountainheads for any individual to drink whatever knowledge they seek and others to participate in providing answers in a democratic knowledge sharing mode. YouTube and Spotify are primarily for media sharing, while Uber and Airbnb are service-oriented platforms that have created the shared economy. An edtech company can create a special purpose learning and development platform that enables career management, skills development, mentoring, peer sharing and coaching within a company or, like NASSCOM's Digital Skills, for four million industry participants across companies within an industry. Similarly, healthcare platforms could be provider-specific, city-specific or even state and countrywide, bringing together pathological labs, clinicians, providers and payers to provide single-window information and services to citizens.

Building Platforms for the Business

A vertical solution built by the company for ease of access by its customers, employees or supply-and-demand side partners will incorporate all critical use cases for the firm and can be developed jointly with consulting or development partners who could potentially become shareholders in the new business spin-out. The platforms could also integrate available platforms that offer adjacencies to the company's core on a revenue-sharing basis based on API calls. The basic idea to absorb is that all platforms will consist of three common layers, the bottom-most being the data layer that identifies users and content as well for the community, the middle layer being the technology infrastructure that ecosystems can reside in, such as YouTube for the online TV show community, and the top layer is the marketplace itself, where the network effects will be most visible, connecting all participants in as many seamless ways as possible.

There are some essential features to make platforms usable by multiple beneficiaries and successful. First is the overall value they offer to potential beneficiaries and their ability to generate network effects by enabling interactions among beneficiaries. The platform itself needs to be highly secure and trustworthy in terms of data and information confidentiality and scalability. Finally, they should seamlessly permit API use to allow other service providers to link and extend the platform's reach and capabilities beyond the original reach of the platform creator.

Overall, platforms are here to stay. As digital transformation becomes an imperative rather than a choice, the platform economy will drive the future of business.

Platforms to Ecosystems

Industry platforms in the last decade and more have been largely developed and deployed by independent service providers. The most celebrated are naturally Amazon, Alibaba, Airbnb and

Uber, who have dominated their chosen markets and disrupted the fortunes of individual product or service providers. However, for the CXO reading this section who has no pretensions of being a tech attacker, platforms provide an opportunity to build their customer and a partner ecosystem that can command amazing long-term loyalty. Let us consider a few examples.

In a study of the ecosystem strategies of hundred incumbent companies, McKinsey & Co suggest that large players who have a dominant position in their chosen business domain can exploit the global move towards data management and digitisation and investments in advanced analytics to personalise products and services and provide ease of access to customers, supply and demand chain partners and other beneficiaries of the incumbent's investment in a truly collaborative digital platform ecosystem that connects all of them.

McKinsey calls the new developments the promise of Ecosystem 2.0 and suggests three principles on which to build a holistic approach. The first is the use of strategic mapping to identify control points and develop a nuanced approach to nurture multiple initiatives by all participants in the ecosystem. The control points will emerge through the mapping of business processes. The second principle is to lock in impact with precise capabilities. These capabilities will be driven by customer demand and journeys and may require the development of innovation in the firm, with capabilities built either internally or provided by new partners. This is where digital marketing and AI providers may find their role. And the third principle is to design the organisation to involve many participants and customers.

This approach, suggested by one of the world's significant consulting firms, opens up a very interesting parallel between the evolution of digital platforms and the evolution of the organisation itself. We have mentioned earlier that platforms should be light and use microservices and apps to connect third-party applications. In a similar vein, future organisation designs will necessitate flexible and nimble organisation structures that can adapt to the availability of new solutions from business partners and even start-up entrepreneurs so that the ecosystem service availed by customers is always leading edge and ahead of the competition.

Building productive and scalable ecosystems calls for every incumbent to approach digital platforms with an attitude of humility and learning. The hungry start-up will always have the alacrity to commercialise technology through demonstrable pilots, but it is only the large organisation with its existing partner and customer base that can provide the sandbox needs for entrepreneurs to experiment and scale their solutions for myriad similar and different customs. For a long time, arrogant market leaders have shunned smaller firms with the belief that their early mover advantage and resultant size will perpetually keep them at the top, but digital will prove to be the big shakeout that will see dinosaurs wiped off the face of the customer landscape. Every worried and forward-looking CEO must recognise the coming paradigm shift and become a paradigm pioneer all over again to retain their market share and build a significant share of new opportunities in changing markets.

RISKS IN PLUNGING INTO DIGITAL

Before exploring the methodology an organisation or institution requires to embrace digital in all aspects, let us reflect a little on the risks that this foray entails so that steps can be taken to mitigate them. The first and the most obvious one is of course the widespread availability of digital technology. Smartphones, tablets and ubiquitous connectivity is still a myth in many parts of India and the world. Targeted beneficiaries of education, healthcare, financial services and retail and even supply chain partners may be unable to participate effectively in the world of digital learning, transactions and commerce. Increased dependence on cloud-based services, with the high risk of accidental or deliberate collapse of data centres and inadequate disaster recovery and business continuity, is a real concern. The lack of manual workarounds and dual supplier arrangements could cause huge business and reputation risks. Cyberattacks and malware in any communication and data storage devices can be the result of high traffic between external entities and private systems. Both people and processes will need to be extremely skilled and prepared for the 24×7 'always available' culture that a digitally reengineered organisation entails. Transparency in policies and expectations, training of supervisors on new ways of dealing with a largely remote workforce and the management of anticipated 'isolation' issues are all important. The risks have to be addressed and addressed well because it is unlikely that the world of work will ever be the same again.

Effectively hastening the process of morphing into a digital business calls for a complete rethinking and reimagining of every aspect of the business. The D-I-K-W quartet, or the transition from abundant data through classification to information, through contextualisation to knowledge and finally through a process of embedding this knowledge to create organisational wisdom becomes more relevant than ever before. With revenue increasingly generated by new business models, ensuring that knowledge forces work together to identify these opportunities will become imperative. Other key performance imperatives for the organisation will include minimising process cycle time and improving overall productivity, the ability to increase lifetime customer value and attract new customers through reach, relevance and reciprocity of value during the customer purchase and service journey and an upskilled workforce completely synchronised to future demands of all stakeholders. Finally, it all comes down to leadership. Are the leaders and you who are reading this book mentally and psychologically prepared for the change yourself and willing to lead the organisation through turbulent times, garnering maximum market and opportunity share in your core and new markets?

DIGITAL REENGINEERING: IDENTIFYING THE CAPABILITIES

The concept of reengineering was first promoted by Michael Hammer and James Champy in the early 1990s when they argued that organisations that just 'put lipstick on a bulldog' would fail to capitalise on the real value of information technology as its processes would not be ready to leverage the potential. In fact, much earlier, in the late 1980s, the Massachusetts Institute of Technology (MIT) did some pathbreaking research that was published as a book titled *The Corporation of the 1990s: Information Technology and Organisational Transformation*, in which they presented a model of transformation that technology would enable in organisations. It consisted of five stages:

1. Localised exploitation, where some departments and functions, typically accounting or materials management, would start using information technology applications for greater efficiency;
2. Internal integration, where the organisation would realise that all interfacing departments would have to participate in the real use of technology. These were the early days of material requirements planning which morphed into enterprise resource planning.

These two stages made up what MIT called the 'Evolution' phase. The 'Revolution' phase would then follow, which consisted of the following:

3. Business process reengineering, where all workflows orthogonal to decision flows would be streamlined to enable quicker processes for delivering the product to the market and customer order fulfilment;
4. Business network redesign, where supply-and-demand chain partners and even customers could become part of the information interchange;
5. Business scope redefinition, where technology would no longer just be a support to business strategy but drive the creation of new products and services and new business models.

If one now looks at the digital discussion that we have had through most of this book, one can see the stunning parallels. The good news about the shrinkage of digital transformation goals to a year or less is that many of the capabilities that organisations will have to develop can be approached in parallel and does not necessarily call for a sequential approach.

For this discussion, let us start with journeys. Customer journeys have already been discussed in detail, but what we need to recall from the relevant chapter is that customer interest may get spiked by any external input and the consideration journey may flow through the physical and digital world with the decision to buy eventually triggered from any place. Supporting the customer journey through persona identification and targeted inbound marketing and providing value propositions at every touchpoint and indeed, creating more touchpoints is what digitally savvy organisations do best.

It may then be worth addressing the next capability, which is technology. Clear business perspectives on every technology in the entire digital stack and a knowledge of when and how to deploy it in every part of the organisation are what will yield maximum results, whether its core cloud and mobility, edge tools such as IoT or virtual reality and even externally focused ideas emerging from blockchains, quantum computing and 5G. Closely coupled with technology is the process (note the movement from evolution to revolution described in the MIT study) and applying decades of knowledge of business process reengineering and business network redesign to the digital agenda, where every entity within and outside the organisation is connected to create agile and simple processes and operating models that anticipate stakeholder needs and meet them with the least pain. Companies such as Apple Computer and more recently Zoom have mastered this to a fine art.

Once the big three—customer, technology and process have been addressed through capability building, at least at a strategy level, the other three must be addressed. Data and analytics and the journey we have described earlier from descriptive to predictive and prescriptive outcomes through an AI and machine learning exploration, culture and competencies with clear tracking of employee journeys and enabling a process of career planning, skills, peer group learning and mentoring and coaching are essential for building an agile organisation with a truly customer-centric culture. Finally, a clear plan to build an innovation ecosystem becomes the way organisations can truly be leaders in digital in their industry segment. We will come back to the six capabilities and also identify stages through which organisations will transition in developing the Digital Capability Maturity Model. But before we go there, let us delve deeper into the art of choosing technologies for the digital journey and managing the innovation ecosystem.

TECHNOLOGY CHOICE AND DEPLOYMENT

The choice of technologies becomes difficult in all organisations aspiring to be leaders in digital because of two seemingly unconnected reasons. The first is the speed at which new technologies are announced, mostly disappearing after a few months and in some cases catching the imagination of early adopters and going mainstream. The second is the lack of a quick appreciation of the value of each technology by business leaders, which hopefully this book should address. The hype around digital and the frustration with the speed at which traditional IT departments were delivering new solutions motivated an industry leader in advisory services to suggest a three-phase model.

The first was for mission-critical 'run-the-bank' kind of applications, where traditional IT departments with their robust evaluation, deployment and security procedures were best equipped to deliver slow but sure systems. The second was under the newly minted chief digital officer, who typically brought in digital savvy combined with a knowledge of the business and quickly introduced digital 'change the bank' solutions with support where needed from the traditional IT folks. And finally, the very impatient chief marketing officer, looking to add some sizzle to the customer touchpoints. has often hired their own technology geeks or external agency to develop these quick solutions in an agile manner with excellent user experience.

As digital thinking has matured and many digital solutions have seen the light of day, the third category has been taken over by the digital folks. But there is still some confusion regarding the process that should be adopted. Let us provide some ideas here. The main goal should be to avoid spaghetti-like strands of digital applications to be developed, which result in chaos when the time comes to integrate and work predictably for mainstream business. Looking beyond seemingly convincing discussions on application programming interfaces and microservices and understanding the implications of technology decisions is essential. The reason the chairman of State Bank of India or the CEO of Bajaj Finance have been successful is the depth of their understanding of what technologies can make their digital processes robust and pathbreaking.

There is a simple must-do set of questions we can provide to ensure that the technology scanning, procurement and adoption processes of the organisation are optimised for success. These can be listed as follows:

1. Are we adequately equipped and staffed to assimilate core technologies such as cloud and master data management and integrate them into the technology mainstream of the organisation?
2. Are enough questions being asked by business users before any new technologies are brought into the organisation and is a fit with existing or future desired processes being established before technology comes in? Buying new technology because it sounds exciting is the worst way to introduce digital technologies into any process or the organisation.
3. Are technologies that come into the organisation simple enough to be assimilated easily and yet not so simple that they add no value?
4. Are we so risk-averse that we are sacrificing opportunity for regulatory or board concerns? A classic example of this is the tendency of financial institutions to adopt private cloud platforms when a robust public cloud would have more security than what can be done internally. Should we not trust

Amazon, Microsoft or Google to be much more security-investment ready than what our budgets permit?

5. Does our technology refresh sound too ambitious with wholesale replacement of legacy but stable systems by the 'latest and greatest' technologies? A judicious mix of incremental changes, with some big-bang high-investment platforms, may be the best approach.
6. Are we excessively reliant on outsourcing and external vendors to create the new digital architecture for the company? It is normally advisable to have internal control on the 'crown jewels' of digital platforms and innovation and use external vendors for consulting and advisory services and also to provide managed services on older applications that are not critical to the organisation.
7. Are we losing focus on the business need in the technologists' push to adopt new gizmos based on promised outputs? Technical excellence may not lead to actual business results, and the correlation must be carefully evaluated and results measured as implementation progresses.
8. Are we building and installing digital platforms for the organisation because they are available and feasible or after evaluating their applicability in the current context of readiness of data, culture and acceptance of innovation?
9. Are we looking at technology as a cost factor or as an investment from which serious returns can and should be expected?
10. Are we building a true culture of digital engineering with discipline and robust development and installation processes to ensure that digital success is achieved and sustained?

FOSTERING AND MANAGING INNOVATION

We are calling out the innovation discussion as we move towards some grand recommendations for the digital business because innovation, despite being a word that gets tossed around just like leadership as a panacea for all ills, remains an essential ingredient for any sustainable major change. Let us consider in some depth what it might take to build a true culture of innovation in the organisation. Why is this a prerequisite to digital reengineering? Because in every success story of digital transformation that we have seen around the world, the most significant ones are those who have built an ecosystem of innovation within the organisation and with external partners, truly something to be harnessed and exploited for significant game-changing success!

Innovation has always had immense value in any organisation. Innovation has occupied centre-stage in the IT sector in the application of information and digital technologies. It started with product innovation, where some companies had some creative designs and could use good manufacturing processes to convert that creativity into commercial success. In India, this was initially largely copycat innovation, but it still enabled the creation of revenue sources for word processing and project management products. The bigger successes happened in the field of process innovation, with the sheer process of moving complex migration and development jobs from global markets to Indian offshore outsourcing centres, thus enabling huge innovation in the way software development. Migration and testing work was performed and delivered with consequent value realisation by global clients. We've also seen input process innovation in India, particularly where companies have used very interesting processes to identify talent and get them into the system just in time to work on mission-critical projects.

The global examples in the last 20 years have seen several firms demonstrating business model innovation. The e-commerce industry is a classic example, where you have multiple cases such as Amazon, Facebook, Google or Alibaba who have all innovated by making assets available from one provider to multiple consumers. In these cases, the company serves as a smart intermediary in the process. Innovation itself over the years has helped many organisations to do breakthroughs as well as to continuously improve their operating parameters. Our own belief is that digital can drive business model innovation at a much faster rate and, conversely, innovation can make digital transformation and its reengineering happen much faster than one could imagine.

To understand how this can happen in an organisation that is seriously seeking breakthrough results through digital, let us understand the models of innovation that exist today. Just to take the three schools of thought that emerged from Harvard Business School, for instance, the first and probably the most significant was from Clayton Christensen. Christensen's theory was that if you have a disruptive innovation idea within an organisation, the best way to capitalise on it through reengineering is to spin out. He always recommended that a great innovation can get stifled in a traditional large organisation, and the innovation team must be completely independent and add value not only to the organisation itself but eventually even become an organisation in its own right. The second model is the one we prefer, which is the work of Michael Tushman, at present still a professor at Harvard Business School. He introduced the concept of ambidextrous innovation, or the ability to work with both hands, which means that while the left hand is focused on incremental continuous innovation, the right hand can conceptualise and bring about breakthrough innovations that are order-of-magnitude transformations.

A McKinsey article mentioned that in 2012 experts recommended creating an innovation portfolio that allocated 10% of the budget to transformational projects, 20% to moderately transformational projects (sometimes called adjacent or substantial projects) and the remaining 70% to incremental innovation. By 2018, their view was that most companies were focusing squarely on transformation, investing as much as 30% of their outlays in major projects and 35% in moderately transformational projects. Only 35% of the budget was being spent on incremental innovation—half the percentage in 2012. Quite a charter for chief innovation officers to take up!

One of the few examples of a company that has implemented multiple large or discontinuous innovations is Amazon, which started off being a humble online bookseller when the internet boom began. But it then very quickly became an enabler of over 50% retail transactions in the US marketplace. Amazon has multiple new spin-off companies to show for its prowess, including Amazon Web Services, which has transformed the way people use software and infrastructure. Finally, the third model of innovation has been the life work of competitiveness guru Michael Porter, with his work on innovation clusters and the premise that innovation happens in clusters of similar companies looking for and deriving collaborative competitive advantage. The leather clusters in Italy or the electronics clusters in Shenzhen, China, and more recently the textile cluster in Bangladesh are all examples of world-class business model innovation in practice.

So how does innovation allow a great digital idea to emanate from an organisation and grow to commercial success? Where does it come from and how is it analysed, understood and matured to enable the company to derive maximum advantage out of this innovation? There are two ways of looking at innovation, and we will discuss both in detail. The first is of course internal innovation, which is having multidisciplinary employee innovation networks come up within the organisation. The second is a much more open innovation approach where one uses both internal capabilities and external disruptive idea providers to make innovation happen in the organisation. If you look at a few examples of truly ambidextrous innovation, you will find companies such as Google which has emerged from the IT company Alphabet. Apple Computer and its multiple innovations, right from iPods to iTunes to more recently the iPhone, has emerged from the work of amazing entrepreneurs such as Steve Jobs, who create products and services for markets which did not ask for them in the first place. Jobs is famous for saying that you can never trust a customer to know what they want, which is the complete antithesis of a traditional marketing logic that says that we are all there to meet the stated or latent demand in the mind of a customer. Michael Tushman also calls this the difference between the exploitative and exploratory approaches.

There are some basic differences between the two models of innovation that can coexist in one organisation. Disparate teams are held together by a strategic leadership that shares a common vision and values while encouraging different pathways in the innovation journey. The strategic intent of exploitation is cost improvement and profit maximisation, whereas exploratory innovation will be truly focused on breakthroughs, much higher revenue and growth and opportunity. The critical tasks to be performed in exploitation will be operations improvement, efficiency and incremental changes. The exploratory mode, however, entails adapting to new opportunities, creating new production services and delivering breakthrough innovation. The competencies needed for exploitation are purely operational, while those for exploration, are very strategic. The structures that drive exploitation are more mechanistic and formal, while structures that drive exploration are much more adaptive, with loose controls and high risks and rewards. Supported risk-taking and high-speed experimentation enable exploratory innovation to truly take root and succeed!

One doesn't have to look far to see how ambidextrous innovation drives digital change. When digital was first coming into the mainstream, people let mission-critical lights-on computing continue to be done by traditional IT folks, who have processes for efficient systems modernisation and ongoing support, while creative teams headed by a chief digital officer were tasked with researching and bringing in digital touchpoints into customer and employee journeys. Also, impatient chief marketing officers were given technology experts as part of their teams to reimagine and develop completely new customer journeys and experiment with ideas which could, if successful, be tossed over the wall to the formal digital team for mainstream adoption. This resulted in three organisations for digital—a functional organisation, a cross-functional digital team and a completely unsupported idea generation and validation. The divisions that were created when people were experimenting with the digital economy led to the coexistence of exploitative and exploratory innovation. These are still two very different aspects of the innovation mindset when considering the model we now see emerging in organisations.

Exploitative innovation is almost always in-house, created within a business unit or by cross-pollination across units. Exploratory innovation can also happen through external collaborators, though converting these ideas into scaled implementations through innovation could and should involve a formal process of selection. There should also be screening and internal evaluation for initial funding and tracking the idea development to its first results. Once that is established, diffusion is possible. This involves the deliberate spread across the organisation. Indeed, the whole process of vaccine development for COVID goes through the same process—an initial screening, multiple rounds of lab testing and then human trials. Only after there is a surety on outcomes and side effects will diffusion be permitted. All these will involve significant and sagacious choices by leaders, of a country in the case of COVID, and at a humbler CEO and CXO level when it comes to digital reengineering.

The critical factor for the choice between internal or external innovation is the capability of our people to generate ideas within their departments and collaboration within the organisation. When the gaze moves to external sources, there is a need to scan the sources outside that can generate good ideas and how the screening process should work. Do we need external help? How quickly can external ideas be internalised and made mainstream within the organisation? A very well-written case study on innovation at Zensar Technologies has been developed by Professor Tushman and his research team, Zensar. Two of the authors embarked on its innovation journey from the year 2001. The motivation for external innovation came from the need to build a differentiated 'point of view' for the enterprise. An entire breakthrough idea of automated software migration and development through solution blueprints and a blueprint foundry came through the acquisition of the intellectual property of one Silicon Valley company that had run out of funding post the dot com bubble burst. The company first tasked the CTO who had suggested the acquisition with building a new Innovative Technology Services (ITS) profit centre for the company. After the exploratory idea was established with a handful of clients, ITS was merged within the core applications management team of the company for ongoing exploitation.

This example of a technological innovation becoming a separate business and then being integrated into the core of the company teaches a lot about the focus on digital that is imperative for every organisation. One of the measures of innovation success in an organisation is the number of quality ideas generated, what proportion comes from outside the organisation, how the ideas are selected and how they then go mainstream. Disney & Company has a well-publicised gong show where people within a new idea are encouraged to present it to a group of peers. Anyone who believes that the idea has no legs can sound a gong which will stop the presentation, a crude but rather effective way of eliminating weak ideas at inception. In companies where we have worked and led innovation, vision communities tasked with blue-sky thinking and generating ideas that have proved to be very useful, again the subject of a Harvard Business School case study by Professor David Garvin and team titled *The Power of Vision Communities*. A contemporary success story of combining internal and external innovation is the premier non-banking finance company in India, Bajaj Finserv, which scouts for new fintech ideas from around the world and selects a few to participate in proof of concept opportunities within the company. Today BFS Direct has been spun out as a separate business that offers products of the three operating companies in financial services, general insurance and life insurance online through a fully digital channel.

Specifically, in the field of digital, there is no better way to understand what can be done and what is being done out there than to study two or three companies that have truly innovated with products, processes and business models. We discussed a digital learning platform called Skills Alpha in the culture and skills chapter. One company that all of us will have got extremely familiar with in the dark months of COVID is Zoom, which crossed IBM's market valuation in September 2020. The company was founded by Eric Yuan after a successful stint at CISCO, where he was part of the team that created WebEx, still a very popular platform for large industry and governments for video-conferencing. In an interview done at an Indian internet event, Eric spoke about his motivation to create a platform that 'everybody loves' after realising that his previous work was not making people happy. In an environment where work from home, play from home and learn from home were going mainstream, Zoom captured the market like no other platform and truly dominates the fairly crowded space even today.

Yuan knows that the original business case was business communications across space, but he is fully preparing for large future use cases in telemedicine and telehealth, higher education and Zoom yoga and Zoom weddings. What excites Eric is the ability to integrate all use cases in life, enable real-time language translation as a discussion is happening and enable digital high fives, digital hugs and digital coffee appreciation. With a large developer community, Zoom's innovation ecosystem is growing, and they will continue to dominate as long as innovation runs through their bloodstream.

Process innovation is an area where Indian IT service providers have excelled. The results in terms of growth and dominant global technology market share are there for all to see. Individual companies have excelled on the strength of their ability to move processes offshore for Fortune 500 clients and design and deploy highly innovative ways of attracting talent, deploying them on large managed service contracts and adding value to the customer's process beyond expectations. In business model innovation, Amazon remains the paragon of excellence, though across many service sectors we see global disrupters and attackers emerge who will redefine the way the world thinks of and does business in the years to come.

How does one compare the benefits of internal versus external innovation? Internal innovation has the advantage of the innovators having access to all the data generated within the company and no fear of data theft or wrongful usage by partners. This should however not perpetuate the 'not invented here' syndrome, which could result in more incremental and less breakthrough innovation happening in the firm. For years, China has offered a valuable partner in their universities, which set up joint laboratories for technology firms in the US and leverages large research funds to co-create new products. As a market leader such as Bajaj Finserv has established, understanding the best in class in the US, Europe, China and Israel helps them to collaborate with the best and bring powerful innovations to the fingertips of the consumer. McKinsey Research points to the fact that smart companies focus on internal core teams for mission-critical innovation pathways but treat external sources of innovation as a way of broadening the portfolio of ideas.

Whatever be the mix, innovate we must, and a programme for sustaining and growing it is essential in any digital journey.

THE CHANGING ROLE OF LEADERSHIP

It's almost a cliché to say that CXOs have to lead from the front when any events that have a substantial impact on the organisation have to be faced, their ill effects mitigated and adversities converted into opportunities. In the aftermath of COVID, leadership is faced with the double whammy of depressed demand in all sectors with the possible exception of e-commerce for food products and new managerial challenges. Social distancing and work from home are becoming the preferred option in all service industries as well as many functions in manufacturing, services and even the agriculture and farming sectors. Add to this the inexorable push of digital technologies, with customers demanding friction- and contact-free transactions and competitors threatening to take the lead in the new paradigm of digitally generated demand and supply compulsions. Leaders are being and will be tested as never before for skills of cash flow management, customer acquisition, demand generation, service orientation, people happiness and technology selection and management. The other big question that will have to be addressed is the innovation imperative and how leaders keep the innovation engines humming during times of crisis.

We have explored design thinking and customer journey management, analysed the potential impact of digital on functions, processes and domains and suggested new ways of addressing skills and culture. It is worth discussing technology choices and assimilation in the organisation, other people issues and the management of innovation in some depth before we build the model for digital capability maturity that is one of the key innovative research areas for this book.

USING THE CAPABILITIES TO BUILD THE DIGITAL FIRM

Earlier in this chapter, we presented the six capabilities that any organisation aspiring to be truly digitally reengineered must demonstrate to lead in the emerging digital marketplace. We recommended predicting and creating customer journeys that would be truly experience-centric, built on seamless technology architecture, a future-focused and insight-driven data and analytics strategy and responsive and streamlined business processes. We have then discussed how to intelligently procure technology, build an internal and external innovation ecosystem that works for the future and unleash the true capabilities of skilled and digitally empowered people with supportive leadership.

One could approach the entire reengineering model as one where there are three parallel pathways to be adopted supported by three foundation activities, Stakeholder journeys, processes and technology are the pathways, while data and analytics, culture and competencies and the innovation ecosystem are the foundation. To reimagine stakeholder journeys, mapping the transformed physical–digital options and creating journey maps with digital touchpoints, fully cognisant at all times of pandemic-induced and human fear-initiated restrictions at all times will be key. Technology optimisation will entail optimising current and future options, evaluating their impact on processes and people and ensuring the highest levels of security. Processes will be redesigned both to leverage the digital touchpoints and new capabilities of core and edge technologies and also to meet changing market requirements and customer expectations and leverage internal and external capabilities in the supply, demand and partners networks.

New technologies will produce data to a great degree of acceleration, and processes will have to leverage data and analytics. This is why the strong foundations of a data warehouse, data lake and data mart and the forward focus of AI and machine learning will have to be thoughtfully deployed. The priority should be to provide a real-time 360-degree view of all stakeholders, with the ability to predict and prescribe buying behaviour and provide early warnings on partner or employee dissatisfaction and potential attrition. A customer-oriented 'always on' culture will require well-honed competencies in all leaders and critical team members as well as the skills to sense and respond to changing market and customer needs in every employee or partner. And finally, innovation, as we have discussed, will need to be a foundation of future success, not just an option for experimentation. This will call for an innovation portfolio approach, with multiple internal and external solutions teams, garages and pods to experiment and create proof-of-concept use cases and an innovation network and a council that thinks anew every day and in every moment of change or opportunity. Future organisations will definitely need a very balanced focus on all these.

GETTING IT ALL TOGETHER: A CAPABILITY MATURITY MODEL

As a precursor to the development of the Capability Maturity Model for organisations embarking on the path to digital reengineering, it may be worth considering the evolution of capabilities in three other contexts—information technology, software processes and knowledge management. Some seminal work in these areas has been done by Professors Nolan and Norton, Carnegie Mellon Institute, and one of our authors Dr Ganesh Natarajan. This research briefly flows as follows.

The first version of the stage theory appeared in 1973 and was built on the premise that information technology undergoes dynamic and continuous development. Nolan and Norton divided the progress within an organisation into several stages—initiation, contagion, control and then, after a period of technological discontinuity, integration, architecture and demassing. Also, the authors developed a growth process model that examined supply factors such as management controls and availability of resources, primarily personnel, technology and demand factors such as user awareness and skills and the application portfolio or the number of automated information systems in an organisation as well as the degree to which these systems support the current work process. The professors concluded that the stage at which an organisation is at is not as important as the balancing of the growth processes, although they did opine that all six stages would have to be passed to reach maturity in the management of information technology.

The software engineering Capability Maturity Model (CMM) was developed by the Software Engineering Institute (SEI) at Carnegie Mellon University in 1987. It has famously been called SEI-CMM by disciples and practitioners in the software industry in India and abroad. Each level of maturity represents a process capability level, starting with 'initial' and moving through 'repeatable', 'defined' and 'managed' to 'optimising'. The model authors have also suggested key process areas—project planning, software quality assurance and sub-contract management at the 'repeatable' level, inter-group coordination and training in the 'defined' level, software quality management and quantitative methods in the 'managed' level and process change and technology change management in the 'optimising' level. The use of this model by large software development and maintenance firms and the proliferation of consultants and lead assessors has made this one of the most sought-after certifications among outsourcing vendors and large internal departments, though the use of agile methods has in recent times taken the sheen off this somewhat regimented approach.

The knowledge management maturity (KMM) model for software and services industries was developed by Ganesh as part of his PhD research at the Indian Institute of Technology Bombay. He also wrote about it in a book he co-authored with Uma titled *Unleashing the Knowledge Force* in 2007. The K-stages identified were pre-knowledge initiation, knowledge management initiation, knowledge management action and finally knowledge management maturity. The research also identified four factors called K-factors—business process readiness, technology infrastructure, human behaviour and leadership, which could hasten or inhibit the progress of the organisation through the KMM stages. In a study of necessary and sufficient conditions for stage transition, the researchers concluded that a balanced approach a la Nolan–Norton growth processes was desirable. Human behaviour is a necessary condition for an organisation to sustain and improve its KM capabilities while in specific stage transitions, established processes are necessary to start the KM journey. Technology deployment enables knowledge action, and leadership is particularly essential for the progress to KM maturity.

In the context of these three studies and consulting recommendations, the digital journey lends itself to the hypothesis that true success in digital business needs customer and other stakeholder journeys to be always at the centre of all digital outcomes, with processes and technology needing a careful balance through the digital journey. As mentioned earlier, the foundational capabilities for the digital journey will be data, culture and innovation. It may be premature to offer a deterministic model for the progress of the digital journey given the nascent stage of digital transformation in many sectors. However, it will certainly be built on these three pathways and three foundational capabilities. Without attempting to develop new terminologies, we could just start with a hypothesis that each pathway, as well as each foundational capability, needs initiation, robust action and then maturity.

MEASURING MATURITY LEVELS AND DIGITAL READINESS

During the research for this book and discussions with many firms in various stages of their digital journey, we came up with some key questions that could be used as part of an initial self-assessment questionnaire for each of the six factors. Digital maturity could be an aspirational stage that emerges from a positive affirmation to all these 48 questions. Let us understand in the context of digital capability maturity modelling how companies could use their assessment base on this model to move up the value chain and attain digital supremacy in their industry segments.

Let us first consider the pathways to success. The ability of all stakeholders to move seamlessly across consideration and usage channels and the digital points available to them to facilitate their journey become the key aspiration for any company. The exploitation of all available digital technologies that sharpen the capabilities of the firm and the exploration into edge technologies make for a heady mix of opportunities.

At a more control level, the predictability and consistency of outcomes delivered through each business process and their seamless leverage of technologies to support every step of the stakeholder journey take the company higher and higher on each pathway. The sequential questions to be ticked off in the maturity journey could be as outlined below.

Stakeholder Journeys

1. Are customers, employees, supply and demand partners and shareholders able to access the firm easily and get the desired response in terms of timeliness and adequacy?
2. Have critical touchpoints for digital adoption been identified at every stage of every journey of each stakeholder?

The first two would define initiation.

3. Is the stakeholder journey being constantly evaluated and improved upon based on formal and informal networks, minimum friction between the stakeholder and the company and optimal efficiency?
4. Is the company continually measuring the interaction of stakeholders across channels and are new journeys being created to maximise satisfaction?

These two would indicate action.

5. Is journey planning and measurement an integral part of the strategic planning and business review processes of the organisation?

This would indicate maturity.

Digital Technologies

1. Has every business process been automated to maximise efficiency and effectiveness for the user and cost minimisation for the company?

2. Is there adequate technology to capture data on interest, service feedback and sentiment in every stakeholder interaction?

The first two would define initiation.

3. Is the necessary security falling into place to protect data, systems and processes from malware and cyber intrusions?
4. Is there a technology refresh happening in every function and process at least once in 12–18 months?

These two would indicate action.

5. Is technology driving the company to think of new strategies and even new products and services delivered digitally?

This would indicate maturity.

Business Processes

1. Has every process in the company been evaluated in terms of digital inputs and automation?
2. Are the operations optimised in terms of speed and usage of digital touchpoints and the use of cloud, mobility and social listening and networks?

These two would indicate initiation.

3. Is there a constant search for edge technologies and a mapping of their use by competition within the industry and similar firms in other industries to reengineer processes and make them more customer and other stakeholder friendly?
4. Are the supply chain and demand chain of the organisation operating at high performance and are all partners fully integrated into the digital network of the firm?

These two would indicate action.

5. Are processes geared towards using predictive and descriptive analytics, social listening and responsiveness and constantly reengineered to delight the customer?

This would indicate maturity.

The foundational capabilities could also be assessed in a similar manner.

Data and Analytics

1. Is the company capturing all data from internal and external sources and storing it in an accessible manner in data warehouses, marts and lakes?
2. Have we ensured that data is analysed and presented in easily understandable information formats through tables and dashboards as appropriate in an efficient and timely manner?

These two would indicate initiation.

3. Are data practices providing actionable insights about customers and other stakeholders?
4. Have we deployed AI and machine learning and getting predictive analytics about the future actions of stakeholders?

These two would indicate action.

5. Are we creating an environment where AI can co-exist with human intelligence and create prescriptive models for customers and employees?

This would indicate maturity.

Culture and Competencies

1. Is every employee fully equipped with the digital and the tech skills needed for the job?

2. Have you identified digital champions in the organisation who can lead digital?

These two would indicate initiation.

3. Is the organisation culture geared for new stakeholder journeys and 24×7 availability?
4. Is the organisation attracting digitally savvy entrepreneurial millennials?

These two would indicate action.

5. Is the organisation skilled for new business models identification and implementation and are the teams innovative and inclusive of new internal and external ideas?

This would indicate maturity.

Innovation Ecosystem

1. Is the firm open to new ideas and better ways of delighting stakeholders?
2. Are there methods to reward innovators who want to experiment with digital ideas?

These two would indicate initiation.

3. Is innovation critical to meeting your future goals?
4. Are you looking at start-ups and external innovation sources?

These two would indicate action.

5. Is there a formal innovation council and a model for embracing incremental and breakthrough innovations to build the digital business?

This would indicate maturity.

APPLYING THE MODEL

We have found during our research that most organisations suffer either because they have not anticipated new customer journeys or have not prepared their teams' and their leaders' mindset to embrace innovation. However, firms have problems with data management, inadequate or excessive unconnected technologies, weak processes or ill-trained people. Bearing in mind that digital will break because of the weakest link, a concerted effort to travel along the three pathways and continuously strengthen the foundation capabilities is the best approach to success.

In our opinion, the new way to building a digital business calls for serious leadership introspection and a fast, focused and flexible approach to creating the digital reengineering strategy. The assessment questionnaires can help establish the baseline and choose specific actions to initiate digital transformation, move towards robust reengineering actions and finally attain some degree of maturity and digital success!

The successful implementation of the digital reengineering model also needs an appropriate choice of partners who can help with the outsourcing of various aspects of digital implementation and with managing the new processes. The service providers themselves will also go through their chrysalis as we explain in the box.

Outsourcing in the Third Wave

The digitally pushed agenda for transformation and reengineering for corporations around the world is not new. Every aspect of successful digital businesses needs to be strategised and managed—stakeholder journey planning, technology selection and assimilation, redesigning business processes and networks around digital touchpoints, using data and analytics to manage internal and external data flows, putting in a reskilling and digital culture-building agenda and creating an ecosystem for internal and external innovation. And all this will need strategic outsourcing partners who recognise the required heavy lifting and can support the company through all stages of transformation.

This is where the third wave if IT and business process outsourcing is expected to kick in. Goldman Sachs in a report has suggested that the real trigger will be the remote-working model for clients and providers, which has suddenly made it irrelevant whether the work is being performed from a home in the US or anywhere in the world. The crown jewels of technology support will increasingly move to offshore locations, and the managed services model will have to be further strengthened to let clients pay for outcomes, not outputs and certainly not inputs.

Industry veterans in IT and business process management companies will recall that the first legitimising trigger for offshore outsourcing was the Y2K problem, when large mountains of legacy software code moved to India to be fixed, modernised and eventually integrated into new applications. The bogey that still prevailed was confidentiality of data and concerns about remote security, which severely limited flexibility in managing technology and processes from anywhere and created the large campuses where people were paid for 'showing up' rather than real productivity. The pool of talent that could be accessed was also limited to folks trained or able to work in the large outsourcing cities. Suddenly vistas of new opportunity are opening up for service providers.

For IT Services Providers

1. Work from anywhere gives the opportunity to employ people from any part of India or neighbouring countries, integrate them through VPN (virtual private networks) and cut costs through lower-salaried manpower, low attrition and minimal office space.
2. Outcome-based pricing finally makes the great promise of taking over complete processes from customers a possibility

and can build even stickier relationships with key customers in any part of the world.

3. The challenge will be to demonstrate even deeper knowledge of customer's domain, intensify marketing to be a true business partner rather than just a low-cost piecemeal transaction outsourcer and even provide research and training support to the client organisation.

For BPM Providers

1. To use AI and Robotics to eliminate the need for most voice processes and build and implement cognitive customer service centres for key customers, possibly on the internet and in the cloud.
2. To take over and manage end-to-end processes and provide a range of analytics and actionable insights.
3. The challenge will be to integrate digital technology in all business process management solutions and emulate their IT counterparts in providing outcome-based solutions.

The industry itself, which today employs nearly 50 million employees directly and provides indirect employment to double that number in construction, facilities management, housekeeping, hospitality and security can be expected to grow at 15% every year, though the reduced use of offices and campuses could lead to indirect employment growing at a slower rate. The Indian market and opportunity share of global technology development and process management can confidently be expected to continue to increase.

Investment banking firm Jefferies, in a recent study of the expectations of investors, has come up with a few forecasts that will determine the success of the services industry to be a true transformation partner for clients. Digital opportunities will abound in every functional area and business domain—from creating completely unmanned factories, energising supply chains through dynamic rerouting of transport to AI in healthcare and friction-free smart contracting in multi-company multi-country transactions.

Getting It All Together

We have reached a stage where we have learnt everything there is to know about digital transformation in organisations. Technology exploration is complete, the opportunities in processes and domains are understood, design thinking and stakeholder journey reimagination have been elaborated upon. We are aware of the foundational capabilities necessary to embark on the pathways to create a digital business. It may be cliché, but there is no doubt that a crisis is too good an opportunity to waste. How the organisation does course correction on wasteful business practices in the post-COVID resilience period and how it leverages the power of digital to completely reimagine its business policies and practices can separate winners from the also-rans.

The first logical opportunity reinforced here is cloud computing becoming the norm, with the deployment of cloud infrastructure expected to peak by 2022 and lend itself to a host of cloud-managed services and true digital innovations. This will lead to bigger and more complex digital projects and will naturally help full-service large players and leave smaller entrepreneurs out of many opportunity spaces. The imperative will be the ability to adapt and grow with the changing digital needs of clients, deepen the knowledge of client domains and context and demonstrate superior execution at all times.

Indian companies, most of whom have stopped reporting the digital percentage of their revenues, have a long way to go before they catch up with early movers in digital services and platforms, such as Accenture, which has 70% of its revenues coming from this segment. Indian providers will have to accelerate their efforts to reskill and upskill employees, embrace automation and artificial intelligence and constantly increase R&D spending. The acquisitions Indian firms make may also have to be stepped up, although this has increased in the past few years with over 2 billion dollars' worth of acquisitions done by just the top five technology services companies in the last five years.

Very similar to the Indian digital economy that has a lot of catching up to do compared to the global 'best in class', Jefferies has suggested that India IT services firms must also learn in key metrics from global market leader Accenture. Apart from the larger digital component of revenues, a more aggressive growth strategy to reach double-digit growth again may be required, although, in organic growth terms, TCS and Infosys are comparable and, in some periods, superior to Accenture. Indian companies also need to retain their superior earning margins with the market moving more towards products, platforms and consulting-led digital reengineering programmes.

The 5G opportunity is also seen as being significant, particularly for Indian services providers such as Tech Mahindra, which have a history of a strong presence in the telecom space. Despite COVID, spending is already sharp in the handset and apps space for 5G while there is a delay in enterprises and communication service providers due to the ongoing pandemic.

This is one industry that can see double-digit revenue growth for the next decade and more if it reorganises its capabilities to serve the current and emerging digital needs of its global clients.

DIGITAL TRANSFORMATION AGENDA

The biggest motivator for a significant transformation is revenue acceleration. A wonderful analysis by the Boston Consulting Group of global business leaders who underwent a recent transformation suggests that in over three-quarters of the companies, at least half the financial impact of the transformation was achieved through revenue growth levers. BCG also found that incremental revenues generated during the early stages of a transformation can be reinvested at least in part to fund the rest of the journey. There are many other obvious advantages of using a revenue lens to measure the success of transformations, including general morale improvement across the company employees and supply and demand chain partners and enterprise value boost through satisfied investors.

The implication for the digital warriors who want to place digital transformation and reengineering at the top of the organisation's consideration set in the COVID recovery phase is that the primary focus needs to be on making customer journeys as effective and delightful as possible so that brand sales multiply and market share in every segment increases. Once this is established, digital can also help in making the six revenue levers identified by BCG most effective for the business.

1. Targeted promotions and loyalty programmes to push sales. The use of digital marketing, persona identification, inbound campaigns and social influencers can play a big role in enhancing brand salience and ensure that the company's brands emerge at the top of the consideration set of the customer.
2. Optimising sales channels and sales coverage efficiency. Here again, the aggressive use of social media marketing and data and analytics to measure the success of every campaign and evaluate the success of every channel will systematically improve the continuous growth of the campaign.
3. Sales force activation. Extensive use of artificial intelligence and machine learning can help support the sales force with just-in-time inputs for every sale. Long-time users of Salesforce, the global market leader in CRM, are willing to pay much more for the licenses for every sales and marketing person in the organisation because the Einstein analytics features help each salesperson to be measurably better in all parameters.
4. Pricing optimisation. Deals are lost too often because of too much hierarchy in the decision-making process. Companies lose money by discounting to a point where the product or service is provided at a loss even as the sales contract is done. Proper data management, evaluation of comparisons, modelling of outcomes and precision pricing are all possible through digital technologies.

5. Contract management. Blockchains are now making smart contracting possible, and proper workflow optimisation and robotic process automation with cognitive inputs can make effective contract management a norm for all large contracting firms.
6. Revenue assurance. Automation and AI can help fix all leakages and also ensure a truly learning organisation evolves.

The combination of all these digital tools in the core areas of revenue acceleration and a further focus on cost minimisation by IoT, robotics and manufacturing and supply chain efficiencies can ensure that organisations of the future are far more sophisticated than ever before. All this and more should be achieved within 12 months of the corporate world making a recovery from COVID. The time to start is now!

What could be a possible 3-6-12-month plan to ensure that the organisation analyses all its options and truly achieves and sustains the potential that digital transformation holds? Let us look at a possible approach through three lenses. The lens of pathways will include customer journeys, technologies and processes. The lens of foundational capabilities will include data and analytics, culture and competencies and internal and external innovation. And the lens of desirable outcomes will include revenue maximisation, profit optimisation and employee and partner enablement.

The first phase should be a full digital strategy exercise starting with an assessment of the foundational capabilities using the provided questionnaire and benchmarking revenue and profits against best-in-class and industry-average performers. A comprehensive strategy for all the pathways can be developed at this stage.

The second stage should see the procurement of chosen technologies, culture and competencies build-up and process reengineering commencement. New customer and partner journeys should be implemented, and early results should be seen.

The final stage is when everything goes mainstream. Culture and competencies should become mainstream enablement programmes, and technology investments and enhancements should take priority. Business process and networks should be optimised to leverage the technologies, multiple customer journeys and innovation interventions institutionalised. The benefits should start in revenue first, spread to cost reduction and resultant profit optimisation, and a truly enabled organisation capable of embarking on a virtuous cycle of innovation should emerge.

For the business leaders who have been with us on this journey, this is your chance. Let's make it happen!

9

The Post-Digital Society: Digital India

India is a country with an amazing past, a rather troubled present and we believe a great future. After having a commanding share in world GDP ten centuries ago, we lost ground, initially to the rapidly industrialising economies of the West and then the surging growth in the East, starting with Japan and moving to the four Asian tigers and in the last decade, a rampaging China. It is debatable whether the long period of Mughal and English rule was responsible for the country losing its entrepreneurial zeal or whether it was the choice of a socialist model of development post-Independence that set the country back. But there is no doubt that in the last 70 years, barring brief periods of excellence, the country has performed below potential.

The opportunity to become the factory of the world, which was initially captured in electronics by Taiwan and later moved to China, was missed to a large extent by India because of our inability to invest in physical infrastructure on the scale that China did and continues to do. Even today, the port and road infrastructure and of course the digital and social infrastructure remain areas of slow improvement, which may be the reason why Vietnam and Thailand have taken a bigger share of manufacturing moving out of China as costs rapidly escalate in that country. Two industries where India managed to scale the peak of global success have been information technology and digital transformation. India's first minister for information technology, late Pramod Mahajan, famously commented that it was the absence of a Ministry for IT or Beauty that allowed Indian enterprises to become global success stories in IT and business process outsourcing and allowed the Indians Sushmita Sen and Aishwarya Rai to become Ms Universe and Ms World respectively. While the success in beauty pageants may have been incidental, the technology industry has grown from a few million in the early 1980s to its current size of over 160 billion US dollars, holding a dominant market share in global offshore outsourcing. This continuing success is truly heart-warming and a pointer to the future, where showcasing Digital India can help us build a multi-trillion opportunity as producers of digital products, services and solutions for the world.

We will explore this further in this concluding chapter of the book.

DIGITAL INDIA: THE FORMATIVE YEARS

Thirty-five years ago, author Ganesh was speaking at a conference in Mumbai where Professor Pankaj Ghemawat of the Harvard Business School said, 'We spent many years in the 1960s and 1970s waiting for a telephone in our homes and then some more years waiting for a dial tone.' This evocatively suggests the many years India lost waiting for infrastructure to be available for serious communications and production capabilities in the country. It was some years later that US entrepreneur Satyen (Sam) Pitroda was tapped by then Prime Minister Rajiv Gandhi and started the revolution of PCO-STD-ISD call booths all over the country. And in an almost unobtrusive manner, the Atal Bihari Vajpayee government in 1999 implemented a key policy reform separating policy formulation and service provision, giving birth to the entity called Bharat Sanchar Nigam Ltd (BSNL), which started building a reasonable telecommunications infrastructure for the country.

From a country where a mere telephone was a luxury item in the 1980s to a reality of over 800 million phones, we have truly leap-frogged to a substantially better status. A burgeoning young and tech-savvy population has reasons to be happy. With the rapid rise of e-commerce and mobile commerce in the country and intense global competition driving down prices of smartphone handsets,

India has far exceeded every target for telecom penetration and teledensity. Just as the Software Technology Parks of India (STPI) scheme in the 1980s gave the policy impetus to the software exports industry, the Telecom Policy has given us the opportunity to leapfrog in mobile telephony, both voice and data to world-class levels.

Watching from close quarters as a participant in industry growth in the skills development and software and business process management services industry in the country, the authors have been heartened to see the number of manufacturing and services firms and even government departments who have benefited from the proliferation of the internet and the availability of mobile phones in most hands in the country. In the computer education segment, where authors Ganesh and Uma had a role to play in the success of leaders like NIIT, APTECH and Zee Education, millions of careers got launched that propelled Indians and India to global success. Even today a large percentage of global software products are engineered in Indian centres owned mainly by global multinationals. It has been possible to launch content and skills development new-model companies such as Global Talent Track and learning pedagogy revolutionaries such as Skills Alpha that have used personalisation and adaptive learning methods in an environment of artificial intelligence to bring peer learning, e-mentoring and career management to digital platforms. They have found adopters not just in large corporations but also in entrepreneurial firms, universities, industry associations and even the social sector. Post-COVID, with the ongoing need for social distancing, one can expect to see every learner, from the age group of five to seventy-five reach out to their smartphones for at least prerequisite, remedial and reinforcement learning. Where will the bottom 100 million of our poorest folk get these devices? That is another story!

Digital has been inexorably transforming all other productive activities in the country. We have already discussed manufacturing, where the introduction of automation, robotics, IoT- and AI-enabled warehousing and transportation has radically transformed the design and implementation of manufacturing execution systems and created data flows from the products on the field, through the shop floor and integrated with process and supply chain data from ERP systems. Large data warehouses, lakes and marts are becoming the norm, with the ability to store, process and disseminate large volumes of disparate data, provide business intelligence and serve up actionable insights on dashboards directly to the concerned decision-makers. Supply and demand chain participants even in remote locations are regularly updated through their phones and can stay connected for any changes that may happen in production and delivery schedules. Even in agriculture, crop data is retrieved by drones and information flows at every stage from farm to fork.

The services industry has truly adopted digital. Some of our banks and financial services firms have become best in class in the adoption of digital in their processes. Innovations such as State Bank of India's YONO online banking has brought enormous convenience to the common Indian. Healthcare has seen telemedicine adoption almost overnight thanks to COVID, and communication services for work-from-home adopters have burgeoned with new apps being launched every week, supported by government schemes and the entrepreneurial opportunity to build solutions for India and the world.

In 25 years of the internet in India, we have seen the opportunities to democratise the availability and access to information. Through its large Smart Cities Mission and smaller but definitive innovations in adopting digital technology through the National Education Policy, National Health and Agriculture Missions and transparency in many government services, the government is paving the way to a truly digital India.

ELECTRONICS INDUSTRY: MISSED OPPORTUNITIES

In all the hype and celebrations surrounding the incredible success of the IT services industry in India, one story of much promise and very little delivery has been in the area of electronics—hardware and consumer. Created by early movers such as DCM,

Wipro, HCL, etc., since the late 1970s when India first started on an independent capability journey, the fledgling industry has been a victim of frequent acts of commission and omission and is only now struggling to find its feet. This history was captured very well in a 2020 article by one of the founders of HCL, Ajai Chowdhry, where he makes a few pertinent points.

1. The ITA Agreement, signed by India in 1996 without industry consultations, led to the decimation of the hardware industry, with WIPRO and HCL shifting their attention to traded products and software products and services.
2. The PM's Task Force for Hardware created by Prime Minister Vajpayee in 1999 created a policy to prepare the industry for 2005, by which year India had committed to bring in a zero-duty regime for IT hardware products. This policy 'never saw the light of day'. A paper detailing the steps to bring the semiconductor and component manufacturing ecosystem to India also floundered.
3. In 2009, a task force set up by the government made pathbreaking recommendations, including setting up a National Electronics Mission, an incentive scheme for semiconductor manufacturing, preferential market access for domestic manufactured products (Vocal for Local?), an ambitious semiconductor FAB, and an Electronic Development Fund to promote R&D in electronics. Much of this was never implemented.
4. In 2011, a core advisory group for R&D in the Electronic Hardware Sector recommended a design challenge that would then give selected designs for high-volume products to Indian manufacturers.

During these years, when the opportunity to become self-sufficient in this critical area has been all but lost, Chinese companies started dominating the import of mobile phones and various other high-volume items into the country. Although Indian domestic telephone brands did get a small boost through the phased manufacturing programme, the low value addition kept this segment from ever having the innovation and cost-effectiveness of the Chinese manufacturers. China surpassed the US as the world's dominant exporter of electronics in 2005 and is consolidating its market position.

ARTIFICIAL INTELLIGENCE: THE NEXT FRONTIER

Prime Minister Modi has set artificial intelligence as one area of scientific research and innovation that this book would like to call out as a key driver of future global competitiveness of nations. A PWC report on the future of AI speaks to the potential of AI to add over 16 trillion dollars to the global economy by 2030, which exceeds the combined current GDP of China and India. China itself is projected to see a value addition of over 9 million dollars, which could be 26% of its GDP, and India has developed a plan to add 957 billion dollars to it GDP, which could be 9–12% of India's GDP, assuming India approaches a 10-trillion-dollar economy by then.

The real question is whether India is prepared to capture this opportunity or will AI also remain a hype component of seminars and rhetoric with very little real action on the ground, given India's COVID-battered economy and weak focus on academic and scientific research. The trillion-dollar AI dream can be realised if AI adds 1.3% to GDP growth annually and a scenario develops of AI applications in every segment of the economy, augmenting human work and adding autonomous value through the creation of new products and services and enabling new shared platforms for education, healthcare, financial services, supply chains and government. There are anecdotal examples of Indian companies rapidly adopting AI and integrating it into their business such as Ola Cabs, which is now tracking traffic and attempting to improve customer experience. Similarly, Myntra is tracking data for fashion and trend prediction, Urban Ladder for optimising intracity logistics and predicting product demand and returns and Paytm for fraud detection and prevention.

One advantage emerging from these use cases is that they stress the power of augmentative AI and dispel the bogey of large-scale job losses which have kept India behind and a late starter in the AI arena. When it comes to AI, policymakers must do two things at once: manage the fears about the impact of AI on society while encouraging innovation. This is being considered and implemented in all the ten and more countries who are exploring the power of AI to transform their economy. While the initiatives are largely led by private-sector companies in countries such as the United States and the United Kingdom, while the government takes the lead in China and Japan, it is essential to ensure that critical elements such as technology, data and people are accessible to all stakeholders of the AI ecosystem. In India, the Ministry of Electronics and Information Technology, working with NASSCOM, has recently created a 'policy group' to work out a policy framework and road map for emerging technologies, including AI, blockchain and big data and analytics. The Ministry of Commerce and Industry has created a 'task force on AI' to explore possibilities for leveraging AI for development across various fields in manufacturing and services. Although these are promising starts, India's policy initiative is not comprehensive yet and lags behind other G20 countries.

For instance, Japan unveiled an overarching AI strategy in 2016 for building its tech-infused, ultra-smart 'Society 5.0'. The manufacturing hub in Germany's Stuttgart-Tübingen area is transforming itself into an AI research hub, with critical support from the country's industrial giants Daimler, BMW and Bosch. Most recently, Amazon committed to contribute 1.5 million dollars to this collaborative research effort and a further 500,000 dollars to funding individual research. The European Commission's SPARC and Germany's Cyber Valley collaboration attract high levels of private-sector funding and participation to execute the region's vision of AI. China embarked on a next-generation 'Artificial Intelligence Development Plan' in July 2017 called AIDP 2017, laying out a three-step plan to bring China's AI industry in line with global competitors in 2020 and reach 'world leader' status in many AI fields by 2025, finally becoming the primary centre for AI innovation by 2030. AIDP has some very specific initiatives: the development of intelligent and networked products such as vehicles, service robots and identification systems, creation of a comprehensive support system including intelligent sensors and neural network chips, development of intelligent manufacturing, which has always been China's forte, and investing in industry training and testing resources and extensive cybersecurity.

China at this stage is streets ahead of India in AI. The controlled environment created by the administration is enabling the country to become a leading hub for AI developments. China controls large amounts of data through Baidu in the country, just as the US has Google in theirs. The ability of these two countries to leverage this data for multiple AI applications will not be easy to beat. With a 2.1 billion-dollar tech park for AI research in Beijing and multiple cities investing billions of dollars in city ecosystems, China is already leading the world in AI research and highly cited papers worldwide.

In India, NITI Aayog's AI policy announced in 2018 called for leveraging AI not only for economic and military growth but also for social inclusion. It touched all the hot-button topics of skills for youth, research investments and developing Indian-made AI solutions for the world. Key sectors for focus are healthcare, agriculture, education, smart cities and infrastructure, smart mobility and transportation, all of which are excellent policy areas. The objective of establishing the country as an 'AI Garage' to enable the development of scalable solutions for India that can be implanted across all developing and emerging economies of the world.

Predictably, where the Indian agenda falls short is the absence of concrete plans and investments that will be so essential to creating a trillion-dollar business opportunity. While China plans on competing with the West through a civil–military fusion and large central and independent city investments, India expects that tighter collaboration between private, government, non-profits and educational institutions will provide a strong AI focus on social development and inclusive growth. India can hope that the present reluctance to support China will make India more attractive to foreign investors and partners and give India access to more data and metadata for analysis and solution development.

India will have to overcome the old bogeys of legal and privacy-related challenges to capitalise on this window of opportunity.

THE FUTURE OF GLOBAL ECONOMIES

Readers would agree that the period 1947 to 2020 has seen rather chequered progress in the development of a digital economy. The progress in electronics hardware has been weak, telecommunications has progressed comparatively well, artificial intelligence holds out a great promise and the success of smart manufacturing, smart cities and even e-government has been patchy at best. In the meantime, many nations in the developed world, such as the USA, Germany, the Nordic countries, Japan, South Korea, Singapore and Israel have assimilated digital extraordinarily well and are on their way to building truly connected societies. China, and increasingly Vietnam and Thailand, have grabbed outsourced manufacturing opportunities. If India can still hold its high in one area, it remains IT services.

Interestingly for India, after this story of weak responses and missed opportunities, COVID and the post-COVID world economy may provide one more opportunity to share and succeed. To understand how a determined Digital India can write a new future for the country and our billion-plus people, let us analyse what is happening in global economies. Most economies are trying to simultaneously address the challenges of relief work and the recovery processes, with a long-term focus on building resilience in case of a future pandemic. The vulnerabilities in each economy exposed by the COVID crisis have to be addressed by monetary, fiscal and policy responses to ensure that a strong economy can be created after the vaccine proliferation in each country.

Large stimulus and furlough schemes launched with the motive of job and wage protection in the US, the UK and other parts of the developed world may have lulled the citizens into a sense of complacency, but these will be temporary. In case of a prolonged recovery period, they can create a trough of weak demand that will have a severe medium-term economic impact. Strong public–private partnerships between the government, corporations and civil society will prepare the ground for a stronger recovery. This will also not run the risk of deepening the rich–poor or digital divide and will deliver equitable growth across social strata.

A McKinsey report on the status of the damage and potential recovery in the US in September 2020 provides an interesting lens through which any country can view its performance on the relief-recovery-resilience continuum and make robust plans for emerging stronger by the end of the next fiscal period. In the US, as indeed in most parts of the world. Small and medium enterprises (SMEs) constitute nearly 80% of employment, and the largest COVID stress has been on this segment. The SMEs are in danger of cash running out, and new start-ups looking for their first or second round of funding can face poor valuations and excessive delays that can make their continuance suspect. This is of course in sharp contrast to the run-up in large technology stocks, thereby underlining the difference in outlook and expectations for many of the SMEs in every business segment in comparison to the large incumbents who have pools of cash and liquidity to tide over the COVID crisis.

We mentioned in the previous chapter that one of the key focus areas for firms seeking to come out of COVID stronger and rise fast on the digital business curve are internal and external innovation. Business funding of R&D tends to decline in times of crisis. Countries like India, where the percentage of GDP spent on research is already substantially lower than 1% could see all or most businesses stop significant innovation initiatives, thereby putting the future of the business itself and country competitiveness in a particular domain or industry segment at risk.

The American analysis reveals that the sectors that were most adversely affected in previous periods of crisis in terms of business efficiency and job creation were hospitality, food services, retail and manufacturing. This also implies that regions in a country whose economy is most reliant on these affected sectors will suffer most in terms of short-term economic loss and delayed recovery. At a city level in the US, Hawaii and Florida naturally show this effect. On a global basis, countries such as Thailand show a significant impact. It needs a strong focus on revival in these sectors on one hand and investments in new sectors on the other to move the country towards a more resilient economic status for the future. Cases in point are Thailand's aggressive move towards contract manufacturing and the UAE's successful migration in focus from oil to tourism over the last two decades.

Each country and region in a country needs to reimagine its dominant industries and also look at new industries whose development can be accelerated to create a substantially different sectoral mix over a defined period that could range from five to twenty years. Sometimes, this also needs focused investments in infrastructure. Dubai made massive investments in infrastructure for shopping and entertainment to attract global investments. China invested massively, just as the US had done many decades ago in physical infrastructure, to become a central part of most global manufacturing supply chains. In developing countries such as India, physical, digital and social infrastructure across the length and breadth of the country has always been inadequate and the rich–poor divide creates a prominent digital divide that drives a wedge into equal opportunity. COVID, with its imperative for social distancing and the need for reasonable speed of data access for education, collaboration and work output, drives an even deeper wedge into the chasm between the digital haves and have-nots and becomes a matter of deep concern for urban and rural development of the economy.

A natural response to these inequities in infrastructure has created the concept of mega-cities—New York, London, Tokyo, Seoul, Shanghai, Bangkok, Mumbai, etc.—in the last few decades. Country planners need to focus on the distribution of jobs so that urban centres can get decongested and many 'smart cities' can emerge. China has done a brilliant job in this context, with over two dozen significant sized smart cities emerging, whereas India has barely managed to make two new cities of any significance merge since 2000. This is particularly true with COVID making urban massing highly avoidable and many urban youths already leaving their apartments and moving to suburbia to continue their work-from-home activities. Globally, this presents the most significant opportunity to identify smart connected cities half the size and twice the number as the mega-cities in each country and make a concerted effort to build out the capabilities in these cities. One only has to step into Hangzhou, Suzhou, Dalian, Tianjin or Zhuhai in China to see how they can be given the same vibrancy and work–life balance as Beijing, Shanghai or Shenzhen. This may well be one of the most significant focus areas for any country seeking to generate a balanced recovery and country-wide resilience for the future.

DIGITAL NATIONS: MULTIPLE VISTAS

The need to go digital, to provide a range of services easily accessible to citizens and to enable country competitiveness has been an obsession for nations in both the developed and developing world for at least the last decade. Less than a decade ago, the Digital Nations or DN group was created as a collaborative network of the world's digital governments with a common goal of harnessing digital technology to improve citizens' lives and work. The DN incorporates both multilateral and mini-lateral collaboration possibilities, enabling small sets of countries to work together in specifically chosen areas that could have an impact on all the collaborators.

While the UK, South Korea, New Zealand, Israel and Estonia were DN's founding members, they have been joined in the last two years by Canada and Uruguay and more recently by Mexico, Portugal and Denmark. Recent collaborative initiatives taken by the DN have been connectivity, open government and coding skills for children.

Connectivity will soon be a global obsession. With the COVID period encouraging more and more social distancing and work from anywhere while digital connectivity has been accelerated by nearly 50 billion connected devices in the world and the promise of 5G, countries are collaborating on infrastructure and the development of standards for seamless connectivity and collaboration. UK's investment in smart cities, IoT and the world's first dedicated 5G testbed centre has enabled a very high percentage of citizens availing e-government facilities. Korea has also focused on IoT, while Estonia has a secure platform-independent data superhighway called X-Road that minimises the cost of transparent digital services.

Open markets have been a core objective of all governments, prompted by the need to have more and more small companies play a role in bidding for public-sector contracts. The collaborators on this theme are exploring cloud services and agile delivery to enable a small part of any service to be procured from independent vendors rather than relying on the old model of getting everything from one large systems integrator. The UK's G-Cloud is being emulated by New Zealand's government cloud initiative and South Korea's e-procurement system. Governments have reported substantial savings in time and costs and significant realised monetary benefits.

Citizen-focused applications are many. Children's coding centres, both online and physical, and integrating coding in the school curriculum has enabled children to move from being only active consumers of technology to creators and also encouraged many girls to take up coding as a key interest area. Every country in the DN has actively embraced this mission, with the UK and Estonia mandating coding from the age of five, South Korea teaching parts of computer science courses in the curriculum and the rest online and New Zealand investing in graduate ICT training schools as well as teaching coding in secondary schools. Israel has gone a step ahead and teaches full computer science courses in all high schools.

With China and the USA continuing to lead in research- and AI-related areas, the race is surely on in many nations to start early, sustain the investments and truly emerge as digital capitals of the world. This is the context in which Digital India has to invest and create a niche for itself in a fast-changing world.

DIGITAL INDIA: MAKING IT HAPPEN

What does the future hold for India and how can the country claw towards some level of symmetry with China? eNAM, a pan-Indian electronic trading portal, suggests that India is the last major emerging market in the world and India's rise in the tech world can be emulated by all industry sectors. Rapid privatisation is occurring as the government exits hitherto 'monopolistic' sectors and creating true oligopolies in ports, airports, telecom, mining energy, etc. Platform plays in healthcare, education and skills around the country can also help India emulate e-commerce and financial inclusion successes and open up opportunities for domestic businesses to scale and invite more foreign investments. More financialisation of savings will open up opportunities for banks, insurance companies, mutual funds, mortgage and consumer finance companies, and the rise of per capita GDP will result in a burgeoning of spends on durables, travel and all forms of discretionary funding.

Prime Minister Modi has set India a target to be an economy with a 5 trillion-dollar GDP by 2024. COVID and the weakening economic situation India has faced since the beginning of 2019 and will continue to face for some time beyond the arrival of the COVID vaccine may make that time frame difficult, but the goal remains laudable and we will get there. What is feasible in the near term is the attainment of a sub-goal in the 5 trillion-dollar agenda, the trillion-dollar digital India. We have had the privilege of working with the Ministry of Electronics and Information Technology on some of the pathways to this dream. The outstanding work done by the McKinsey Global Institute (MGI) is worth summarising here as a prelude to our discussion on the opportunities and challenges.

The vision for a trillion-dollar digital India is not just the 160-billion-dollar IT and IT-enabled services companies growing at that speed. At best, this segment and also electronics hardware and e-commerce could grow from the current level to 410 to 510 million in the period up to 2025. What is interesting is a new and emerging ecosystem encompassed by a whole gamut of digitally enabled services. These services can scale to a level of 500 to 600 billion in the same period and drive new hopes and opportunities for the digital economy in the country. MGI has outlined nine themes around which this new digital India can develop,

The first of course is infrastructure and software for connecting the country from Kashmir to Kanyakumari. This government and the previous government has talked about the National Optical Fibre Network and the creation of the ambitious BharatNet, which would ensure high-speed connectivity and internet access, connecting not only the main cities but potentially even the 240,000 *gram panchayats* and the 600,000 villages and make the common service centres hubs of local business activity integrated into the national mainstream. The second theme is the Make in India Mission, which in essence can mean not just make in India for India but make in India for the world. Three segments will become important focus areas—consumer electronics and defence, digital supply chains enabled by artificial intelligence and ubiquitous connectivity and finally, the internet of things, with its ability to generate data flows from every inanimate object and even wearable computers. IoT will energise information and knowledge capture, processing and dissemination to productive resources within and across manufacturing enterprises.

The third priority area for Digital India is agriculture because doubling farmers' income is imperative. Any member of a rural family will realise that the present-day landholding of a farmer is so small that they tend to be in poverty most of the time. We need to ensure that better productivity methods are made available to them to make them viable participants in the economy. Precision know-how shared from the best in the world with our farmers in every part of India will be enabled, digital marketplaces will be created where the best price can be acquired for the produce and total transparency can prevail across the supply and demand chains.

Next-generation financial services will need to be developed as well. We in India are extremely proud of what we've done with the JAM trinity, which are Jan Dhan, Aadhaar and Mobility.

The success of JAM and the Indian stack will have to be replicated in healthcare and multiple other domains so that friction-free information interchange can happen everywhere, connecting up various constituents and making sure that contracting across people and businesses is friction-free. Blockchains will proliferate, and synchronous and smooth flow-based lending will become the norm. Digital India will finally see healthcare for all, where anybody can go anywhere and get treated. The onslaught of COVID has accelerated the growth of robotics in healthcare and telemedicine. Diagnostics are now happening from anywhere in the country, and 3-D printing, where even equipment can be printed on the field, is becoming the norm.

Another great evolution will be energy availability for all with grid automation, including alternative energy sources, automation and balancing of the grid and creating energy marketplaces. Digital India must not only impact urban governance, which is happening through the Smart Cities Mission but also common service centres, fully powered with broadband in every part of rural India. The migrant labour crisis showed the need to de-urbanise and have widespread job availability in all parts of the country, which will only happen physical and social as well as digital infrastructure is uniform in all parts of the country. Rural job exchanges that connect the entire availability, employment and entrepreneurship ecosystem will be an essential component of this. Digital will also provide platforms for prerequisite, remedial and reinforcement learning for all students and adult learners.

The good news is that this is already beginning to happen. The India stack in financial services is being replicated in education and health. DIKSHA in the education sector will provide an open digital public infrastructure with comprehensive educational content and tests. It has already been rolled out in several states and is being used in Tamil Nadu and Maharashtra quite effectively. The limitation, which has already been witnessed in moving all school teaching online, is that many children from disadvantaged communities cannot access education comprehensively from their mobile phones. In healthcare, the success of telemedicine in COVID times and the extension of the Ayushman Bharat mission should enable a massive platform to be launched. This could be the largest coverage provided by any digital platform in the world, totally enabled by AI and cognitive patient relationship management.

Electronics manufacturing is a race in which India has remained far behind China. However, the recent change in the geopolitical situation and the reconfiguration of global supply chains presents India with its biggest opportunity. The government has recently announced a production-linked incentive (PLI) scheme aimed at attracting five global champions and five domestic champions and giving them incentives to start high volume manufacturing. Mr Ajai Chowdhry warns that they should close out with interested parties quickly and also suggests that this may be the right opportunity to revive the SME backbone and cover printed circuit boards and IT products under the ambit of PLI. He also believes creating a fab in India is no longer an option but an imperative. A fab can either be acquired second-hand to take care of current electronics needs or installed in India by one of the large companies such as Samsung.

Many industry veterans such as Roopa Kudva, Managing Director of Omidyar Network India, have also pointed out the huge opportunity the country has with the National Urban Innovation Stack. The first layer of the stack, called DIGIT, is a platform that is already being implemented in municipalities. With the efforts of the National Institute of Urban Affairs, it could become the standardised approach for all Indian urban municipalities. The India Urban Data Exchange, which is already under implementation in Pune, aggregates all data emerging from the city and makes it available to entrepreneurs who can use it to solve pressing issues of the city. Open data exchanges implemented in other critical areas—agriculture, land records, law and justice—will all ensure that data flows through the system. Proper intelligence tools and good governance will create hundreds of billions of dollars of new economic value and pave the way for a transformed India in the not-so-distant future.

India will exploit digital when two significant components of the Indian landscape become digitally smart—smart cities and smart villages all enabled by 5G and country-wide connectivity.

When that does happen, what can we expect to see on the ground and what will be the benefits?

The Smart Cities Mission

An ambitious programme started by the Ministry of Housing & Urban Affairs, Government of India, in 2016, this is possibly the most comprehensive initiative for digital value creation in urban spaces in the world. A programme that is envisaged to invest over 14 billion dollars, this is one area where the objectives of jobs and prosperity distribution can be achieved. With a strong mission director at the helm, this mission can truly catapult India in the global leader status amongst digital nations.

The objective of smart cities is to create both city-wide and locally concentrated changes in smart infrastructure and drive initiatives ranging from command and control centres to sustainable livelihood acceleration to environment protection, which are all important for sustainable cities. Water and electricity supplies, solid waste management, healthcare and education, affordable housing and public transport systems are all being transformed in a hundred and more new and old cities in India. The primary goal is to ensure that economically weaker sections of the city are positively impacted and, in the process, the entire city develops into a more liveable, resilient and sustainable place. Best practices in digital and information technologies, public–private partnerships and policy development are being developed every month as this major mission unfolds. The execution of the mission has been divided into four broad categories. and cities are being encouraged to choose some which they implement in entirety to provide maximum citizen satisfaction.

1. Physical infrastructure, including power and water supply, solid waste management, multi-modal transport, physical and cyber connectivity, housing and disaster management
2. Economic infrastructure, including skills development, incubation centres, industrial parks, trade and service centres and export processing zones with the specific objectives of

enhanced jobs and livelihood creation, market and GDP contribution
3. Social infrastructure, including education, healthcare and entertainment and inclusive planning for socially or financially 'othered' segments of society
4. Institutional infrastructure focused on better city governance, including simpler and citizen-friendly taxation, institutional finance and banking services and speedy delivery of services, transparency and accountability, citizen advisory committees and citizen participation in decisions for the good of the city.

Environment protection should also be a big component of the smart city development agenda. The focus is very much on efficient use of resources, waste reduction, renewable energy and ongoing steps to alleviate the impact of climate change.

Smart cities would not reach their potential if digital technologies are not extensively deployed. All the technologies, core and extended, find an application here, from cloud and social media access to mobility, IoT, AI, machine learning to the management of large open data platforms to enhance the timeliness and quality of governance. Operating efficiency and targeted investments based on citizen convenience become very feasible through the application of technology. A massive digital literacy effort is needed to ensure that at least one member of every family in a city is comfortable with the use of digital and finance. Smart citizens will automatically create smart cities.

Smart cities alone will not build a Digital India. We need a widespread network of hubs, starting with large urban conglomerations as well-connected as New York, Shanghai, London, Hong Kong or Seoul, moving to at least 50 geographically dispersed next-tier smart cities and finally spokes with reliable connectivity extending to each of the 200,000-plus *gram panchayats*. That will open up opportunities for distributed job creation, e-employment exchanges in every district and extensive use of digital technologies for industry, agriculture, healthcare, education skills, entertainment and every aspect of 'Jaan aur Jahaan'—life and livelihoods. This will set the stage for a return to 7–10% sustained GDP annual growth and a tryst with the prosperous destiny that this nation so richly deserves,

THE ROAD AHEAD

Paul Saffo, a futurologist and singularity expert from Stanford University, in his keynote at the National Management Conclave of the All India Management Association, spoke about the need to create an exponential wave to counter the exponential COVID challenge, which has battered every country like a tsunami since early 2020. Saffo argues that in such exceptional situations, where the large problem is being met and has to be overcome and normalcy restored by digital reengineering, the important idea is that we have to ask the right questions, not questions like 'Do robots want to take away our jobs?', which is self-defeating in articulation, but a curious question like 'What will be the future of work?'. We also consider how our AI can be trained to be ethical and how a moral economy can still be sustained in the digital age. Or else we will be like the story about the man in the bar of the doomed ship Titanic saying, 'I know I asked for ice, but this is ridiculous.'

The road ahead for the world, for countries, for companies and citizens everywhere will be full of new questions to ask and new answers to discover. There is a lot of learning to be done from early science and space fiction movies like *2001: A Space Odyssey* and early internet start-ups like Second Life, which permitted every player to create her own avatar and wander through a make-believe world on a voyage of discovery. With technology evolving all the time, our voyages into the future will be assisted by gadgets like 3-D head-mounted displays, shared virtual reality, physical workplaces fully integrated with cyber and a complex cocktail of new technologies and customer expectations redefining the boundaries of reality. And Saffo gets it right when he says, 'Don't use technology to pave your cow path, use it for deep innovation to build new pathways to the future.'

Reimagining the future needs clarity on the threats of complacency, the opportunities of digital, the intrinsic organisation strengths and of course the Achilles' heel that could come in the way of progress. At an organisation level, we accomplished this by recommending foundational capabilities and pathways to be created. At the level of a nation, with particular focus on India, a similar Capability Maturity Model could be erected comprising the following foundational capabilities and transformation pathways.

Digital Nation Capabilities

One could argue that there are so many capabilities that it would be impossible to list just a few. But we are taking the liberty to broadly suggest three capability categories:

1. The network, which enables high-speed connectivity and flow of data
2. Access devices that enable easy use
3. Aware and digitally savvy citizens of all ages and vocations.

The first two are obvious and easy, though they will need significant investments from the government and public–private partnerships. It is a strong focus on the third that will create both the post-COVID push and the digitally enabled pull in all aspects of the community to enable the pathways to the digital nation to be built on truly fertile ground.

Digital Nation Pathways

Again, at the risk of over-simplification, let us list just three categories that could be addressed:

1. Digital government, including adequate citizen–government interfaces in smart cities and villages
2. E-marketplaces for financial services, manufacturing and agricultural supply channels, skills, education and employment
3. Accountability, sustainability and outcome measurement for all digital missions to ensure that the benefits are realised and are widespread.

These have been great focus areas for successful digital nations—Japan, China, South Korea, Singapore, Dubai and of course the Western world. Building incubation centres to create a true innovation ecosystem and ensuring the ecosystem for digital transformation comes together will be critical for future success. Taking a leaf from the US book, citizens in every part of the country should have equal access to education and work opportunities. It becomes a key responsibility of policymakers to ensure that skills for the new world are made available through formal and non-formal universities and other digital platform capabilities. Recent innovations supported by the Ministry of IT in India for enabling ongoing skills development for ASHA workers for healthcare missions and SMEs to spur the smart manufacturing ecosystem are examples of levers that will truly lead to success.

Investment in physical, digital and social infrastructure remains a key responsibility of the government. The surge of capabilities that will be offered by quantum computing and 5G will support global investments if a high-quality workforce is made available in every part of a digital nation. In the wake of COVID, far-sighted governments as in Singapore are increasing investments in digital infrastructure and entrepreneurial ecosystems. All nations will have to do this to get the engines of economies running again. Most importantly, all cities, towns and even villages should build transparency—between farmers and large buyers, SMEs and their OEM partners, students and universities and every citizen with the providers of opportunities for education and livelihoods.

It would be appropriate to end this book with an exhortation to every leader of the new world which is enshrined in the famous words of Indian sage Swami Vivekananda: 'Arise, awake and stop not till the goal is reached.'

Index

C

I

J

K

Q

R

S

About the Authors

Ganesh Natarajan is Co-Founder and Chairman of 5F World and Lighthouse Communities Foundation and a director of State Bank of India, GTT, Skills Alpha, Kalzoom Advisors, Principal Center for AI & Advanced Analytics, Hinduja Global Solutions, SVP International, Educate Girls, the Asian Venture Philanthropy Network. He is the author of *Business Process Reengineering*, *BPR—A CEO Guide*, *Knowledge Management*, *Knowledge Force* (with Uma Ganesh), *Winds of Change*, *Through the Corporate Lens*, *What We Really Want* (with Lavanya Jayaram), *Inspired* and *From Start-Up to Global Success.*

Uma Ganesh is Co-Founder and Chairperson of Global Talent Track, which provides live training and digital platforms for talent development in Asia. She is also a board member of Skills Alpha, Centre for Advanced Analytics and AI and Emoha Elder Care. She was earlier the CEO of Zee TV's Education business. She is the co-author of the book, *Knowledge Force*.

Lavanya Jayaram is a high energy marketing and strategy professional with 20 years' experience in defining and delivering differentiated brand experiences and helping build customer loyalty. Lavanya was previously Chief Marketing Officer of Zensar Technologies and is currently a passionate change agent focused on driving innovative business strategies and business improvements for technology companies. She has co-authored another book, *What We Really Want—Aspirations of Gen Y.*